Reading the Puppet Stage

Drawing on the author's two decades of seeing, writing on, and teaching about puppetry from a critical perspective, this book offers a collection of insights into how we watch, understand, and appreciate puppetry.

Reading the Puppet Stage uses examples from a broad range of puppetry genres, from Broadway shows and the Muppets to the rich field of international contemporary performing object experimentation to the wealth of Asian puppet traditions, as it illustrates the ways performing objects can create and structure meaning and the dramaturgical interplay between puppets, performers, and language onstage.

An introductory approach for students, critics, and artists, this book underlines where significant artistic concerns lie in puppetry and outlines the supportive networks and resources that shape the community of those who make, watch, and love this ever-developing art.

Claudia Orenstein is Professor of Theatre at Hunter College and the Graduate Center, CUNY, USA.

Reading the Puppet Stage
Reflections on the Dramaturgy of
Performing Objects

Claudia Orenstein

LONDON AND NEW YORK

Designed cover image: *Paper Story*, created by Blind Summit Theatre, Mark Down, and Nick Barnes. Puppeteers (from left) Sarah Calver, Ivan Thorley, Mark Down, and Sean Garratt. Photo by Nick Barnes for Blind Summit Theatre.

First published 2024
by Routledge
4 Park Square, Milton Park, Abingdon, Oxon OX14 4RN

and by Routledge
605 Third Avenue, New York, NY 10158

Routledge is an imprint of the Taylor & Francis Group, an informa business

© 2024 Claudia Orenstein

The right of Claudia Orenstein to be identified as author of this work has been asserted in accordance with sections 77 and 78 of the Copyright, Designs and Patents Act 1988.

All rights reserved. No part of this book may be reprinted or reproduced or utilised in any form or by any electronic, mechanical, or other means, now known or hereafter invented, including photocopying and recording, or in any information storage or retrieval system, without permission in writing from the publishers.

Trademark notice: Product or corporate names may be trademarks or registered trademarks, and are used only for identification and explanation without intent to infringe.

British Library Cataloguing-in-Publication Data
A catalogue record for this book is available from the British Library

Library of Congress Cataloging-in-Publication Data
Names: Orenstein, Claudia, author.
Title: Reading the puppet stage : reflections on the dramaturgy of performing objects / Claudia Orenstein.
Description: Abingdon, Oxon ; New York : Routledge, 2023. | Includes bibliographical references and index.
Identifiers: LCCN 2023006749 (print) | LCCN 2023006750 (ebook) | ISBN 9780367561475 (hardback) | ISBN 9780367561444 (paperback) | ISBN 9781003096627 (ebook)
Subjects: LCSH: Puppet theater.
Classification: LCC PN1972 .O74 2023 (print) | LCC PN1972 (ebook) | DDC 791.5--dc23/eng/20230406
LC record available at https://lccn.loc.gov/2023006749
LC ebook record available at https://lccn.loc.gov/2023006750

ISBN: 978-0-367-56147-5 (hbk)
ISBN: 978-0-367-56144-4 (pbk)
ISBN: 978-1-003-09662-7 (ebk)

DOI: 10.4324/9781003096627

Typeset in Goudy
by MPS Limited, Dehradun

For all the puppeteers, past and present, who have devoted themselves to this wonderful art.

And for Sophie and Caleb, blossoming in their own endeavors.

Contents

List of Figures — *viii*
Acknowledgments — *xi*

Introduction — 1

1 A Puppet *Being* and a Puppet *Doing* — 19

2 The Dramaturgy is in the Object — 32

3 The Image Aspect of the Puppet — 57

4 Humans and Objects — 84

5 Notes on Sounds and Words — 116

   Conclusion: Choices We Made — 124

   A Selective and Selectively Annotated Puppetry Bibliography — 141

   Index — *173*

Figures

Cover	*Paper Story*, created by Blind Summit Theatre, Mark Down, and Nick Barnes. Puppeteers (from left) Sarah Calver, Ivan Thorley, Mark Down, and Sean Garratt. Photo by Nick Barnes for Blind Summit Theatre. The photo shows the performance's use of pictures and words on paper as performing objects	
1.1	*The Woodsman*, Off-Broadway. The beast, with the head of a tiger and the body of a bear, built in several parts, performed by different puppeteers working together to create a whole figure. Directed by James Ortiz and Claire Karpen	24
1.2	*Charcoal Boy*. A close-up of Charcoal Boy showing the real tree branch from which he was crafted. Sarah Provost—creator/writer/director; Eric Novak—creator/writer/puppet and set designer; Elyas Khan—creator/writer/composer	28
2.1	Carpenter Dwarka Prasad Jangid opening his traditional *kaavad* box. Bassi, Rajasthan, India, 2013	33
2.2	Tony Miyambo contemplating the blocks standing on the table in *The Cenotaph of Dan Wa Moriri*. Written by Gerard Bester, Tony Miyambo, and William Harding, directed by Gerard Bester. Wits Amphitheatre, Johannesburg, South Africa, October 2014	40
2.3	The ice puppet of Oedipus in Théâtre de L'Entreouvert's *Anywhere*	44
2.4	"Idee-Fixe" from Figurentheater Triangel. A blindfolded puppet with a stick hovers above the large open head, another puppet emerging from it	46
3.1	A diagram showing the many connected realms of object performance	59
3.2	A diagram showing the connected artistic realms of both object and image	60
3.3	A performance of *Pabuji ki phad* by singer-storyteller Pappu Bhopa (and his wife Kamla Bhopi, not pictured) with a scroll painted over fifty years previously by the uncle of Kalyan Joshi, an artist from the last family painting in this tradition.	

	Performance at Devena Singh's Art Inn Jaipur. Rajasthan, India, April 2014	61
3.4	Left, Rani Chitrakar sings the story, unrolling one panel of her *pattachitra* scroll as her daughter, Shushana, points to the images, and her granddaughter, Shima, looks on. Right, Hazra Chitrakar displays her scroll on the theme of the destruction of the 2004 Indian Ocean tsunami. Here the image, not painted as discrete panels, spreads from top to bottom in the style of a painting or wall hanging. Naya, West Bengal, India, 2013	63
3.5	Ono Shunjo, head priest of Dōjōji Temple, Wakayama, Japan, performs his temple's famous scroll story. (He wears a mask as the photograph was taken during the worldwide COVID pandemic.) January 2022	65
3.6	Left, performers at Wat Khanon temple in Thailand dance their *nang yai* puppets in front of the screen. Right, a *nang yai* shadow puppet displayed in the museum at Wat Khanon temple showing the Demon King of Lanka, Thotsakan (Ravana), and his captive, Nang Sida (Sita). Photaram, Ratchaburi, Thailand, January 2018	69
3.7	Les Anges au Plafond's *Le Cri Quotidien*. Political figures emerge from the morning newspaper	72
3.8	Tortoise in a Nutshell's *Feral*, directed by Ross Mackay, set design by Amelia Bird, lighting by Simon Wilkinson, performed by Arran Howie, Ross MacKay, Alex Bird, Jim Harbourne, and Matthew Leonard. The scene shows the paper city set and three of the puppeteers, below, and a live feed projection of the main family of characters inside their house, above	74
3.9	Clare Dolan displays the full expanse of her picture storytelling dress. Before a performance at the Detroit Institute of Art, 2015	77
4.1	Little Amal walks across the Brooklyn Bridge during her visit to New York City. October 2022	86
4.2	The large Mocco puppet standing against the Tohoku landscape, with control apparatus and crew, alongside another puppet: a helmet Mocco wore that came off and transformed into a flying bird	87
4.3	*Hakomawashi* performer Nakauchi Masako offering blessings with her puppet of the god Ebisu while Minami Kimiyo accompanies her playing a small drum. Nishinomiya, January 2022	93
4.4	*King Kong* on Broadway. One of the most powerful moments in the show, when the gorilla breaks the fourth wall and confronts the audience	98

4.5 Hachioji *Kuruma Ningyō* performer Nishikawa Koryū V with his Sanbasō puppet. The photo shows the unique manipulation method of this tradition and the master puppeteer's evocative facial expression — 104

4.6 *Disfarmer*. The puppet of Disfarmer pays for his purchases by handing money to a puppeteer, who now acts as a character. Conceived, directed, and designed by Dan Hurlin; music by Dan Moses Schreier; text by Sally Oswald; presented by St. Ann's Warehouse; Brooklyn, NY. Photographed Monday, January 26, 2009 — 108

5.1 *Diagram* of the many interconnected realms of puppet performance — 118

6.1 *Hairy Ape*. The puppet of Yank's torso (operated by Diana Benigno and Chris Wilson) combines with machine parts (operated by Nick Beach) during Yank's long speech in praise of technology. Hunter College, New York City, August 29, 2017 — 130

6.2 *Hairy Ape*. The Aunt, made from dough and dressed up, performed by Holly Hepp-Galván — 132

6.3 *Ubu Roi*. Designer Bonni Benton and performer Holly Hepp-Galván demonstrate how the small Trump version of Ubu emerges from the unzipped head of the larger figure — 135

6.4 *Dante's Inferno*. Designer Bonni Benton demonstrates the small, toy theatre version of the Devil puppet — 137

6.5 *Dante's Inferno*. The final image of the large three-headed Devil, featuring the full company of puppeteers. Dixon Place, May 9, 2018 — 138

Acknowledgments

I am grateful beyond measure to the many people and organizations that have, in big and small ways through the years, supported my puppetry pursuits and helped to bring this book to fruition. These include puppetry scholars and artists around the globe too numerous to name, but they are all included in my thoughts, and many are mentioned throughout the book. UNIMA, the international organization for puppetry, has connected me with a large, supportive network of people, institutions, and publications that are ever-ready to help those dedicated to puppetry arts. Each and every one is a treasure.

Thanks always to Hunter College and the Graduate Center at CUNY for the resources that have contributed to the development of my work, including time and space for research activities, Presidential Travel Awards, PSC-CUNY research awards (jointly funded by The Professional Staff Congress and The City University of New York), supportive colleagues, and inspiring, engaged students. I am fortunate to have been afforded opportunities to grow as a scholar and artist. My thoughts on what I hope students will understand about puppetry have been a guiding force in writing this book. My 2021–2022 Fulbright Research Fellowship and host institution, Sophia University's Institute of Comparative Culture, allowed me to study ritual puppetry in Japan. Some of my research from that time appears in these pages. I am eternally grateful for the support of the Fulbright Foundation.

Ben Piggott was the original Commissioning Editor at Routledge for this book and a welcome advocate there for publications on puppetry. Ben has since moved on but left me in the very capable hands of Steph Hines, who has tirelessly kept me on track. I am grateful to both and to all the anonymous Routledge reviewers for their time and very useful comments on the proposal and first draft as well as to Routledge's copy editors, Urvi Sharma and his team, and my indexer for their work on the manuscript.

Dassia N. Posner, Larry Switzky, Gabriel Levine, and Jane Taylor's positive responses to a portion of the book presented at LoKO: Laboratory for Kinetic Objects gave me the confidence to move forward with this project. Participants in the American Society for Theatre Research Puppetry and Material Performance Working Sessions also provided valuable feedback and inspiration. An early version of one chapter was presented as part of Ben Katchor's Comic and Picture Storytelling Symposium.

Enormous thanks to Colette Searls, who graciously gave her time to read an early draft and allowed me to bombard her with frequent, random questions, and to Tim Cusack for his thorough reading of the final draft, lending his incomparable editorial skills to the project. Enormous thanks to Liz Laurie as well for her editing work.

Leslee Asche, Cariad Astles, John Bell, Alex Bird, Edna Bland, Blind Summit, Jeroen and Henk Boerwinkel, David Buchen, Barbra Busackino, Bradford Clark, Roberta Colombo, Pattara Danutra, Clare Dolan, Melissa Flower Gadney, Kathy Foley, Holly-Hepp Galván, Kristin Haverty, Martin Holman, Conrad Koch, Jim Lasko, Tom Lee, Bruno Leone, Reay K. Maxwell, Alissa Mello, Tony Miyambo, Noémie Montagne, Atasi Nanda Goswami, Ono Shunjo, James Ortiz, Raphael Pares, Tarish Pipkins, Sarah Provost, Lori Reese, Paulette Richards, Noriyuki Sawa, Chrstine Scarfuto, Devena Singh, Theodora Skipitares, Nancy Staub, Richard Termine, Stephen Thomas, Gretchen Van Lente, Liqing Xu, and Janni Young are among those who shared their work with me or helped me with questions, sourcing photos, connecting to artists, or finding other information. I am grateful for their generosity and their assistance.

Thanks to my mother, Gloria Orenstein; my father, Stephen Orenstein and his wife, Susan Fox; my sister, Nadine Orenstein; my children, Sophie and Caleb Carman; and their father, Taylor Carman, for everything they do.

Introduction

The word "puppet" inevitably brings to mind figures associated with childhood—characters from *Sesame Street* and other beloved television shows; live performances for children in schools, parks, and libraries; and the toys and playthings of youth. Puppetry, however, has never been solely a form of children's entertainment, and in recent decades it has gained renewed prominence and recognition as a multidimensional, sophisticated art form. Within the United States, but also across the globe, there has been an explosion of talented puppetry artists experimenting with innovative styles and techniques, a growth in puppetry festivals, and the infiltration of performing objects into every form of live and mediated performance. In New York, one of the world's major theatre capitals, the appearance of puppets on stage has become so ubiquitous that, in May 2017, renowned culture magazine *the New Yorker* ran a Bruce Eric Kaplan cartoon attesting to its unavoidable presence in the contemporary theatre: a couple sits in their living room; the wife peruses the newspaper, and her husband responds to her apparent query about what shows to get tickets for. The caption reads: "I'm sixty-six—I don't want to see puppets in anything."

In contrast to Kaplan's cranky cartoon husband, it has been my great joy for nearly two decades to have grabbed a front-row seat to the exciting re-genesis of puppetry performance in New York and elsewhere. I have made it my project to not only see *everything* I can with puppets in it but to think through puppetry as an art form, both in response to and with the help of—even led by—the rich proliferation of performances taking place around me.

This book attempts to capture and articulate some of the more forceful views that have emerged and settled with me during that time, relating to how we read, experience, and understand puppetry. I acknowledge that many important artists and scholars have already lent their considerable talents to express their ideas and observations on this art. I hope that my own years of watching, thinking about, and, whenever I can, doing puppetry have generated some useful insights to share. This book does not profess to be any kind of definitive or programmatic delineation of what puppetry is or how we should consider it but is instead one gal's view from my own vantage point. I hope it will offer a dramaturgical and critical orientation to the art, especially for those newly connecting with it, whether as critics, artists, scholars, or spectators. There are surely ideas and references

DOI: 10.4324/9781003096627-1

important to puppeteers that I may fail to address, but hopefully the ground I do cover will reveal some interesting terrain.

This book also clarifies my personal journey of coming to comprehend various facets of puppetry as much as it offers critical tools and perspectives for analyzing the art. For many years I hoped to write a "Poetics of Puppetry," an intricate breakdown of the elements that make up the form, showing how they operate, following a kind of Aristotelian model. I don't believe this book exactly achieves that now subsided ambition. My work and focus over the years have taken other paths and a growing cultural awareness of puppetry generally perhaps makes that original goal less necessary. Also, my thoughts have never conformed easily to Aristotle's rigorous analytic style. However, I do take some methodological cues from Aristotle here by thinking about the particular "pleasures" this art form affords and that are unique to it, in contrast to other arts, and, with that knowledge, dissect the theatrical experience of puppetry and the various elements that contribute to it. I allow myself to write in a more discursive manner than we find in Aristotle, winding in and out of the diverse paths of observation I have followed and the myriad experiences and performances that have helped elucidate for me puppetry's nature and artistic potential.

My journey to puppetry

People often ask me how and why I came to be so immersed in the world of puppetry. My answer, while personal, also offers a general map of significant landmarks in the puppetry world at least from my own encounters with them and admittedly from my own very New York–centered view. It can provide an orientation to or mapping of the puppetry world that exists all around us, with its own networks, connections, and landmarks. My personal story also, I hope, expresses a helpful model to any who are academically inclined, of how one might pursue and develop a critical passion, to find it emerge as one's field of study. In fact, I intend the mix of personal and critical material throughout the book to show the importance of *process* and personal inclinations as part of developing research and coming to new ideas. This sometimes relies on serendipity, keeping an open mind, staying troubled by questions, and having indulgent or generous friends. An academic life doesn't need to be confined to or defined only by the books one writes or the classes one teaches but is more aptly an all-encompassing profession that expresses how we encounter and help shape or reshape the world around us. Each individual determines what that means, manifesting that understanding through their actions, as well as in the thoughts they eventually put down in writing. I like to underline for my students something they might easily forget: the fact that every critical book they read has a person behind it who has their own sensibilities, passions, inclinations, points of view, and a journey that brought them to their understanding of their material. While this may not sound like the "objective attitude" we are taught to seek in academic material, within the humanities and the arts it is a value to be savored. It exists in any case, so best to put it up front and enjoy it. So, who is the person who writes this book, and what are her interests and inclinations?

Since first discovering my love of theatre in childhood, I have always been drawn to highly stylized models of performance, in contrast to the psychological realism that dominates the American theatre. This predisposition led me to focus on Asian theatrical traditions and political protest theatre in my early scholarly and creative work, both fields in which puppetry has a strong presence. But I plunged fully into the world of puppetry, yet to reemerge from it, starting in the 1990s, inspired like many others in New York by the series of Henson International Puppetry Festivals produced biennially at New York's Public Theatre between 1992 and 2000, curated by Leslee Asch.[1] These festivals introduced New York audiences to a vast array of puppet forms and new works from around the globe, showcasing the diversity and reach of the art. The festivals included works like *Gesell Chamber* by Argentina's El Periférico de Objetos, which used broken, turn-of-the-twentieth-century dolls to tell the tale of a young boy's violence, and Handspring Puppet Company from South Africa's *Woyzeck on the Highveld*, which set Georg Büchner's nineteenth-century German drama in South Africa and combined evocatively carved wooden puppets with artist and director William Kentridge's animations. While many local performers were galvanized by these festivals to explore fresh artistic models in their own creative work, my response took a critical bent. I became interested not only in what I was watching but *how* I was watching. The successes and failures of these shows seemed to land differently from those in the human-actor theatre I knew so well. A presentation might draw audiences in by focusing on a beautiful, captivating figure but lack traditional markers of dramatic structure. Eloquent Shakespearean poetry might hang uncomfortably in the air next to gorgeously crafted puppets. Unusual objects, surprising forms of manipulation, and mixed-media combinations of crafted figures, film projections, dancers, and live actors lit up the stage in novel ways. The festivals offered some of the most exciting *theatre* I was seeing, and I wanted to understand what made these shows effective and how I was watching or *being asked to watch* puppetry differently from other kinds of performance.

As I was beginning to ponder these issues, I was excited to be asked for the first time (in 2000), as part of my appointment at Hunter College, to propose a course for the CUNY Graduate Center's Doctoral Program in Theatre. I immediately proposed a class on puppetry. I had already been nurturing a vision of gathering theoretically astute graduate students together, going with them to the next Henson festival, and, in lively critical discussions after the performances, wrestling with the provocative ideas the shows inspired. What better way to answer my questions than to pick the brains of smart graduate students? A course at the Graduate Center, which would include our Hunter MA students as well as PhD candidates, seemed like the ideal opportunity. So, I proposed the course for that fall semester, fully anticipating the next edition of the Henson festival to run on the same biennial timetable as the previous ones. Unfortunately, I found out late in the summer, as I waited patiently for the festival schedule to come out, that not only would the festival not run that year, but there would be no further festivals at all. Not only was I (as so many others) devastated by the news that we could no longer look forward to these rich, inspiring cultural events, but my central plan for the course was torpedoed. Instead of having the resource of this festival, with all its exhilarating, unusual, innovative puppetry performances available to spark discussion and critical thinking, I found myself having to construct, from scratch, a PhD level course fully devoted to puppetry—surely the first of its kind in the history of the world it seemed to me. Maybe it was? I spent that summer scouring the library for every critical text I could find in any way relevant to puppetry. Many resources were familiar to me from my work on political theatre and Asian performance traditions, but others were in fields like anthropology or linguistics and were less interested in the questions I was asking than in things like kinship relationships within puppetry communities in Africa or how puppeteers in traditional forms pass on their vocal training and linguistic inflections. It became apparent that there was little or no critical literature, at least in English or that I personally saw available to me at that time in the United States, that was shedding light on the interesting, innovative puppet productions I had been seeing at the Henson festivals. A special issue of *TDR*, edited by John Bell, which came out about the same time as one of the festivals and was subsequently published as its own volume under the title *Puppets, Masks, and Performing Objects* (MIT Press, 2001), became an invaluable resource; yet it didn't cover all the terrain I perceived stretching out before me.

In teaching that graduate course, I hoped to answer two main critical questions: "How do we watch puppetry differently from other forms of theatre?" and "Why is the culture so interested in puppetry—why is it becoming such a strong, visible artistic presence—at this historical moment?" Looking through the literature on the art, it seemed that the last time puppetry, a generally marginalized art form in the West, had taken major focus in artistic circles was during the modernist period in the early twentieth century. What was it about that period, and then about our own moment historically and culturally, that made people interested in puppets and turn to puppets as a way of expressing something vital? And what were the differences between what these two cultural moments saw in the puppet and how artists used the form? Although I stressed these issues during the class and had some wonderful students in the course, I now realize that perhaps my questions were simply not theirs. By the end of the semester, these queries had failed to take focus in discussion and elicit answers from my brilliant students. So, I was left with the burden of having to pursue them on my own.

I began to tackle them by trying to see as much puppetry as possible and doing my best to describe, in thick descriptive writing, what I was watching and how different aspects of puppet performances took focus or created meaning on stage. Jan Mrazek's *Phenomenology of a Puppet Theatre: Contemplations on the Art of Javanese Wayang Kulit* came out in 2005, just as I was heading into my first sabbatical from teaching. Since it is nearly six hundred pages, I was lucky to have leave time to devote to it. In turning to phenomenology as a critical methodology, it offered a truly useful approach for my investigation. Prague School Theory adherents Jiří Veltruský, Peter Bogatryev, and Otakar Zich had, in the twentieth century, been among the rare scholars to give critical attention to puppetry. Their semiotic approach to the art had bequeathed one of the few critical tools being applied to puppetry analysis at the time. Within both theatre and puppetry circles, it could sometimes seem as though the writings of their two most prominant predecessors—Heinrich Von Kleist and his eighteenth-century essay "On the Marionette Theatre" and Edward Gordon Craig's 1908 essay, "The Actor and the Ubermarionette," both foundational critical texts for the field—were the only critical writings on puppetry at all. Semiotics, however, didn't speak to me, in spite of my having taken a course entirely devoted to it in graduate school with the impressive and somewhat intimidating scholar and critic Martin Esslin. Semiotics, with its meticulous analysis of sign systems, felt too mathematical in its approach, antithetical to the emotionally complex experiences I wanted to investigate and reveal about the work. It was perhaps also not in synch with my own methodological or analytical temperament.

I have since grown to have a deeper appreciation of the usefulness of semiotics as an analytical tool for puppetry, spurred by working as dramaturg on the puppet show *Shank's Mare*, a collaboration between US puppeteer Tom Lee and Japanese *kuruma ningyō* (cart puppetry) master, Nishikawa Koryu V. This show combined new and traditional puppets with projections and premiered at La MaMa in New York in 2015, subsequently touring to Japan and elsewhere. In order to play to both American and foreign audiences, *Shank's Mare*, like many puppet productions, used no language and expressed its story—a merging of two tales of characters who each go on a journey and face death in contrasting ways—primarily through visual means. In my role as dramaturg, watching rehearsals to determine if the stories could be read clearly by the audience, I felt I had unwittingly taken on the position of "semiotics police," continually pointing out to the artists moments when signifiers onstage might mislead or confuse. Semiotics suddenly seemed like a really useful tool for understanding and creating puppetry. However, in 2006 I was more interested in how all the various aspects of puppet performance that were communicating to audiences, on both intellectual and emotional levels, could be thought through, analyzed, and expressed to bring out the full depth of the art and reveal the myriad ways it functioned. Mrazek's book and its meticulous, step-by-step process of attending to every aspect of a Javanese *wayang kulit* shadow puppet performance felt like a revelation. Mrazek begins his analysis with a description of the puppets themselves as objects and images, whose large eyes and profile stance allow alternately for both cinematic-style long shots and close-up visions of the character. He then investigates the puppeteer's connections with those objects as he brings them "trembling" to life on the screen. Next, he analyzes how music and cues from the gamelan orchestra work in conjunction with shadow-puppet action on the screen, and so on. This process offers a comprehensive, detailed investigation of the performance event and all the meaning-making and expressive individual and networked elements onstage.

I must acknowledge that other important critical works on puppetry were out at that period, but I did not encounter them at the time, so they did not have a strong influence on my own critical journey in this realm, although they have been foundational for the field as well. These include Steve Tillis's *Toward an*

Aesthetic of the Puppet: Puppetry as a Theatrical Art (Praeger, 1992) and Henryk Jurkowski's *Aspects of the Puppet Theatre* (Puppet Centre Trust, 1988).

Other important resources from that time include Michael Meschke's *In Search of Aesthetics for the Puppet Theatre*, which offers many useful insights drawn from the perspective of creating puppetry. With the support of UNIMA-USA (the American branch of an international organization for puppetry, which I will discuss later), Laurence R. Kominz and Mark Levinson published their coedited collection *The Language of the Puppet* (Pacific Puppetry Center Press, 1990) packed with interesting, if relatively short, essays. The six volumes of *Puppetry Yearbook*, published from 1995 to 2005, edited by James Fisher, collected a range of diverse essays on puppetry across the globe. UNIMA-USA's *Puppetry International* (PI), a semiannual magazine rather than an academic journal, offers interesting, generally brief articles that are not specifically scholarly, addressed as they are to a more general audience, especially professional puppeteers. In recent years, however, *Puppetry International* has begun to accept scholarly articles for peer-review spots within its pages, edited by Dassia N. Posner. Husband-and-wife team Andrew and Bonnie Periale, puppeteers themselves among their other talents and professions, are the founding editors of *Puppetry International* and were at the helm of this inspiring publication from the first issue in 1995 through 2022 when husband-and-wife team Alissa Mello and Mike Kelly took up the reigns. Knowledgeable scholars, like Nancy Lohman Staub, have also contributed important writings. Despite all these resources available at that time, I was still searching for more critical scholarship in this area.

In investigating how to write about puppetry, I also had the nagging feeling that I was missing an appropriate vocabulary for discussing an art that was so very visual. The tools for dramatic analysis I had studied didn't provide language for describing objects, their construction, or their visual elements, let alone their kinetic qualities. Moreover, so much of the new puppetry I was looking at—I offered "New Puppetry" as a term to apply to this work in the papers and articles I was writing—was borrowing from cinematic techniques, using certain puppets to express close-ups and others to show wide shots, creating a dynamic, shifting environment such that a cinematic vocabulary also seemed necessary. With critical resources on puppetry scarce, I started to look for and assemble a library of non-puppetry critical works that might speak to puppetry and help me articulate what I was seeing.

Material culture as a field and object-oriented ontology as a critical perspective were still emerging and didn't infiltrate theatre criticism fully until later. Jane Bennett's *Vibrant Matter: A Political Ecology of Things*, published in 2010 (Duke University Press Books), coming out of the disciplines of political theory and environmental studies, eventually became an important critical text for me and the field of puppetry at large. Bennet's work replaces a human-centered ontology that views people as dominating and acting *on* the material world with one that understands the combined agency of humans and objects in collective action. She proposes the idea of *vital materialism* to reveal matter as more than inert and the concept of *assemblages* of humans and nonhumans in describing them as collective *actants*. This new ontological model parallels the replacement within puppetry of a view that sees the puppeteer as a god-like figure dominating the puppet to one that acknowledges the interchange that takes place between human performer and object, with puppeteers giving themselves over to the material of the puppet and its possibilities. Kathy Foley describes this model as following Asian traditions in "The Dancer and the Danced" (*Puppetry International* 8: 14–28, 2001). This Asian view has taken over in current puppetry teaching and practice in the United States and more accurately describes how puppeteers master working with their material performers.

Bennet is just one theorist within the growing critical fields of New Materialism, Object-Oriented-Ontologies, and Posthumanism, which all displace a central critical focus on human agency with investigations into objects, materials, and materiality. Studies from these critical viewpoints, coming from various disciplines, have now created a rich body of academic literature with which puppetry has come into conversation. These critical ideas began in philosophical literature with scholars like Bruno Latour, whose writings on actor-network theory have been particularly influential, notably through his book *We Have Never Been Modern*, first published in English in 1993. Object-centered perspectives have now become commonplace throughout theatre and performance studies scholarship.

However, as I continued investigating puppetry back in the late 90s and early 2000s, these views were not as widespread, and the number of disciplinary discourses I thought I ought to absorb to get a better critical grasp on puppetry kept expanding. Because of the strong choreographic nature of the puppeteer's movements of and with objects on stage, as well as the necessary choreography of puppeteers themselves amongst each other during performance, dance also seemed like a field of study that could contribute to describing puppetry. Was a dance vocabulary also necessary? And within technological frameworks puppetry was drawing not only from cinematic techniques but also from animation and robotics. Did I need those methodologies and terminologies as well?

To dig further into these questions, I eventually started a little puppetry reading group with two PhD students and one undergraduate who were interested in the puppetry work I had been doing and who were engaged in their own research in adjacent fields. As I was to be a faculty adviser on the field exams for both doctoral candidates, this was a useful way for us to explore some texts on their reading lists together and think about the application of these materials to puppetry. One of these students, Deborah Hilborn, was focusing on medieval material culture. Her article, "Relating to the Cross: A Puppet Perspective on the Holy Week Ceremonies of the *Regularis Concordia*," which began as her MA thesis in our Hunter College MA program, was later published in *The Routledge Companion to Puppetry and Material Performance*, the volume Dassia N. Posner, John Bell, and I coedited. In it, she applies what Hilborn calls a "puppet perspective" (165) to analyzing how medieval congregants may have experienced the presence of Christ through their various and changing relationships to the cross used during Holy Week ceremonies. The other doctoral student, Lisa Reinke, was interested in video games, a realm I knew (and still know) next to nothing about, though its use of manipulated avatars undoubtedly points to its relationship with puppetry. Undergraduate Maria Tsalpina, coming to Hunter after leaving a program in animation that had not fully satisfied her interests, was just beginning to delve into puppetry in her creative work. She has since become a professional puppeteer and writes on performing objects within the fields of medical health and disability justice. For the reading group, we each proposed different critical texts we thought would shed light on approaches to puppetry, as we met weekly to discuss them over cookies and tea in my living room. Drawing from fields such as material culture, anthropology, art history, as well as prosthetics, cyborgs, and video gaming literature, our readings included David Freedberg's *The Power of Images: Studies in the History and Theory of Response*; Daniel Miller's *The Comfort of Things*; Stephen Pattison's *Seeing Things: Deepening Relations with Visual Artefacts*; W.T.J. Mitchell's *Iconology: Image, Text, Ideology*; Michael Nitsche's *Video Game Spaces: Image, Play, and Structure in 3D Worlds*; Susan Stewart's *On Longing: Narratives of the Miniature, the Gigantic, the Souvenir, the Collection*; Peter Schwenger's *The Tears of Things: Melancholy and Physical Objects*; John Berger's *Ways of Seeing*; Stephen Pattison's *Seeing Things: Deepening Relations with Visual Artefacts*; as well as Jane Bennet's *Vibrant Matter* previously discussed. Other favorite critical texts I turned to, especially as I began looking in-depth at traditional puppetry in India, were Diana Eck's *Darśan: Seeing the Divine Image in India* and Richard H. Davis' *Lives of Indian Images*. Gaston Bachelard's *Poetics of Space*, which I had enjoyed in graduate school, also held the promise of helping to understand the power and emotional pull of objects in theatrical spaces, as did Sherry Terkel's books, *Evocative Objects: Things We Think With* and *The Inner History of Devices*.

Besides reading works that could help elucidate[2] puppetry critically, I set out to see as much puppetry as possible, looking especially for productions that used novel techniques and were directed primarily at adult or mixed audiences, rather than children. As the mother of two young kids at the time, it was somewhat awkward always to be seeking childcare so Mommy could take herself to see some puppet shows. It would surely have been more productive for me to focus instead on productions I could bring my kids to, and I did occasionally find happy convergences of our interests, as my article "The Danish Festival at the New Victory Theatre: Puppetry and A New Perspective on Family Entertainment" (*TDR/The Drama Review* 52.3 (2008): 187–195) attests. Encouraging my kids to come with me to experimental adult work was sometimes successful, but too many such excursions eventually earned the following diplomatic response from my young daughter (said in her most mature, patient voice), "Mom, that's your thing, not my thing," and from her older brother the more revealing, skeptical inquiry, "Is this one of those 'one night only, work-in-progress, no reviews' kind of things?"

In New York, one could find these shows at several venues. Some had become especially active, inspired by the Henson festivals, often attempting to fill the gap left by their termination. HERE Arts Center inaugurated their Dream Music puppet program in 1998 with Basil Twist's *Symphonie Fantastique*, a provocative production showcasing the lyrical movements of lengths of cloth and other objects in a huge tank of water to the accompaniment of Berlioz's music played live by pianist Christopher O'Riley. Devoid of any figurative objects, this piece of abstract puppetry surprisingly became a popular hit and the mainstream face of avant-garde puppetry, with Basil Twist, a third-generation puppeteer, emerging as a nationally recognized artist outside the often-insular puppetry world. In 2018, HERE revived this production to mark the twentieth anniversary of their Dream Music puppet program, which annually commissions new full-length works of puppetry using live music. HERE also showcases other works in development through their Puppetry Parlor and Puppetopia programs. St. Ann's Warehouse in Brooklyn was and continues to be another venue welcoming to puppetry, especially in hosting its annual Labapalooza, a presentation of works in progress from its Puppet Lab. In the Lab, a chosen group of artists meet weekly over several months as they develop new work. Like HERE, the St. Ann's Puppet Lab, started by Janie Geiser, actively supports the development of experimental puppetry work, especially by including artists from outside the puppetry community. Both venues are interested in interdisciplinary collaborations and have helped encourage the innovative directions the form has taken in New York and inspired other venues in the city and around the country to take up their models. Over the years a Who's Who of significant puppetry artists have run the Lab, usually in pairs, including Dan Hurlin, Theodora Skipitares, Tom Lee, David Neumann, Matt Acheson, Lake Simons, and Robin Frohardt. The Object Movement Puppetry Residency and Festival at the Center at West Park, a church on Manhattan's Upper West Side, is a relatively new venture, started in 2017, following in the footsteps of the St. Ann's model and curated by Maiko Kikuchi, Rowan Magee, Marcella Murray, and Justin Perkins. La MaMa ETC has also started a similar program for emerging artists called Jump Start. La MaMa has, since 1962, included puppetry in its programming and continues to feature puppetry in the new work it presents. In 2021, LaMaMa celebrated the ninth edition of its own puppet festival, curated by Denise Greber, and LaMaMa continues to host an annual slam, curated by Jane Catherine Shaw. Dixon Place's Puppet Blok offers yet one more presentation series.

It is also important to mention that Disney's *The Lion King*, premiering on Broadway in 1997 and winning six of its eleven Tony Award nominations, introduced generations of mainstream audiences to a whole new way of appreciating how objects and performers can work in concert to embody characters on stage. *Avenue Q*, *War Horse*, *Hand to God*, and *King Kong* have since then all shown Broadway audiences how puppets can be at the center of adult, as well as family-oriented, entertainment.

While I am on the subject of puppetry venues, I will here fill out a short roll call of some representative US organizations and institutions that support and present puppetry as a further resource for readers and as an acknowledgment of the hard work and devotion of puppet lovers to the art. The Puppet Slam Network, spearheaded by Jim Henson's daughter, puppeteer Heather Henson and her Ibex Puppetry company, connects underground cabaret-style events and showcases across the country, offering short-form puppetry—usually late at night—for adult audiences. With Sam K. Hale and Alex U. Griffin, Heather Henson and Ibex have also created Handmade Puppet Dreams, a traveling film series featuring puppetry on film. The Carriage House, on New York's Upper East Side, once used for filming and editing Jim Henson's Muppet projects, has, through the work of the Henson Foundation, offered puppeteers short residencies for developing and presenting works-in-progress to a small audience of aficionados, who give feedback during guided post-show discussions. Theatre for the New City, Bushwick Starr in Brooklyn, and the Tank are other New York venues that give space to contemporary puppet performances for adult audiences. Brendan Schweda has developed puppetry programming under the name Puppets Come Home! at a small museum and performance space at Coney Island. New York is also home to the New Victory Theatre, the Central Park Marionette Cottage, Puppetworks, Inc., and Teatro SEA, all presenting puppetry for families and young audiences. The Henson Foundation's online Puppet Happenings provides easily accessible, continually updated listings of puppetry events taking place in New York and across the country, while UNIMA-USA's annual Citations of Excellence in the Art of Puppetry recognizes high standards of puppetry work. Cities around the country have a growing number of venues devoted to puppetry, such as Automata Arts in Los Angeles, cofounded and codirected by Janie Geiser and Susan Simpson; Puppet Showplace Theatre in Boston, from 2010 to 2021 under the direction of Roxanna Myhrum and now headed by Leslie Burton; Northwest Puppet Center, Carter Family Marionettes in Seattle under the direction of Dmitri Carter, which also houses an international puppet museum; and, most importantly, the Center for Puppetry Arts in Atlanta, Georgia, a pioneer in the field, established in 1978 under the direction of Vincent Anthony. The Center, with museum exhibitions and extensive programming, especially in the area of education, is also the headquarters of UNIMA-USA. Bread and Puppet Theater in Glover, Vermont, invites volunteers to work with the company as they present their own performances annually, and their buildings accommodate a museum featuring objects from the troupe's fifty-plus years of work. More venues continue to introduce audiences to sophisticated puppetry work as the popularity of the art increases. During the COVID pandemic, a variety of online platforms offered puppetry shows and workshops, bringing the art to even more new audiences and crafting further means of creating, presenting, and sharing all aspects of puppetry.

In the past, there were few international puppetry festivals in the United States. The first major festival, before the Henson series in the 1990s, was held in Washington, DC, in 1980, under the direction of Nancy Lohman Staub in conjunction with UNIMA's thirteenth congress meeting . This was the first UNIMA congress held outside of Europe and a major, successful undertaking that those who were lucky enough to be part of—I was not among them sadly—continue to remember with joy and admiration. But it was followed by somewhat of a dry spell of US festival offerings. Today, however, puppetry festivals are taking place at regular intervals around the country. These include the formerly biennial, now annual, Chicago International Puppet Theater Festival, held each January under the direction of founder Blair Thomas, with the goal of "establishing Chicago as the Center for the Advancement of the Art of Puppetry" (https://www.chicagopuppetfest.org/about/); the Nashville International Puppetry Festival, which has had three editions in 2008, 2011, and 2013; and, the biannual International Puppet Fringe Festival, NYC, established by Manuel Moran and his bilingual theatre company Teatro SEA. Teatro SEA's festival takes place at the theatre's home base, the Clemente Soto Velez Cultural and Educational Center on New York's Lower East Side, and had its inaugural edition in 2018. A second edition, postponed by the COVID pandemic, finally took place in the summer of 2021, and included both in person and online offerings. A third edition is set for 2023. The Chicago International Puppet Theater Festival now also produces events all year round outside of any specific festival offerings, including an online workshop series. Teatro SEA also offers its own puppetry events year-round. Like so many puppetry projects, the initiative for creating these festivals has, in each case, come from puppeteers themselves, who have put in the hard work required to make these events a reality in order to promote and share their art. I am continually amazed at the energy, resourcefulness, and commitment of puppeteers the world over, who are the driving force behind supporting, sustaining, and growing all aspects of their profession. Across the globe, puppeteers have not only produced their own festivals but formed professional organizations, inaugurated training exchanges, and founded performance venues, museums, and publications. In the United States, the Henson Foundation has been particularly helpful and appreciated for the financial and other support it continuously provides to a variety of puppetry ventures. The Henson Foundation's annual grants for the creation of new productions have been invaluable in supporting puppetry's creative development.

Within this orientation to puppetry venues and hubs, I will add some words about puppetry training. In the United States, puppeteers have tended to come to their work through their personal discovery of their passion for the art, which often leads them either to start experimenting on their own, learning new skills and picking up tricks of the trade as they go, or to apprenticing with other puppeteers to learn on the job. These continue to be important ways puppet artists are formed. Many countries in Europe and elsewhere have national puppetry training programs or academies. The only degree-granting puppetry training programs in the United States are at the University of Connecticut's Storrs campus, which offers both a BFA and an MFA in Puppetry Arts as well as a Puppet Arts Certificate, an online graduate program. Frank Ballard initiated what is commonly referred to as the UConn program in 1962 and was the sole puppetry teacher in it for many years. Bart P. Roccoberton Jr., an alumnus of that program, took over as director in 1990. In recent years, the program has continued to grow with an expanded faculty and its own campus facilities. It partners with the Ballard Institute and Museum of Puppetry in downtown Storrs, under the direction of John Bell, offering shows, exhibits, online forums, and other programming related to the art. The Ballard is itself attached to the downtown branch of Barnes and Nobles's UConn bookstore, which stocks a respectable selection of books on puppetry in a designated puppetry section and, initially, had a coffee shop selling puppet-themed sandwiches.

Despite the lack of puppetry degree programs, the art has infiltrated academia by virtue of performers, researchers, and advocates who are on the faculties of many institutions. The founders and many of the artists involved in the Object Movement Puppetry Residency and Festival in New York, for example, all studied at Sarah Lawrence College, where Dan Hurlin initiated a strong puppetry focus within the Theatre Department for both graduate and undergraduate students. He has mentored a generation of important practitioners. Puppetry artist Tom Lee has also taught there, bringing students into his professional productions; more recently Lake Simons has continued in their footsteps. Even though its arts program is not singularly focused on puppetry, Sarah Lawrence has developed a good number of innovative puppet artists. California Institute of the Arts has incorporated puppetry work by virtue of the presence on campus of filmmaker and puppetry artist Janie Geiser, part of the Experience Design and Production faculty, as well as Susan Simpson, who taught there from 2000 to 2014. Colette Searls has brought puppetry to the Theatre Department at the University of Maryland, Baltimore County. Bradford Clark at Bowling Green State University and Kathy Foley at the University of California, Santa Cruz, have both given puppetry a focus at their respective institutions with a special concentration on Asian forms. I have myself made puppetry a prominent offering within the Theatre Department at Hunter College, CUNY. There are a growing number of other dedicated faculty throughout the country, Amanda Petefish-Schrag at Iowa State University, Deborah Hertzberg at Brooklyn College, and Heather Jeanne Denyer at California State University, Fullerton among them, bringing puppetry to their curricula. UNIMA-USA maintains a list of people researching and teaching puppetry within academic institutions that is accessible through their website.

A lot of puppetry training, of course, still takes place more informally, with puppeteers teaching each other, especially by bringing novices or emerging puppeteers on during productions whenever there is need for an extra pair of hands. Puppeteers also pass on the training to each other through organizations like the Puppeteers of America (P of A), which offers workshops and skill exchanges through the many activities of its regional guilds and national festivals. P of A connects and supports puppeteers in a variety of ways. The Eugene O'Neill Theater Center's annual Puppetry Conference, taking place every June in Waterford Connecticut under the direction of Sesame Street puppeteer Pam Arciero, has, since its inception in 1992, made important contributions through its development of new puppetry productions and by enhancing the skills of puppeteers. Participants can take part at various levels of expertise, both studying with master artists and creating their own work. Attending a summer program at the O'Neill stands almost as a rite of passage into the puppetry world. The Chicago International Puppet Theater Festival; Sandglass Theater in Vermont, founded by Eric and Ines Zeller Bass; NYC Physical Theatre, founded by Richard Crawford; and Kevin Augustine's Lone Wolf Tribe are some other prominent organizations that have regularly offered puppetry workshops.

In my own continued pursuit of seeing puppetry in the early 2000s, as I was just connecting with all these resources and learning my own way around the puppetry network, I was fortunate to get a small grant from the Professional Staff

Congress of the City University of New York (PSC-CUNY) to travel to the International Puppetry festival in Charleville-Mézières in the Ardennes region of France. The small town of Charleville-Mézières[3] is a kind of mecca for puppetry artists the world over. It is home to the puppetry research center L'Institut Internationale de la Marionnette (the International Institute of Puppetry), as well as to ESNAM (L'Ecole Nationale Superieure des Arts de la Marionette), which is France's national puppetry training school, and is also the base of operations for L'Union Internationale de la Marionette, or UNIMA, the international organization for puppetry. UNIMA, founded in Prague in 1929 with the mission of promoting international understanding through the art of puppetry, is the oldest international arts organization in the world, and now boasts 85 national centers across the globe. Its headquarters moved to Charleville in 1981, a town that had already been hosting an international festival every three years since 1961. In 2011 the festival became a biennial event. Charleville's huge international puppet festival is run with major support from local volunteers, and every inch of the town, inside and out, is given over to (or taken over by) performing objects. This small municipality devotes itself wholeheartedly to puppetry. Each festival kicks off with a large-scale puppet performance in the city's central square, the Place Ducal, followed by ten days packed with puppet events of every kind. The first time I attended, it took me the whole summer of combing through the hefty festival program to organize a schedule that allowed me to see fifty shows in ten days. I spent those days joyfully crossing back and forth over the Meuse River, which divides the city's two centers, as I tracked down the various performance sites in theatres, community centers, town halls, and tents. The fact that most performing object shows run for about an hour was helpful. This general performance time frame also reflects puppetry's ability to express itself in an immediate way through visual means. The Charleville festival introduced me to a host of extraordinary performers I had never heard of, even though many, like puppeteer-dancer Duda Paiva, based in the Netherlands, and Ilka Schönbein of Germany, already had strong reputations in Europe. I came to understand that Europe at the time had a generally more developed understanding and appreciation of puppetry as a sophisticated, adult art than the United States. At the festival book stalls, there were critical journals like *E Pur Si Muove* (*And Yet It Moves*), published by UNIMA in three languages; *Puck; La marionette et les autres arts* (*Puck: Puppetry and Other Arts*) from the International Institute of Puppetry, published annually from 1988 through 2012; and a series of thematic publications from Theema, France's national association of puppetry and associated arts. Like so many other puppetry lovers in Charleville, I knew I had landed in puppet paradise.

At this time, at the prompting of my friend and colleague Kathy Foley, Professor of Theatre at the University of California, Santa Cruz, who is also an accomplished *dalang* (puppeteer) in the Indonesian wooden puppetry form *wayang golek* (wooden rod puppets), I accepted a nomination and was then elected to the Board of UNIMA-USA. I embarrassingly confess that before Kathy Foley nominated me, I knew little to nothing about this organization. I knew Kathy through our shared research interests in Asian theatre and our work for the Association for Asian Performance, and I have always looked to her as a role model. She has and continues to serve, for me and many others, as a generous resource on all things Asian theatre and puppetry, so I had been in touch with her about my growing interest in this field. She must have felt somehow that I would be a good addition to the UNIMA board, either for their benefit or mine. Or maybe it was an act of desperation? Or a leap of faith? Or maybe she understood that it was a way of pulling me further into the heart of the puppetry world, which it did.

At the first board meeting I attended, we went through the, to me, terrifying process of assigning members to various leadership roles or to head different committees. When they asked for nominations for treasurer, I sank down in my chair trying to be invisible. To my surprise, many other board members, who were all puppeteers running their own theatre companies, unafraid of budgets and accounting, raised their hands vying for the job. When the time came to appoint someone to head the publications committee, however, mine was suddenly the only hand up, and I was elected. The board then discussed what projects UNIMA-USA should engage in during the forthcoming year, and someone suggested that it would be great to have a book on American puppeteers and that perhaps the publications committee should get to work on this venture. Being new to the board, not being a puppeteer, and not wanting to be seen as disparaging the history of American puppetry, I was reluctant to reveal that this was not currently at the top of my own research and publication agenda. However, when I later met for lunch with scholar, professor, and puppeteer John Bell, the other member of my committee, I voiced my reluctance to embark on this suggested project, however worthy it might be. We both agreed that what we as scholars both really wanted and needed most at that time was a book that would address the critical questions I and others had been asking about puppetry, one that would bring robust, contemporary scholarly discourse to bear on this art. This book should also bring together the research people were doing in related fields like robotics, dance, animation, etc. It should be the book that didn't exist but was needed for that first graduate puppetry class I had taught back in 2000.

How would we find material for this volume? We decided that perhaps a conference would be the best means of generating papers. John Bell had been active in UNIMA's Research Commission, which had held a series of small conferences, usually somewhere in Europe, and he had already been thinking about the possibility of hosting one at UConn. So, we embarked on creating a puppetry conference there. Dassia N. Posner, who was also teaching at UConn at the time, came on board; Bart Roccoberton, Janie Geiser, Susan Simpson, and UConn puppetry graduate student Nicole LeDuc Graziano (then Nicole Harrington) all collaborated in various capacities. We sent out the call for papers and assumed that, as with the previous research commission meetings, maybe forty-five people in the world would be interested in coming to a scholarly conference on puppets. In the end, however, to our shock and joyful surprise, so many people signed up for the event that we were forced to close down registration when it reached two hundred, as we were at capacity. A snowstorm hit at the beginning of the conference, but people defied the weather, driving, flying, and traipsing through the Connecticut snowdrifts to gather in the UConn theatre buildings. There was an unmistakable buzz of excitement everywhere. There were scholars and puppeteers and puppet scholars and scholar puppets, and everyone was going around expressing with breathless enthusiasm just how excited they were that this event was taking place. Apparently, an interest in critical discussion of puppetry was not just something to entertain a few academics. The world of US puppetry was hungry for this kind of conversation. Puppeteers themselves were frustrated that newspaper reviews of their work by critics unfamiliar with puppetry might only say something like, "The puppets were very beautiful," but wouldn't attempt to understand the work on a deeper level or the thought that went into it. These artists were eager to engage in thoughtful dialogue about their productions and their artistry. The conference demonstrated to us that there was indeed a deep yearning for this exchange and a desire beyond the classroom for the book we wanted to publish. This book became *The Routledge Companion to Puppetry and Material Performance* (2014), a collection of twenty-eight essays, offering, as the cover states, "a wide-ranging perspective on how scholars and artists are currently re-evaluating the theoretical, historical, and theatrical significance of performance that embraces the agency of inanimate objects," which aimed "to advance the study of the puppet not only as a theatrical object but also a vibrant artistic and scholarly discipline." The book, I hope, both drew from and gave back to the puppetry community.

Since I first began asking critical questions about puppetry, about two decades ago, it has been inspiring to see the field of scholarship grow with the publication of new books and forums for scholarly exchange and to find many graduate students and young academics enthusiastically entering the conversation alongside veteran academics. Eileen Blumenthal's *Puppetry: A World History* (Abrams, 2005) was early on a watershed book, scoping out a wide terrain of artistic expressions, historical and contemporary, that could all gather comfortably under an expanded idea of "puppet," with aluring photographs on every page of photographs on every page to manifest the visual vibrancy of the form. Kenneth Gross's *Puppetry: An Essay on Uncanny Life* (University of Chicago Press, 2012), in beautiful poetic prose, elucidates Gross' personal encounters with puppets and puppeteers, showing the powerful effect this art has on individuals while meditating on the form's salient artistic features. Other important publications include *Handspring Puppet Company* (David Krut Publishing, 2009), edited by Jane Taylor, with essays offering an inside view of the history, work, and thoughts of the artists in this important puppet troupe from South Africa. The company is best known popularly for devising and creating the horses that take center stage in the UK National Theatre's international hit *War Horse*. Significantly, some of their most recognized productions, *Woyzek on the Highveld* and *Ubu and the Truth Commission*, were done in collaboration with the brilliant South African artist William Kentridge, whose creative endeavors, expanding across printmaking, animation, and opera and theatre design and directing, as well as other visual and performing arts, echo the wide realm puppetry inhabits today. *Aspects of Puppet*

Theatre, in its reprinted 2014 edition from Macmillan International, has made the critical work of lauded Polish puppetry scholar Henryk Jurkowski more accessible internationally. *Puppetry: A Reader in Theatre Practice* (Macmillan Education UK, 2011) by Penny Francis serves as a useful pedagogical handbook for puppetry courses in higher education, while John Bell's *American Puppet Modernism* (Palgrave, 2008) offers insightful critical and analytical views on performing objects in the United States throughout the twentieth century. This list names just a few prominent books, but the collection continues to grow. I have tried to provide a more comprehensive, though not exhaustive, bibliography at the back of this book to serve as an additional resource. Furthering scholarly work on the subject has been an ongoing project of the American Society for Theatre Research (ASTR) Working Group on Puppetry and Material Performance, which Dassia N. Posner, Alissa Mello, Lawrence Swtizky, Dawn Brandes, and I have co-organized over several iterations, and which, over the years, has included dozens of participants, all producing exciting new scholarship. Recently, we have seen more practicing puppeteers join this academic forum as well. The Puppeteers of America's biennial National Festival now includes the Critical Exchange, an event that John Bell and I co-organized in three editions beginning in 2015. It follows in the footsteps of the UNIMA-USA symposia that had previously been part of the National Festivals but offers more extensive programming. I recall the name, "Critical Exchange," coming to me one day as John and I were shaping the first event, and it aptly characterizes the program's goal of connecting scholarly discourse and the world of puppetry practice, a necessary (critical) dialogue (exchange). The Critical Exchange on each occasion offered a week of morning panels, papers, and conversations about select critical topics in puppetry that address current themes of interest to the art and its practitioners. The program has seen a growth in attendance and enthusiasm from puppeteers at the festival, even while being scheduled against creative workshops. Important scholarly journals like *Critical Stage/Scenes Critiques*, *Journal of the Oriental Society of Australia*, and *Asian Theatre Journal* have all devoted special issues to puppetry. As I write, UNIMA-USA is in the process of masterminding the creation of a new, online, peer-reviewed scholarly journal devoted to puppetry, masks, and related arts, *Puppetry International Research*, for which I will be the editor. Critical discourse on object-oriented ontologies spreading throughout theatre scholarship has helped make puppetry and academic investigations into other roles of objects in performance a thriving area of study generally.

As part of my own continued critical examination of puppetry arts, Alissa Mello, Cariad Astles, and I coedited the anthology *Women and Puppetry: Critical and Historical Investigations* (Routledge, 2019), and Tim Cusack (who assisted on my previous two co-edited collections) and I are coediting the two-volume anthology *Puppet and Spirit: Ritual, Religion and Performing Objects*. I have followed my long-held interests in Asian theatre through research into puppetry in Asia, notably with a focus on ritual puppetry in India, Japan, and Southeast Asia. I have now taught puppetry courses to BA, MA, MFA, and PhD students—often in the same class—at my home institution, Hunter College, and created several performances with students and wonderful puppet designer, Hunter alumna, Bonni Benton, enjoying opportunities to put theory into practice. Throughout my work, I have had the amazing good fortune to connect with puppeteers across the globe, the most generous, kind, and creative people I have ever met. Perhaps devoting oneself to an art that requires the artist to take second place to the material creations they bring to life fosters a giving attitude toward the world. Artists and scholars in puppetry are continually educating me on how to be a kinder and more compassionate person in all my endeavors.

In spite of what appears to me as a lush, flowering world of contemporary puppetry arts and scholarship, people continue to ask me, sometimes with surprise as well as interest, how and why I became involved in this art. And many people I meet and speak to about my interest in puppetry continue to identify puppetry solely with *Sesame Street*. While I am certainly a Muppets fan, puppetry aficionados know that this type of entertainment is only the tip of the iceberg of the craft and creativity that define puppetry. As I sometimes say to my students, you don't need me, someone who has devoted so much of a scholarly career to thinking and writing critically about puppetry, to help you understand or appreciate or even become aware of the Muppets. I hope instead to expand their view. Likewise, for readers of this book. I also find that there are many artists and scholars who, suddenly discovering the world of puppetry and excited by its potential, wonder where to turn next to learn more, to dig more deeply into thinking about this work. This book is for all these people, to bring them, through my own personal critical perspective, to the heart of what I feel animates and defines the vast, creative world of puppetry arts.

What I have done in this book is to try and assemble under a few different topical umbrellas important thoughts, ideas, views, and rules of thumb that have arisen for me over my years of engaging with puppetry and that shape my understanding of the art of performing objects and guide my critical excitement about the work. It is without a doubt a personal, somewhat idiosyncratic perspective. Some of the views I present have sprung up here and there in my other writings but may have appeared in out-of-the-way publications or may not have been put forward as being as essential as I actually believe they are. When a student or artist or colleague comes to the world of puppetry and wants to pick my brain about this form, this is the book I hope to hand them as a way of offering the fruits of my years of thinking, now harvested and gathered in one place.

As I mentioned previously, I am well aware that I am not the only scholar or artist who has done critical thinking about puppetry. I owe a great debt to those who have come before me, and many of the views here have been echoed elsewhere. Certainly, many puppet artists already know intuitively or have discovered things I discuss, which is not surprising as my interest in puppetry has always been led by the creative work that has captivated my thoughts. And my idea of puppetry is very much focused on an extremely broad view of what counts as a performing object, as well as the extensive time I have spent studying Asian puppetry forms. In these pages, I may also intentionally skirt some ideas or subjects that are widespread within puppetry in favor of offering others that I hope might add to or expand thinking on this topic from my own unique vantage point. Puppeteers and scholars may wholly disagree with my observations. But I hope my attempt to articulate these views in a single, somewhat comprehensive place can be of value to those who have long cared for and about this art, as well as to newcomers discovering this intriguing world for the first time.

When I worked as dramaturg on director Stephen Earnhart's multimedia production *Wind-Up Bird Chronicle*, based on Japanese author Haruki Murakami's novel—a show that included puppets alongside human actors and projections—Stephen would periodically call me up, sometimes monthly but occasionally weekly or daily, asking if he could "borrow my brain" as he tried to think through a problem in the show, seeking how to conceptualize what would happen onstage or the way it would come across or how audiences would interpret it. I always said yes. I am more than happy to put my brain and whatever particular skills it may have at the service of those interested in creating exciting art or analyzing it. Consider this book my way of making my brain available to a few more people, for whatever it is worth. I hope you might find borrowing it worthwhile.

Notes

1 In 2020, Asch, who was Producing Director of the festivals, published *Out of the Shadows: The Henson Festivals and Their Impact on Contemporary Puppet Theater* through Inform Press. It offers a full account of these festivals, the artists involved, and their legacies.
2 Full citations and brief descriptions of these texts can be found in the annotated bibliography at the end of the book.
3 The town is actually two small towns, Charleville and Mézières, that merged into one municipality in 1966.

1 A Puppet *Being* and a Puppet *Doing*

Puppets, animated inanimate objects, grab our attention. It is the very fact of seeing inert matter come to life that initially draws us to them, and it is this aspect of puppetry that many who discover a new sense of wonder in the art first strive to articulate. If you have ever witnessed a master puppeteer pick up a lifeless character of any kind—hand puppet, rod puppet, marionette—and watched as a bundle of materials—cloth, wood, string—gradually takes shape into a figure, activated limbs progressively organizing themselves into a coordinated form, a head lifting and turning to look, and, in looking, starting to consider the world, then I imagine you have a visceral understanding of this fascination that puppets can exert. These initial moments of a figure coming into being are most illustrative of something that is constantly at work in the viewer's engagement with the puppet and clarify how one attends to puppetry: spectators persist in watching such objects' ever-renewing coming-into-being, their ongoing striving to maintain the illusion of life, whatever else they do. Basil Jones, co-founder and executive producer of South Africa's Handspring Puppet Company, takes this understanding a step further when he states that the puppet's struggle to maintain its life onstage is the central story of every puppet performance. In contrasting the work of the puppet to that of the actor, he says, "The puppet's work, then—more fundamental than the interpretation of written text or directorial vision—is to strive towards life" (62). He continues, affirming that "the puppet's *Ur*-narrative is something quite different to, and more fundamental than, storytelling. It is the quest for life itself ... this quest ... forms the impulse behind every move and every gesture the puppet makes" (62–63). By "ur-narrative," I believe Jones means the puppet's most primal, original, central story, present with and undergirding every other tale a puppet is enlisted to tell. In other words, the act of becoming animate, being alive, is the story that is always being told or enacted by the puppet within or alongside any other plot of a puppet show.

Why does this act of animating material draw people to it? Pia Banzhaf brings theories of human cognition to bear on the study of performing objects in investigating the whys and hows of the human attraction to puppets. Her studies on the neurological response to performing objects suggest that people do not see the inanimate object as animate but rather that the human mind moves back and

DOI: 10.4324/9781003096627-2

forth between acknowledging these two states of existence—animate and inanimate—and this oscillation excites us. She says,

> The audience becomes captivated because the mind is activated in a highly specific way. In the end, there is no need for precarious "leaps of faith" or the "suspension of disbelief." All we need are neurons lighting the firework of perception, as if by magic. (23–24)

Whether one prefers to relish puppetry's wizardry through Jones's artistic lens or Banzhaf's scientific approach, or take pleasure in contemplating both, the presence of the puppet and watching its repeated affirmation of matter as something that is alive is undoubtedly the starting point for coming to and thinking about puppetry. It is surely what initially first drew many of us to the beloved, familiar puppet figures of childhood. Importantly, however, if we recognize the animation of inanimate matter as the essential interest in and excitement of puppetry—as what lies at its very heart and creates the states of wonder and magic so often associated with it—then we can also understand how this idea moves us beyond the relatively confined world of familiar childhood puppet characters and traditional notions of the puppet to a broader realm in which there can be a multitude of ways all kinds of materials are brought to life and enlisted to perform. This is the more expansive idea of puppetry at stake in this book and that has pervaded the world of puppetry performance in recent times. One overarching goal of mine is to help readers become sensitive to the many ways matter is and can be expressive. This can involve a fundamental shift in thinking, a substantial reorientation of one's perspective on performance and materiality, which I call "thinking like a puppeteer." It involves seeing all the matter that surrounds us as potentially alive and dramatically meaningful. Warning: this transformation of perspective can make the simple act of picking up a cup of coffee or spying cardboard boxes put out for recycling into a complicated experience, a new negotiation with, reappraisal of, or exciting, maybe even troubling, renewed engagement with matter. It can give you what I call, affectionately, "puppet disease," an invigorating "pathology" in which the sufferer sees and at times enacts everything around them as a puppet.

A worldview akin to this is not, in fact, unusual but deeply ingrained in many cultural contexts that understand the world as full of spirit or spirits. Such perspectives, evident in archeological excavations of the earliest civilizations, as well as in more recent historical and contemporary belief systems and practices, may view material elements, especially those in the natural world—trees, rivers, even rocks and mountains—as having their own spiritual, animating energies. They may also, or alternatively, not specifically see matter itself as animate but rather as something providing a place for disembodied beings to alight and thereby manifest within the visible world. The widespread human practice of using crafted figures or objects representative of deities as points of worship embodies this notion and is certainly an important ancestor to puppetry. There are even examples of deliberate animation of venerated figures, in what could be considered puppet-like ways, moving them or making them appear to speak or cry as more forceful exhibitions and physical evidence of the spiritual presence within them. In *Puppetry: A History*, Eileen Blumenthal recounts that in medieval Europe "Crucifixes were rigged so that Jesus could move or bleed, and statues of the Blessed Virgin were made to weep" (4). Victoria Nelson tells us that in ancient Greece, "Statues were filled with sympathetic herbs and plants, then brought to life, at which time they often lit up first, then laughed or smiled or (most important) began prophesying" (36).

By contrast, later Western European models of thinking and philosophical perspectives that culminated in eighteenth-century Enlightenment ideologies stressed the primacy of scientific ways of knowing, setting spirituality in opposition to logic and rational inquiry. In such contexts, inanimate matter is not understood as capable of being alive or enlivened by spirit, but strictly separate and distinct from living things. Moreover, these views have valued human intellectual capacity not only as a way of understanding the natural world but also as a means and rationale for dominating it. Modernity is undergirded by this faith in science over spirituality and embraces material evidence and explanations of phenomena devoid of spiritual views or belief in anything unseen, clearly positioning what is inanimate what is inanimate in opposition to what is not. Sigmund Freud, in the early twentieth century, along with other contemporaries, brought such scientific models to considerations of human psychology. His psychoanalytical perspective identified and categorized views about or fears of inanimate matter becoming animate, and the "uncanny" apprehension of such perceived phenomena, as a return of repressed notions defined as primitive. In "Playing with the Eternal Uncanny: The Persistent Life of Lifeless Objects," John Bell provides an illuminating view into Freud and Ernst Anton Jentsch's theories about the uncanny their relationship to puppetry. In 1991, philosopher Bruno Latour in his book *We Have Never Been Modern* deconstructed such binary divisions within modernity, questioning the dominance of science and especially modernity's conceptualized split between nature and culture. He and others have since set a renewed foundation for a more hybrid, integrated conceptual model that regards human beings and our rational faculties not apart from but as part of and deeply embedded within nature and the natural world. It is a necessary conceptual shift that can help us address current environmental crises, acknowledging our position as both impacting and impacted by the environment.

These various positive or negative views of the notion of animated matter have at various historical periods and in different cultural contexts influenced both perceptions about and the place of puppetry and related forms within their societies. Yet as Freud's and Latour's work suggest, even in modernist settings, preoccupations with and interest in the animation of the inanimate have always been present in one way or another. One might conclude that this is ultimately a very human, if not fundamentally human, tendency.

If we are captivated by inanimate matter appearing to be alive, then how does a puppet, of whatever kind, do this? Express life? A puppet *being*—being alive—is in some sense always a puppet *doing*—doing actions or movements that indicate life. For the puppet, the state of just being alive onstage is not something defined by stasis but is continually enacted through subtle movements and motions. Take, for example, some of the most familiar puppets—Sesame Street characters. These figures, with their large mouths that open and close, tend to do a lot of talking and engage with each other and their human costars in dialogues through which we apprehend their personalities and identify their familiar voices. They seem, in this way, to be on par with actors portraying characters, even if they appear nonhuman—dark blue with googly eyes or orange and hairy. But look closely. While we may recognize their voices, since these cannot come directly from the puppets themselves but only from their human performers, we also, either consciously or subconsciously, identify which character is speaking by noting how each one moves and, more importantly how even when silent these figures always remain slightly in motion, bobbing their heads, shifting, doing small gestures that keep them dynamic and mimic human indicators of life. Human beings, likewise, are rarely so completely still that we make no movements at all. Even when lying fast asleep, our chests rise and fall with our breath. When we watch human actors onstage, the tiny motions of breathing, rustling shoulders, and shifting weight many, understandably, strike us as inconsequential, although good actors make use of all these resources in their art. But we expect the living actor to breathe and move, to remain alive, to do gestures that strike us as human and familiar. In fact, it is generally only when a character dies in a production that we become attentive to breath and small movements, searching for the continual play of these signs of life in the living actor striving to perform as dead. And while a particular actor, director, stage moment, or style of acting many rely on or draw attention to breath and small gestures in performance, the fact that the actor will take a next breath is rarely in doubt. For the puppet, however, somewhere in our minds the question of whether it will continue to stay alive, to resemble something living, is perpetually present; the puppet answers that question anew at each moment, affirming its enacted life through its physical actions.[1]

Basil Jones further emphasizes the important role of breath in keeping the illusion of the puppet's life at play throughout a drama, even in stasis, in what he calls a "breathed stillness" (66). Handspring Puppet Company favors puppets that require several puppeteers to manipulate a single figure, as in the life-sized, cane-framed horses they created for the National Theatre's production of *War Horse* in London. Each horse figure calls for three puppeteers: one standing beside it, working the head, and two inside the horse's frame, one on each set of front and back equine legs. Handspring stresses that these multiple puppeteers working in concert need to breathe together, as well as with the movements of the puppet, to generate a cohesive, living puppet presence. This is a practice now widely adopted in puppetry circles. So not only are the movements that make the puppet appear to breathe and be alive important, but equally essential is the breath of the puppeteers linked to each other and to the puppet's actions. Even in the case of a figure manipulated by a single puppeteer, the link of breath between object and performer is central to the sense of presence and life of the puppet. Just as breath is the source of human life, the illusion of breath through movement, connected to the real breath of the performer, is the initial source of the illusion and maintenance of puppet life.

Jones's emphasis on the puppet's breath in stillness is part of his larger understanding of puppetry's means of storytelling. He writes that, if a puppet is still and perceived as breathing through small movements, "the audience is able to read its thoughts" (66). In the absence of further actions, we see the still, breathing puppet as a living creature and begin to project onto it an internal life, providing an added dimension to its existence. When the puppet then moves from stillness into motion, we connect its physical actions with the projected internal life and thoughts, rounding out the sense of a living, engaged, intentional presence. In doing this, we are also instinctively crafting narratives that make sense of these elements as we bring them together.

Human beings are, in general, habitual story makers, seeing or devising relationships between events, reading intention and consequence into sequential, adjacent, or juxtaposed actions. In *Understanding Comics: The Invisible Art*, Scott McCloud shows how comics also draw on this human tendency. The images in comics set out one next to another invite readers to fill in the actions that take place in the gutters between the pictures and understand the visuals as part of a continuous progression. He traces models of sequential image storytelling as far back as the wall paintings on tombs from ancient Egypt. Human beings are, overall, good at making links between sequential elements, creating rational connections, and, in this process, forming stories. In comics, the distinct components are static images. In puppetry, an art that takes place in time, they are the stage events that happen from moment to moment and include everything set out and enacted before and around the spectator through the course of the show. Puppetry invites us to participate actively in creating, reading, and apprehending the emotions of characters and the narratives of their actions. It does so through many means that do not rely primarily on language and dialogue.

The act of pulling adjacent actions or images together to find the links between them is not only something done in the creation of a puppet's narrative but also is contained intrinsically within the concept of the puppet. As Jan Mrázek points out, puppetry is necessarily an art of montage (27). Spectators, as we have seen, maintain a sustained belief in the object's life through its various movements from one instance to the next. For speaking puppets, we bring voice and object together to create the sense of a cohesive, living whole. Some characters and productions lean into the montage aspect of puppetry, using it as an opportunity for additional creativity and, in so doing, mine a rich field of possibility. In the Off-Broadway show *The Woodsman* (2012), directed by James Ortiz and Claire Karpen (Figure 1.1), with music by Edward W. Hardy, lyrics by Jennifer Loring, and book and puppet design by Ortiz, the puppet figures include an enormous beast with the head of a tiger and the body of a bear built as three distinct parts: a head, a set of front legs, and a set of hind legs with a tail. Each piece is carried and manipulated independently by a different performer; all three puppeteers move in unison with their part of the figure to create the illusion of a unified animal. Spectators clearly see the three different performers visibly at

24 A *Puppet* Being *and a Puppet* Doing

Figure 1.1 The Woodsman, Off Broadway. The beast, with the head of a tiger and the body of a bear, built in several parts, performed by different puppeteers working together to create a whole figure. Directed by James Ortiz and Claire Karpen.
Photo: Michael Kushner.

work within the beast. The puppeteer in front holds the tiger-like head out ahead of her, standing in full view of the audience and in front of the creature's middle part. Rather than feeling horrified at this chopped-up animal figure, spectators become engaged in doing the work of bringing the pieces together in their minds to watch both the full creature in motion and, simultaneously, the actions of the performing artists who are creating the illusion of a single, living animal. This effort also allows audiences to appreciate the art of the puppeteer and the puppet designer. Viewers actively work to see the illusion. This direct involvement in the act of creation offers extra excitement in watching the show.

The Woodsman draws on this process in other ways as well. Its story, drawn from Frank L. Baum's Oz books, is about the woodsman Nick Chopper whose axe, cursed by the Wicked Witch of the East, gradually cuts his limbs off one by one. With each dismemberment, he substitutes his missing human part with a metal replacement, until he becomes a man made entirely of tin—the Tin Man, familiar from *The Wizard of Oz* film. Throughout the production, audiences see the human actor progressively transform into a full puppet, with an increasing number of prosthetic puppet limbs, until he is replaced by an entirely crafted figure. The audience is asked to piece together the material elements that progressively work with the human actor and the human form and see all of it as one slowly transforming character. The indulgence in montage here is not just an act of inventiveness or mere practicality but an expression of the show's central theme. It becomes a deeply interpretive element as, within the plot, Nick Chopper's human heart and soul remain somehow alive within his increasingly inorganic, material being. Some of the most powerful puppetry happens in situations like this, one when the material nature and presence of puppets thoughtfully intersects or interconnects with or concretely illustrates or communicates a story's themes and narrative, allowing puppets to tell their tales through the very materiality of their beings. In these cases, the puppet's *being* and the show's larger *doings* are united. In *The Woodsman*, the Tin Man puppet's "ur-narrative," its "quest for life itself," lines up directly with the larger story of the character's struggle to stay both alive and soulfully human while his organic parts are gradually replaced with tin.

The mixing of human performers with crafted materials in unusual ways births compelling, imaginative puppet figures from the intrinsic montage character of puppetry. For example, the type of puppet called a "humanette" uses the puppeteer's own head placed above a crafted body to create a full figure. Disney's production of *The Lion King* (1997) on Broadway, directed by Julie Taymor, incarnates giraffes through performers walking on stilts with both their hands and their feet to form the animals' four long legs while wearing long-necked mask headdresses on their heads; the performers' own torsos fill in the rest of the animal in between. Peruvian puppeteers Hugo Suárez and Inés Pasic, known by their company name Hugo y Inés, specialize in playing with the unusual, yet simple, ways their bodies interconnect with material elements. In one iconic piece, Hugo pulls a button-down shirt over the bottom part of his leg and places a red clown nose on a string around his bent knee. Putting his arms through the shirt sleeves, he instantly creates a character, with his knee serving as the head and his hands working as the character's own hands. In a similar vein, the Italian company Teatro Dei Piedi specializes in puppetry that enlists the bottom of the puppeteer's foot, with crafted nose and eyes attached, as their puppets' heads: the puppeteers' own hands standing in for those of the character. Teatro Dei Piedi puppeteers Laura Kibel and Veronica Gonzalez lie on their backs, feet up in the air, to achieve these illusionistic, contortionist puppet feats.

It may be taking you a moment to visualize each of these examples, which are also difficult to describe clearly, as they each upend common expectations of how human bodies and objects appear, intertwining them in novel ways. If, as Banzhaf tells us, the animation of a traditional inanimate puppet figure makes our neurons fire excitedly as our brains oscillate back and forth between the views of animate and inanimate, how much more energetic this brain activity must be in witnessing these more complex interminglings of living and nonliving materials uniting to incarnate unified, animated beings. We don't require a scientific investigation to instinctively appreciate the fun and complexities at work in these acts.

Scholar Margaret Williams provocatively asks whether all the different kinds of creations and their enactments that count as puppetry today, many using only objects and no figurative characters at all, constitute "a mode of spectatorship rather than any specific theatrical form, that identifies puppetry and links those unspecified related arts to 'the puppet'" (27). In other words, is it necessary to have a specific figurative character, a character that looks like a person or animal, called a puppet at the center of what we call puppetry? Or is puppetry, rather, an art that invites us *to watch* in a way that sees life and additionally character and maybe anthropomorphic (or perhaps zoomorphic in the case of animal characters) actions and incarnations in material or human and material combinations? Even abstract forms in motion are part of puppetry.

The work we are invited to do as puppet spectators—of seeing the inanimate as living, of bringing disparate elements together to perceive a unified creature—is at the heart of puppetry and its unique pleasures. Puppeteers play with the art form in devising new ways to engage us in active watching, summoning us to participate in the very act of creation during performance. Audiences take the indicators they see, the montage of elements—respond to them, and do the work of filling in what's absent, in the process apprehending complete characters and their rich stories. Puppetry continually calls on these human proclivities and asks audiences to be active as they watch.

Basil Jones again takes us a step further into thinking about how a puppet's being is linked to its doings, its storytelling. He says that the thoughts we read into the puppet in stillness, "an unwritable text, one that is 'authored' by the puppeteer manipulating the puppet and, to some extent, by the designer/maker who engineers such subtleties into the puppet's mechanism" (66). In other words, the story of the puppet is not primarily written out in dialogue by a playwright, but first in the materiality of the character, how it is designed and built, which will circumscribe what it is able to do and then how a puppeteer can put the figure into action. A puppet's size, shape, and any jointed or flexible parts it may have and how these move all contribute to our view of a character and the kind of performance journey it can enact. A moveable jaw will allow a puppet to speak, and joints establish what parts of the puppet's body can bend. These features and others can all have implications for character and storyline. For example, Kyounghye Kwon analyzes the difference between two female characters in a traditional Korean rod puppet play as performed by the Seoul Namsadang company. In this traditional folk puppet show, a husband takes a second, younger wife, angering his first wife. The first wife's jointed jaw with string mechanism allows her to speak her mind and scold her husband. The mouth of the younger woman, by contrast, only painted on, leaves her a silent, disempowered figure in this marital drama (54–55). A puppet's design informs our *reading* of a character's personality as well as its possible story.

The casting of characters that takes place in design involves not just *how* a puppet is built but the very materials used to make it. Cloth, wood, metal, rock, paper, cardboard, plastic—puppets can be made out of any of these, indeed any material at all. Each choice of material has both practical and associative implications. Practically, each will move differently and need to be dealt with in its own particular way, both in the building process and in performance. Paper can tear easily while metal is strong and durable. These facts about materials also help articulate aspects of character. What does it mean for a character to be made of paper? Does that mean they are flimsy and insubstantial? Easily torn? How is such a figure different from one made of metal? Or plastic? Or cloth?

Each possible material also brings up certain kinds of responses from spectators, based on its tactile qualities and the webs of association connected to it. Wood can feel warm, handcrafted, and organic in contrast to plastic and its connection to the world of commercially produced products. Paulette Richards describes how Tarish "Jeghetto" Pipkins thoughtfully employs fabric in his performance of *A Conversation with Frederick Douglass*, noting the old denim jeans used for the character's hair:

> Denim took its name from Nîmes, a French port that was heavily invested in the slave trade. The sturdy fabric woven from cotton cultivated by slave labor served to make sails for ships that plied the triangular trade routes. Dyed with indigo produced by enslaved laborers in the Carolinas and the Caribbean, blue denim jeans became the quintessential uniform of the American workingman. The Douglass puppet's hair therefore signifies on how integrally the legacy of slavery is woven into American identity—everything you own, owns you. (31)

Choice of material can go a long way in already describing a puppet character and its story. A paper might invite a puppet to become torn or written on during the drama, a natural, associative extension of its materiality that describes a journey. In *The Adventures of Charcoal Boy* (2006), created by Sarah Provost, Eric Novak, and Elyas Khan (Figure 1.2), the main character is a tree branch that has been broken off its mother limb by a lightning strike. It searches for a way to belong until it discovers its ability to use its burnt charcoal ends to draw. The puppet, built generally to echo a human figure, was crafted from an actual found tree branch with charcoal drawing sticks inserted in its feet. At a point a long roll of white paper unfurled on the tabletop stage allows the figure to glide across it, drawing beautiful swirls. The material fact of burnt wood transforming into charcoal becomes the basis for a crafted figure and its tale.

There is no obligatory material for a puppet; there is instead the choice of every and any material depending on what one wants to create and express. The choice, therefore, with all its possibilities and implications, is an essential part of crafting the object, its expressive meaning, and its story. The choice of puppet construction material is an important way a puppet character and its tale's meaning can manifest. Building a puppet is, therefore, part of crafting its drama and can be rich with numerous interpretive implications.

Many puppeteers, instead of building new puppets, avail themselves of the objects already proliferating around us, adopting them as the stars of their shows. Such objects are already rife with the stories, connections, uses, and associations we have with them from daily life, which puppeteers can draw on. Paul Zaloom appropriates discarded, commercial objects from American consumer culture as characters in his satirical shows that comment on social and political issues. An Ivory Liquid Soap bottle, with its feminine curved form, plays a schoolteacher while also exuding ideas of whiteness and purity in a scene about American education; a bucketful of old paint brushes of different sizes and shapes, their worn hairs splaying out in various directions, play beleaguered, edgy, downtown artists in a piece about

Figure 1.2 Charcoal Boy. A close-up of Charcoal Boy showing the real tree branch from which he was crafted. Sarah Provost – creator/writer/director; Eric Novak – creator/writer/puppet and set designer; Elyas Khan – creator/writer/composer.

Photo: Jordan Provost.

political attacks against the National Endowment for the Arts.[2] These objects serve as characters while visually presenting comic, social critiques.

Puppeteers then offer a next level of character development and storytelling in the ways they play with and within a figure's range of movement to express further personality traits and storytelling. This is the area attended to by the many books and workshops on puppet manipulation. Each kind of puppet and even each individual figure, with its own crafting and unique personality, requires its own means of being put into action. The puppeteer experiments with a figure's movements, seeing how the tilt of a head or the shake of a limb will read to spectators. Does this figure require large sweeping gestures or smaller, incremental ones? What is the particular rhythm for this character in its walking and breathing? Even a mature, skilled, professional puppeteer will take time working with a new puppet to discover how it wants to move and what kind of work the puppeteer should put in to bring out those movements for different expressive intentions. Mervyn Millar's *Puppetry: How to Do It*, (Nick Hearn Books, 2018) is a wonderful introduction and guide to the practical work of paying attention to and discovering an object's unique way of expressing itself. His process leads the artist from the initial discovery of an object's material qualities to engaging it in small, fundamental actions: waking, rising, sitting, looking. His puppeteers also explore an object's range of emotions, investigating how it might express joy, sadness, or fear, before building all of these into simple puppet scenarios.

All the while, in performing a puppet's actions and emotions, the puppeteer is attending to the primary story: that of keeping the puppet alive. Jones tells us that what he calls a puppet's "micromovements"—actions of daily life that become captivating precisely because of the puppet's struggle to be alive, such as "reaching for a cup just beyond one's grasp"—turn into "micro-dramas"; these, he says, "trump the macro-action onstage" (63). They grab the attention of spectators and draw in their empathetic responses. Small movements of a puppet's doings become the focus of the stories at hand, as they center on the puppet's continued quest for life.

But what of the larger "macro" stories a puppet show is trying to tell? Jones concludes his essay by stating that, because the true dramas that happen for the puppet are in the continued action of striving to seem alive, the work of the puppeteer—creating a story through movement—can be at odds with that of the traditional playwright, who primarily uses language and dialogue as their means of expression. In puppetry "meaning is created more by process than by content, more by movement than by words" (67). If that is the case, what kind of processes and what kinds of movements create the *larger* performance stories on the puppet stage?

Thinking about this question puts us on the precipice of a vast terrain of questions regarding how to create compelling puppet performances. While puppets are crafted objects in distinct materials with particular possibilities for movement that are expressive and whose continuous action of becoming animated is their primary story, they are also enlisted into storytelling beyond the fact of performing their liveness, looking beautiful or enticing, or displaying their materiality and mechanisms. Their small doings somehow add up to larger doings that are the plots or emotional journeys of performance. For puppetry, these stories may not end up in the purview of traditional playwrights. Still, how do the micro-dramas of animated matter add up to macro-dramas that don't just capture our attention but move forward, develop, and come to an ending in ways that are unique to or uniquely suited to what animated matter can best express? How can all the elements of a performance with animated matter as their center express meaning, progression, and/or an emotional journey that is appropriate to the world of puppetry? How do micro-actions accumulate to support, rather than trump, macro-actions? What kinds of stories can material performance tell and how?

While our fascination with the magic of puppetry's ability to bring the inanimate to life remains the essential pivot point on which all other aspects of puppetry hinge and is the essential beginning point for thinking about puppetry, discussion and analysis of puppetry need not end there. The attraction of the animated object is so strong that thinking about puppetry can sometimes stall at this idea. This experience, however, is just the beginning of analysis. We may start with this idea but also need to consider all the other aspects of thinking through the puppet to get a comprehensive view of the art and how stories are told and meaning created on the puppet stage.

For the duration of your reading here, sweep away any reflexive associations of the idea of "puppet" with cute childhood characters and give yourself over to further investigations into how attraction to animated matter becomes the heart of performative storytelling and meaningful expression. While a puppet being is always a puppet doing, let's investigate how this evolves into the larger doings of puppets that can become powerful, dramatic productions.

Notes

1 Those who are critically inclined might profitably compare this view of the enactment of life in puppets to feminist critic Judith Butler's influential views on the performance of gender. Butler argues that cultural expression of male and female gender (as opposed to biological sex) is not something natural or innate but rather affirmed through continual performance of the markers of gender, those ways of being, the learned enactments of gendered behavior associated with masculinity or femininity. They say gender "… is an identity tenuously constituted in time—an identity instituted through *a stylized repetition of acts* … gender … must be understood as the mundane way in which bodily gestures, movements, and enactments of various kinds constitute the illusion of an abiding gendered self" (519). Similarly, the puppet's bodily gestures, movements, and enactments constitute the illusion of an abiding living creature.
2 This piece responded to the 1990 controversy over the "NEA Four," artists Karen Finley, John Fleck, Holly Hughes, and Tim Miller, whose NEA proposals were vetoed by NEA Chairman John Frohnmayer, an appointee of former president Ronald Reagan, for controversial controversial subject matter, although the proposals had been approved by peer reviewers. The politically charged case went to the Supreme Court and led to changes in the NEA.

Works Cited

Banzhaf, Pia. "The Ontology of the Puppet." *Dolls and Puppets: Contemporaneity and Tradition*, edited by Kamil Kopania, The Alexander Zelwerowicz National Academy of Dramatic Art, 2018, pp. 8–27.

Bell, John. "Playing with the Eternal Uncanny: The Persistent Life of Lifeless Objects." *The Routledge Companion to Puppetry and Material Performance*, edited by Dassia N. Posner, Claudia Orenstein, and John Bell, Routledge, 2014, pp. 43–52.

Blumenthal, Eileen. *Puppetry: A World History*. Harry N. Abrams, 2005.

Butler, Judith. "Performative Acts and Gender Constitution: An Essay in Phenomenology and Feminist Theory." *Theatre Journal*, vol. 40, no. 4, 1988, pp. 519–531.

Jones, Basil. "Puppetry: Authorship and the *Ur*-Narrative." *The Routledge Companion to Puppetry and Material Performance*, edited by Dassia N. Posner, Claudia Orenstein, and John Bell, Routledge, 2014, pp. 61–68.

Kwon, Kyounghye. "Women, Marriage, and Femininities: 'KKokdu Gaksi Geori' (or the Love Triangle) in the Korean Traditional Puppet Play." *Women and Puppetry: Critical and Historical Investigations*, edited by Alissa Mello, Claudia Orenstein, and Cariad Astles, Routledge, 2019, pp. 50–65.

McCloud, Scott. *Understanding Comics: The Invisible Art*. Harper Perennial, 1993.

Millar, Mervyn. *Puppetry: How to Do It*. Nick Hern Books, 2018.

Mrázek, Jan. *Phenomenology of a Puppet Theatre: Contemplations on the Art of Javanese Wayang Kulit*. KITLV, 2005.

Nelson, Victoria. *The Secret Life of Puppets*. Harvard University Press, 2001.

Richards, Paulette. "Living Objects: How Contemporary African American Puppet Artists "Figure" Race." *Theatre Symposium*, vol. 29, 2022, pp. 16–34.

Williams, Margaret. "The Death of 'The Puppet.'" *The Routledge Companion to Puppetry and Material Performance*, edited by Dassia N. Posner, Claudia Orenstein, and John Bell, Routledge, 2014, pp. 18–29.

2 The Dramaturgy is in the Object

In January 2012, I was in the south of India leading an Education Abroad program on Indian performance for Hunter College with a colleague. On one excursion with the students, we made a brief stop at a crafts fair set up in an open field. One of the booths had some beautiful Rajasthani string puppets hanging in it, along with other wooden items. But what ended up captivating me most at this stall were not the puppets but a group of cabinet-like painted boxes set up on a table. While the bold colors and intricately designed figures decorating these objects caught my eye, what truly excited me about them was the way they opened … no … unfolded. On the front of each were two door-like panels that could be parted to each side, like French doors, revealing another painted image behind. This illustration was itself on a panel hinged to a series of others folded in behind it. These could all be unfurled, to one side of the box, in an extended series, revealing stretches of painted images, like comic frames, across the length of the wood. Tucked behind this was yet another similar group of folded panels that could also be pulled out and unfolded toward the opposite side. When both sets of panels were fully displayed, flanking the box, one more set of painted doors appeared at the back. Parting these, the viewer beheld either two or three carved, three-dimensional figures set inside a *niche*. The figures in some of the boxes were the Hindu hero-deities from the Ramayana epic: Rama, his wife Sita, and his brother Lakshmana; or in others, Krishna and his consort, Radha. Opening and reopening these unusual boxes, I knew that what I had before me was a performing object, that is, an object used in a performance or presentation of some kind. These cabinets had action and drama crafted into them. The Rajasthani string puppets, beautiful as they were, were familiar to me. They have become emblematic of Indian puppetry, even while India is home to of puppetry forms of every kind—shadow, rod, string—as well as to many scroll and object storytelling traditions. Rajasthani string puppets are usually the first thing people imagine when they hear "Indian puppetry," and they are part of a beautiful performance tradition. Nazir Ali Jairazbhoy's *Kaṭhputli: The World of Rajasthani Puppeteers* (Rainbow Publishers, 2007) is a wonderful book for learning about this form. The cabinet boxes, on the other hand, were completely unfamiliar to me; yet they cried out that they too were part of India's rich performing object heritage.

DOI: 10.4324/9781003096627-3

The Dramaturgy is in the Object 33

Figure 2.1 Carpenter Dwarka Prasad Jangid opening his traditional *kaavad* box. Bassi, Rajasthan, India, 2013.

Photo: Claudia Orenstein.

I later discovered that these boxes, called *kaavad*, are also from Rajasthan (Figure 2.1), and built primarily by wood craftsmen in the small town of Bassi for traveling storytellers, *kaavadiya bhats* or *ravs*, who take them into Rajasthan's desert regions as a form of traveling altar or temple. As described by Nina Sabnani, an expert on the tradition, the process of opening the *kaavad* mimics the experience of moving into and through a Hindu temple to eventually be surrounded by images of the gods (82).[1] Seated on the ground, a *kaavad* on his lap, the *kaavadiya bhat* points with a peacock feather to the different characters depicted on the box panels—deities from the Hindu epics, such as Krishna, or local saints like Meera Bai—as he recites the figures' tales and exploits illustrated in the painted images. These storytellers also serve as genealogists for the people of this region, keeping track of births and deaths in their patron families as they make their annual rounds and connect family histories to the boxes' mythic characters. A small drawer at the bottom of the *kaavad* is where patrons put money, both as offerings to the gods sculpted at the back of the box and as payment to the storyteller for his religious teachings. If a patron is too parsimonious one year, he might find himself painted upside down in the imagery the following year as a not-so-subtle coercion to increased generosity.

What captivated me about these *kaavad* boxes is something that is not really or at least not centrally part of the original tradition but something that I believe holds thoughtful ideas for contemporary puppet practitioners. While the *kaavadiya bhats* tell their stories by pointing to the pictures, and the box may have evolved as a convenient means for carrying these altar surrogates and a large number of story images out into the far desert regions, the box itself I feel has dramaturgy built into it. By *dramaturgy*, I mean a dramatic structure that takes a spectator through an emotional journey. The ancient Greek philosopher Aristotle, whose *Poetics* is the oldest and primary text on play analysis in the Western European theatre tradition, on play analysis, famously said that a good tragedy should have a beginning, a middle, and an end. This seems like a basic, straightforward idea, barely worth mentioning, but questions about how we start, develop, and end stories, especially in performance, are complicated ones that playwrights, scholars, and puppeteers spend a lifetime exploring. These, what I am going to call "dramaturgical moments" (beginning, development, end), and others—plot twists, rising action, climax, red herring—can be built into an object. Or I might say, more forcefully, if the center of a puppetry performance is our focus on the action of objects and materials onstage, then an interesting puppet show can take advantage of this by having the dramaturgical structure come from the material itself, revealed in and through materiality.

As we explored in the previous chapter, the animated object captures our attention and is the heart of puppetry. Puppetry scholars have, understandably, theorized a good deal about how animated objects engage us, often with a focus on how puppets differ from human actors. But beyond just captivating us, how do and can objects express and take us through a story? What can we discover when we shift our focus from puppet actor and character to plot and storyline, while keeping the important understanding of animated matter within puppetry in mind? When we use a puppet, we don't just replace a human actor with an object; we shift from one art, one aesthetic sphere, to another. Because of its use of objects and material, puppetry directs the audience's attention to things differently from the human-actor theatre. A marionette walking can seem like an astonishing bit of magic whereas a human actor doing the same action is generally unremarkable. Bringing animated matter to life in a puppet performance constructs a world where theoretically, and sometimes actually, any material on stage might come to life, even the stage itself. Puppetry changes our experience and expectations of the performance world, and so it changes what and how we watch. It is only natural then that if we are watching puppets or objects express a story, how that story happens and the important elements within that story will take a different form than in the human-actor theatre. Seeing puppet theatre is not just a matter of watching captivating objects instead of human beings but rather of watching animated objects unfold some kind of emotional journey. How do they do that? We need to take the object or puppet into account and, beyond talking about it and its manipulation as arts in themselves, look at how those objects in and of themselves, connecting with other objects and humans, accompanied by language or music, express meaning over the course of a performance.

I would like to say a few words here about the terms "dramaturgy" and "dramaturgical." I have been warned by colleagues that some people, even (or maybe mostly) theatre people, hate these words or find them daunting or incomprehensible. I, however, find them useful, at least in this context. This book is, in fact, investigating a dramaturgical approach to puppetry. Understanding dramaturgy can be as essential to puppeteers as learning to build and operate puppets. Contemporary puppeteers are habitually called on to create their own shows and, therefore, act as authors, as well as builders and performers. We have already seen how Basil Jones links the puppeteer's performance with the idea of authorship of a puppet performance text and shows how it can "trump" the work of a playwright. Many puppeteers are already in the position of creating and crafting stories by working with and through their puppets. Nonetheless, we can ask: if the traditional notion of a text by a playwright does not adequately support puppetry, what kinds of structures do? There are many more books, workshops, and classes on building puppets and performing them than on constructing what I'll call here "stories," for lack of a better word, for puppetry. "Story" falls short because I don't mean to imply only a traditional, linear narrative structure but rather some kind of meaningful, shaped sequence of performed events that hang together, taking the audience through a variegated emotional experience. A more widespread, common, traditional notion of story, however, can be a helpful reference point for this discussion. As creating puppet stories is one of the primary tasks of contemporary artists making new work, embracing an exploration of dramaturgy can be very helpful.

While the term dramaturgy has multiple uses and implications, for me the term here refers primarily to two important things: 1) How the elements of a stage performance create meaning and 2) The structures that help shape the expression of this meaning. I am tempted to write "dramatic structures," and I do think I am talking about dramatic structure to some extent, but that doesn't mean to confine this topic to how structure is conceived within traditional models of dramatic theatre. I am referring more broadly to all the performative elements that can make something into a compelling performance. I am also tempted to use the term "storytelling," but again, I do so allowing the term to swing free from strictly linear, literary, or narrative-based models. In its structure and means of meaning-building, puppetry can follow models drawn from many artistic forms—music, dance, poetry—and need not be confined to traditional theatrical forms. It is precisely my intent to emphasize here that objects can express stories in their own way. Yet I think all these terms drawn from traditional theatre studies can still be helpful in pointing to and pulling apart different aspects of a puppet performance. As I tell students in my play analysis and puppetry classes, these ideas provide "tools not rules" for analysis. A tool can help you dig into something, take it apart, or see what it's made of. It can also be like a cookie cutter that allows you to place it on something to determine what fits the shape of the cutter and what falls away. What doesn't fit can tell you as much about your dough or cookie as what does fit. My thinking is, of course, formed by my theatre training. But I do believe these theatre-derived terms can serve as a good starting point for this discussion and can be particularly helpful to people coming from a theatre background who are discovering an interest in puppetry. I invite people well-versed in other art forms to extend this conversation and extrapolate on other models. What I can do here is lend my own background and knowledge of theatre to the dissection of puppetry and show some important approaches useful for analyzing (or constructing) a performing art with objects at its center.

So, dramaturgy it is. Or "puppeturgy" if you prefer. No need to go running for the doors. These words can become your friends.

The experience of a performance is primarily an emotional journey through time. In creating a show, artists shape this journey through what they put onstage or into the event; this includes not only the actions of people or objects but also sounds or music, interactions with the audience, etc., basically anything that happens during the time span of the artwork. Of course, other elements outside the work proper, such as posters, marketing, venue, etc., can also affect the performance experience, as can the audience's own background or expectations of the work. But let us stick first with what artists are crafting as part of a show when they build it, whether it be theatre or puppetry or any other form of performance. Dramaturgy for me here is a term that points to the question of how elements in a performance are creating events that are cumulatively adding up to a performance experience.

For a performance to be an emotional *journey*, there need to be shifts in the quality and tenor of different events so that the work is not all of a single piece. Just as actors would be boring if they acted one passion or sentiment for a whole play, a show of any kind is a strain if it remains at the same affective pitch throughout. The shape of those shifts is the structure, or the dramatic structure, which here signifies that there is a compelling nature and a sense of purpose to the form. I am going to add the term "dramaturgical moment" to define the markers where emotional tenors shift. These can also be moments in which a world or set of possibilities open up or close down, helping to give shape to where the journey is headed. To give a classic example from theatre, in the ancient Greek play *Oedipus Rex* by Sophocles, the title character left his home in Corinth many years before the play begins to escape a prophecy that he would kill his own father and marry his own mother. During the play, as Oedipus searches for the killer of Laius, the previous king of the city Oedipus now rules, a messenger arrives and tells Oedipus that the man he believed to be his father in Corinth has died. Since Oedipus was nowhere near Corinth, at that moment he breathes a sigh of relief that he has escaped the awful prophecy. That is, until the Messenger, seeing Oedipus' reaction, reveals that he never had any reason for concern since the man he knew as his father in Corinth was not his biological father. With this disclosure, a whole new world of questions and possibilities opens up, some of them awful, such as the worry that the prophecy might still come true. Oedipus is also transformed at this moment from someone who thought he knew all about himself and was confident in his ability to make wise choices to someone whose very fundamental understanding of who he is and the life he has led are put in question. This is a dramaturgical moment that shifts the tenor of events and moves us to another point in the story, or progression of the experience.

Here dramaturgical moments that shift the emotional experience and help move events forward toward their conclusion form a plot. In human-actor versions of this play, this moment of revelation constitutes a psychological upheaval for the main character, who sees that his life is completely different from what he had previously believed and on which he had staked his whole identity. Although there have certainly been wonderful puppet versions of *Oedipus*, puppetry is a different beast from theater, and its way of storytelling doesn't necessarily need to be oriented primarily toward these human, psychological constructs. How can an understanding of something like this psychological shift work in puppetry, in a way that is central to the objects onstage or expresses the shift through materiality? How is new information brought into a story within puppetry? How are new worlds disclosed? What would it mean for a new world to be revealed? For events to move forward? We don't have to be attached to plays, actors, or traditional narrative storytelling models to ask these questions and investigate how performing objects can answer them. What constitutes a dramaturgical or "puppeturgical" moment in puppetry?

The *kaavad*, if I may borrow this object to speak about something not specifically intrinsic to its own tradition, is an excellent object for illustrating the idea that *dramaturgy can be in an object*. Whether the original tradition is interested in this idea or not, the object itself reveals a dramatic structure and can instruct us about or sensitize us to how material can do this. The *kaavad* box provides its own beginning as it starts fully closed, with all the panels—stories, storylines, plots and subplots, etc.—folded away inside it. The object contains all its tales and reveals them piece by piece, in time, as the reciter unfolds it. The fact that the full extent of the story possibilities is already contained inside the box from the very beginning is dramaturgically satisfying, in the sense that the trajectory of what the object has to offer—its own material dramatic tale—doesn't seem haphazard but pre-crafted; the end is contained in the beginning.

The first two doors that open strike one as a visual introduction. It is a small beginning. As the panels unfold further and further, we see and experience, physically, sensorially, phenomenologically, the development of the object's tale. The object manifestly grows and expands as its storytelling progresses. The final set of doors heralds the conclusion, which is ultimately realized in the vision of the carved, three-dimensional gods situated behind them, at the very inner depths of the object. The conclusion here literally and figuratively takes us to a new dimension, replacing painted two-dimensional images with three-dimensional carved figures. In so doing, it seems to physicalize a kind of epiphany, a final revelation with such a sense of change and impact that it is difficult to imagine where else we could go from here. The vision of the carved gods offers a sense of completion. The cabinet, splayed open, panels unfurled wide on either side, has offered up all its contents, all it has to express. Its tale is fully told, something that we can visibly and physically apprehend. Again, I stress that I am not referring necessarily to how these boxes are actually used in their tradition nor to the storylines of the tales that are painted on the panels, but to how the physicality of the object itself expresses a dramatic structure that takes the viewer through an emotional journey.

While the *kaavad* traditionally encases Hindu tales, today's *kaavad* artists have adapted it to a variety of different stories, mostly to cater to tourists who buy them as souvenirs. Their original use in educating about religious stories has also expanded to teaching about other subjects like ABCs or ecological concerns. A *kaavad* of the story of Jesus Christ that carver Dwarka Prasad Jangid made shows the events of the story of Christ's Passion on its panels and eventually opens to a final image of Christ crucified as its conclusion. The backside of this box is also cleverly painted with the image of Christ on the cross as seen from the back, with the other crucified sinners to each side, as if we are just witnessing what is painted inside the box from behind. In all these choices of where to put what image, the artist is exploiting the physicality of the box's structure to support the dramatic trajectory of the Christian storyline. Here, the painting on the back serves almost as a coda to the tale, one small added note underlining the final event. In truth, it offers two concluding images, with an additional scene of Christ taken down from the cross, surrounded by his followers, below the backside vision of the crucifixion.

If when you think of "puppet," you only imagine a marionette or a Muppet, then the observations I have made here about the dramaturgical structure of the *kaavad* box might strike you as maybe bizarre or irrelevant. What they point out, however, which I think is useful within a broad understanding of puppetry, is how objects and materiality can have their own emotional trajectories constructed into them, and we can experience these physically. If, as we looked at in the previous chapter, what makes puppetry a particularly interesting and intriguing art is the fact of seeing inanimate material brought to life, then when we watch puppetry, our focus is necessarily directed toward the inanimate material onstage. It is here, in the material, where the action and the drama take place. Simply using puppets as characters to replace human actors does not fully take advantage of what bringing puppets or material performers onstage has to offer. As already noted, our interest in a crafted character is very different from our interest in a human performer; almost the opposite. We look for signs of humanness in the puppet that are taken for granted in the human actor. Edward Gordon Craig even proposed that the actor's humanness was obstructive to artistic storytelling, not allowing human performers to express theatrical tales in their purest, unadulterated forms. He felt actors brought too much of their own personal emotions to the stage. So, if the center of the puppet performance is the material onstage, it is here where the power of the drama can be expressed most forcefully, where the story can be told. By understanding how materiality can express dramaturgical structure, a puppeteer can use puppets not just to reveal character but to relay story. Developing a strong grasp of dramatic structure or of the kind of creation and expression of dramatic structure that exploits the possibilities offered by and the power inherent in objects and materials can be as important to the construction of performance as learning to build beautiful, functional puppets.

The *kaavad* box, as I have described it, of course expresses just one model of a dramatic structure.[2] Imagine how a tale might unfold in various directions, with wooden panels opening on all axes. Or how main plots and subplots might take off on different paths, panels folded within or below other panels. Or how plot lines might intersect. Envision any kind of dramatic storytelling path, progression, or journey, and then think of how it could be concretized in a crafted physical object that could embody that form. In theatre when we talk about dramatic "structure," we sometimes create two-dimensional diagrams, like the famous Freytag pyramid developed by Gustav Freytag for describing novels in the nineteenth century, to try and visualize what that structure, which takes place in enacted scenes with actors in space and time, might look or feel like. In puppetry, one could concretely manifest that structure in three dimensions by building it.

Granted, not all or even most (or really any) puppetry is an unfolding box. What else can this focus on materiality tell us about how a story can be built into a puppet? Or about how the building of a performing object can also craft or circumscribe the parameters of a show's dramatic events? When building a show, puppeteers often ask themselves, "Why use puppets?" "What can puppets do for this show that human actors can't?" A puppeteer friend once recounted taking a workshop at the puppetry training center in Charleville-Mezières, France, where the teacher, a famous performer, gave the students the challenge to only use puppets in the work they did for the course if they *had* to, if puppets were necessary in some way. These devoted puppeteers, working with an important puppet artist, at the heart of the puppetry world, ironically spent most of the workshop doing creative projects *without* puppets, at a loss to adequately address this question. But puppets unquestionably can do a lot of things that human performers can't. They can fly, transform, come apart, and have disconnected pieces come together to create a single body during the course of a show. They can be built from materials that offer their own associations and provocations and unique physical possibilities—the ability to stretch, spring, crumple, and blow up. All of these aspects of a puppet can be used both to express character and to create drama. If a puppet can reveal a new or unexpected side of itself during a performance, like its ability to come apart, how much stronger it is if this material transformation occurs at or becomes a significant point in the story, a dramatic climax, or a plot twist. The physical reveal itself is, in fact, creating the climax or plot twist, enacting onstage in a material way a dramatic shift. To bring this element together with whatever storyline one wants to convey exploits the offering of the art form and brings the spectator added artistic enjoyment and critical understanding.

In 2019, as part of LoKO, the Laboratory of Kinetic Objects established by Jane Taylor at the Humanities Research Center at the University of the Western Cape, I had the pleasure of seeing *The Cenotaph of Dan Wa Moriri*, a one-man show performed by the talented South African actor Tony Miyambo,[3] who has worked with Handspring Puppet Company (Figure 2.2). This intriguing show offers interesting examples of the use of materiality onstage in dramatic storytelling. The show is about a young man coming to terms with his father's death. The set is minimal, a stage with only a table, covered with small, simple, unpainted, wooden, rectangular blocks, the kind children might play with. The actor uses these blocks powerfully throughout the show, never anthropomorphizing them but rearranging them frequently, in his desperate attempt to recapture

Figure 2.2 Tony Miyambo contemplating the blocks standing on the table in *The Cenotaph of Dan Wa Moriri*. Written by Gerard Bester, Tony Miyambo, and William Harding, directed by Gerard Bester. Wits Amphitheatre, Johannesburg, South Africa, October 2014.

Photo: Erica Luttich.

memories of life with his father. At several points, he rearranges the blocks to represent the street that led to his house, the house itself, and his parents' bedroom. At times, he picks up a single block to represent his deceased father as he talks about him. Since the show memorializes an ordinary man and his struggles, the profusion of identical blocks onstage appropriately reveals the many common lives also worthy of celebration, as well as the difficulty of distinguishing and lauding the individual amidst the crowd. The show could be said to live between two performance genres: it is basically a one-man show for an actor, but by bringing the blocks on as the only fellow performers onstage and giving them such focus, also makes it object theatre. If one is watching the trajectory of the blocks and their story, the most powerful dramaturgical moment for them is when the actor comes to the table and, remembering his thirteenth birthday, enacts blowing out his birthday candles. He does so by building candles out of a few of the blocks strewn across the table and then lifting the table up as he blows the candles out, sending all the blocks crashing to the stage floor. For the material onstage, this to my mind is the climax of the play, its most emotionally powerful, affecting material event. In the character's journey, his thirteenth birthday was also an important turning point in his life, after which his mother left the family and his father later died. The physical event of the falling blocks echoes that dramatic personal moment of transformation for the character. In the empty box setting, with only the table, the actor, and the blocks onstage, once the actor overturns the table, he completely and powerfully transforms not only the space but all the possibilities it holds for action, event, and story. Whereas before the table stood "so it parallels" after being overturned it is suddenly revealed as a dynamic object, capable of movement, even violent action, since its flipping causes the forceful crash to the floor of the cavalcade of blocks. One exciting thing about puppetry and object theatre, as mentioned previously, is that once you show materiality to have life, any material thing on stage, even the stage itself, holds the potential to become animate. With the turning over of the table, a whole set of new possibilities of action and movement come alive. We can ask, "What else can the table do?" "What other movements or dramatic actions is it capable of?" This type of action is the equivalent of the Messenger telling Oedipus that the man he thought was his father wasn't. With the turning of the table, the world established in this show has *literally* and *physically* transformed and become a whole new, possibly unknown place, left to discover. An audience at this juncture doesn't only feel the emotional impact of the moment but understands through it all the new questions it opens up, which helps lead them into the subsequent set of events.

Structure is not just about creating impactful moments onstage but also giving them a sense of shape, a sense of how one leads into the next, and even more importantly perhaps, how one event might *demand* the next event or events to come (or at least put into place the setup that invites them or, as here, offer the questions and possibilities that clamor to be addressed). Miyambo used the overturned table ingeniously to acrobatically reconfigure his body over it as he played a scene of getting a haircut, an important theme within the play since the father was a barber. However, in this piece, the climactic object moment was the end of the story of the table, which, sadly for me, had no further actions to perform. Its major life transition, from inactive set piece to dynamic, violent *actant*, didn't lead to any further exploits. This might leave object-oriented audiences feeling a lack of completion to this part of the tale. Miyambo concluded the show as actor-centered rather than object-focused. "Now the tables have turned" is a powerful idiomatic expression, here concretized through physical materials onstage that might be exploited for further dramatic expression. The blocks, however, did continue their journey in the piece, making for a moving ending. The final action of the show has Miyambo taking the time to place every single one of the many blocks scattered across the stage into a standing rather than prone position, a simultaneously metaphorical and concrete tribute to and resurrection of his father and his father's memory.

While this example is not from a puppet show but from a one-man show for an actor that also uses objects, it gives an excellent illustration of how materiality expresses itself onstage and how paying attention to that can shift our focus and interest. It shows how storytelling in a traditional dramatic model needs to shift to express itself through what objects are doing to be powerful.

An understanding of object performance can, in turn, speak to actor theatre. One semester when I was teaching my puppetry class, I ran into two of the graduate students who were in it at a play at a New York City theatre dedicated to developing new theatrical work. At intermission, they shared how being in the class was teaching them to look at all theatre differently and remarked on the show at hand, in which the set, which represented a one-room studio, had an abundance of furnishings, with a refrigerator, sink, couch, table, chairs, etc. Yet the major scenes ended up staged with all the actors bringing their chairs into a semicircle downstage, in front of all the furnishings, to carry on their conversation. The show repressed all the possibilities the material held for being expressive, leaving the objects onstage standing silent, unmoving, unused upstage. One of the students added "And what about that coffee mug?!" with a sense of injured pride for the cup that an actor had poured coffee into in one scene and then just left on the table for the remainder of the act. On the other hand, we had all also seen Walter Meierjohann's production of *The Emperor*, adapted by Colin Teevan from Ryszard Kapuściński's nove at Theatre for a New Audience (2018), starring the amazing British actress Kathryn Hunter. The show, about Ethiopia's Emperor Hallie Salassie, featured Hunter playing all the characters, people who knew or worked for Salassie. But the great man himself was represented only by an empty throne center stage. This physical object, even with no movement, served as a strong co-actor. The success of this production, as with any good show involving objects in performance, whether puppetry or not, comes from paying attention to what materiality is expressing, how it does so, the journey it makes, and what it reveals.

Some people in the puppetry world have strong feelings about making distinctions between what is called "puppetry" and what might more appropriately be termed "object theatre." For them, "object theatre" deals with objects found in daily life that are not, like puppets, crafted specifically for the theatre and focuses less on manipulating them as characters and more on their metaphorical and evocative qualities, the resonances they bring with them as they appear, often uncharacteristically, within theatrical spaces. Agnès Limbo, writer, director, and performer of the Belgium Cie (Company) Gare Centrale, is a masterful performer and teacher of object performance. In her workshops, she encourages participants to apprehend these differences and discover objects in ways that are distinct from enacting them as puppet-style characters.

I appreciate these categorical definitions and the work of performers invested in the unique, separate qualities of each form. I confess, however, that I use the term puppetry in a very broad way, with other terms like performing object or material performance being equally valid. However, here is an example to show why a distinction between puppet and object theater might be important to me, but maybe not in the way some puppeteers care most about. By a strict view, Miyambo's use of objects was not puppetry but object theatre. He never anthropomorphized the blocks or manipulated them like characters; he used them primarily as supporting illustrations for his story, as objects through which he expressed his struggle to come to terms with his father's death. However, had he wanted, he might have changed his use of them to something more recognizable as puppetry and in a way that could have been *dramaturgically strategic*. For example, imagine if the man who is using deadweight children's blocks to tell the story of his father's death and absence (a life that had disappeared) had a dream in which his dead father came to speak with him. Suddenly, in such a scene, these "object theatre" blocks could become puppet-like, that is, be manipulated and made to move and speak as if they were characters. Suddenly, material that seems dead, might come to life in a new, unexpected way. This could be a powerful shift, as could a subsequent scene of the man waking up from the dream to find the blocks once again empty of a certain kind of performed life. I'm not suggesting Miyambo and his colleagues should add these scenes; I am only illustrating that the distinction between puppetry and object theatre for me is less essential as two different camps of performance but rather offers an opportunity for pointing to different ways of using objects and materials onstage that can also be exploited for their ability to express story or meaning. Such shifts would have been, in my language here, dramaturgical moments that changed the world we were inhabiting and the possibilities it exposed. There might be productions in which such choices could be more exciting for a dramatic experience than a show staying confined to a single idea of a performance genre and the nature of its use of objects. So in the end, creating good performance with objects, whether they be puppets, strictly speaking, or something else, is really all about understanding what materiality has to offer onstage as expressive, how it can create dramaturgical moments and shifts to express meaning and structure events, and making wise, thoughtful, inspired artistic choices.

The very broad notion of puppetry that I embrace, and that has become widespread among contemporary puppeteers in New York, as well as with many puppeteers around the globe, understands puppetry as a highly eclectic art form, mixing all kinds of objects, materials, and means of manipulation, even alongside human actors, animations, and other kinds of technology. Interestingly, these productions do not usually end up as postmodern pastiches but bring these various elements together within a unified aesthetic. In this landscape of puppetry, with so many options, each element onstage will express meaning through its very presence, materiality, category of manipulation, etc., before it has even done any action or revealed any story. This situation describes a different scenario from a more traditional model that employs only a single type of puppet, for example, in which *all* the characters are marionettes or hand/glove puppets. In this more homogenous model, spectators become accustomed to the kind of puppets telling the story and subtle differences in painting, costume, and movement help to express character. However, in the more multiplicitous model prevalent in much contemporary puppetry, there exists so much choice in the variety of objects and media available to mix onstage, that it is important for artists to understand the meanings that these different choices bring with them, and how their materiality and other qualities are expressive, and what they express. No one really wants to see just a hodgepodge of objects thrown together in performance, even if each is uniquely beautiful or well crafted. What unites them does not necessarily need to be conformity to a single idea of what a puppet is or even what kinds of performing objects will be commandeered for a particular show, although this can help, but rather the thinking behind the choices and how that leads to a coherent, comprehensible stage world. Artists should embrace having constructively critical conversations around their work to clarify this kind of thinking and may even seek out perspectives from people outside their design and production teams who can provide fresh eyes on productions in development. Sometimes these people are called dramaturgs. Or this kind of work, done by any helpful person whose perspective one trusts and wants to hear, can be called dramaturgy.

The choice of object and materiality can be particularly powerful when a puppet expresses a dramaturgical trajectory linked with storytelling. A wonderful example of this is the choice of Théâtre de L'Entrouvert, based in the south of France, to use puppets crafted from ice in their production *Anywhere*. This kind of object is compelling and suggestive on its own because of the transformative nature of ice, something that looks solid and yet can easily melt into a puddle or disappear completely in the case of dry ice. *Anywhere* is based on Henry Bauchau's novel telling the tale of the ancient Greek king Oedipus' wanderings in exile with his daughter Antigone and his final apotheosis as he disappears in a clearing, taken up by the gods. As the show progresses, the ice melts, until Oedipus' transformation into mist is physically enacted through the natural process of the transformation of the ice. The use of ice puppets (Figure 2.3) here is not just an intriguing novelty, although that aspect should not be denied, but an expressive choice. France's Théâtre du Fust had previously used ice puppets as well in their 1996 production of *Un Cid*, based on Pierre Corneille's French neoclassical tragedy (Blumenthal, 14). This was another instance in which ice melting captured the tragic dimensions of the story. Ice is captivating precisely because it doesn't just show character but tells a story, shows progression, and

Figure 2.3 The ice puppet of Oedipus in Théâtre de L'Entreouvert's *Anywhere*.
Photo: Vincent Beaume.

signifies transformation. Ice is the story of firmness melting over time into liquid or sublimating into air; that is a drama in and of itself, perhaps the very incarnation and manifestation of the idea of tragic fate. In *Anywhere*, the drama of Oedipus' tale is illustrated by and physicalized in the natural action of the material of the puppet. The end of the story is also contained here in its beginning as spectators can anticipate what will happen to the ice through the course of the show, although not necessarily how that will be used to dramatic effect or how those dramatic moments will strike them emotionally. An ice Oedipus is the embodiment of vulnerability itself. We can experience an extra degree of excitement, of pleasure in engaging with a puppet show when the center of our focus—the materiality—has a journey to undergo, a story to tell, a drama to express. This drama could be about conflict, transformation, coming to stasis, opening up, expanding, or any other number of ideas that in traditional theatre might only be metaphors but in puppetry can more easily be both metaphorical and concrete. In the case of the *kaavad* box, it is the crafting and movement, the mechanics of the hinged panels, that is narrational. In the case of *Anywhere*, it is the transformation of the substance that has been used to craft the figure that tracks a story. In both cases, however, the objects and materials that take focus as the center of our attention describe the action. These objects are not merely characters moving through a dramatic plot—they embody the dramatic plot.

Stop and enjoy the puppets

There is another facet to the materiality of performing objects that can offer us further dramaturgical insights, and I have long turned to a short puppet piece by the Dutch puppeteer Henk Boerwinkel of Figurentheater Triangel (Figure 2.4) as an illustrative example. I was lucky to catch Boerwinkel's performance of *Metamorphoses*, a series of short puppet works, in San Francisco when I was in graduate school in the late 1980s to early 90s, and the piece can be found in an episode devoted to Boerwinkel from the 1985 television series, *The World of Puppetry*, hosted by Jim Henson. Each of the six episodes in this collection focuses on the work of one remarkable puppeteer active at that time and features portions of their performances, behind-the-scenes glimpses of their lives and creative processes, and conversations between them and Henson.

Boerwinkel's shows, which he originally performed for local audiences in his converted farmhouse in Meppel, Holland[4] and toured internationally, generally use no language. Accompanied only by music, the characters don't just enact but delineate their storylines, which can be deeply fantastical, poetic, or metaphysical. Boerwinkel says of his own work,

> I cannot conceive of the puppet as an illustration of a text or music. With my puppets I try to communicate a certain atmosphere, mood or a sensation to the spectator just by means of rest and motion: long forgotten dreams, visions from the subconscious full of magic and poetry, always connected with life and death. (Jurkowski, "Henk Boerwinkel")

Figure 2.4 "Idee-Fixe" from Figurentheater Triangel. A blindfolded puppet with a stick hovers above the large open head, another puppet emerging from it.

Photo: Henk Boerwinkel.

The short show I examine, like many of his others, is performed within a traditional-style puppet booth, similar to those used for outdoor Punch and Judy hand puppet shows except, fully draped in black cloth. Boerwinkel and his wife Ans, who performed with him, hid within the booth as they manipulated various types of performing objects in any single piece, sometimes working them from below and sometimes from above, often in the same scene, at the service of producing surprising images and transformations within their small stage frame.

In this piece, a small black curtain draws open to reveal a large head, eyes closed, and bandages wrapped over its face. Soon, a smaller character, a blindfold tied around its eyes and carrying a long rod, descends into the frame from above. He attaches the rod he carries to the end of the bandage on the large head and begins to pull the rod around the head, removing the bandage and simultaneously winding it onto the rod in the process. This slow, deliberate action continues until the head is free of the bandage, now neatly wrapped around the rod. This unusual, meticulous operation is captivating in and of itself. The virtuosity required to pull the cloth off with a rod held by a puppet is remarkable and is one reason spectators willingly give it their sustained attention. But I want to bring focus to the next moment in the show. The small puppet hangs in midair, static for a moment, simply holding out the rod with the cloth wrapped around it. The cloth then gradually begins to unravel from the rod of its own accord, falling off, first slowly, then faster, following the momentum of gravity, until it drops fully to the ground.

This spellbinding event is instructive in several ways. For one, the action we watch is the natural effect of gravity on cloth. In puppetry, again, our focus is on material, usually inanimate material brought to life by the skilled manipulations of a puppeteer. Here, however, we focus on the material onstage brought to life seemingly on its own, through the simple facts of physics. Boerwinkel ingeniously exploits our interest in and excitement at seeing inanimate material appear animate and surprises us, because our expectation is to witness this only as the result of a puppeteer's actions. Instead, we are offered an added artistic pleasure by watching the liveness of matter take place without motivation from a human force. This moment also illustrates the point I have already mentioned that in puppetry, a realm where the inanimate comes to life, anything, any material on the puppet stage, can potentially be animated. Nothing is "safe." To know that and use it to good, surprising, and even dramatic effect enhances the artistic experience. Boerwinkel's show gives us two anthropomorphic figures—the large head and the small character coming from above. Yet it is the falling bandage that both surprisingly yet somehow expectedly—given our internalized understanding of physics—takes focus for a moment as an animate presence.

One more reason I love this moment is because of what it teaches us about dramaturgical ideas in puppetry. We have been talking about storytelling and the need for a dramatic structure. This doesn't need to be a linear structure or any traditional storytelling model. Art and puppetry are not limited in this way of having to follow traditional forms. A puppet show doesn't need to be literal, but like Boerwinkel's pieces, can take us into poetic dreamworlds. Even such productions, however, have structure, just as dance and music performances have structure. We shouldn't confuse the idea of structure with only a prosaic notion of "and then, and then, and then" storytelling. Structure provides a format for the emotional journey of the show. Knowing and thinking about structure helps us understand how we are moving forward in time through an artistic experience and a strong structure makes us feel that everything that takes place onstage is there for a reason, even if we can't immediately articulate what that reason is, even if it doesn't answer the question "What happens next?" The reason for including a moment onstage structurally doesn't always have to be plot-related in that it moves the story or emotional journey forward. While we are within the emotional, artistic trajectory of the show, there are pleasures that we want to partake in that are intrinsic to the form. In this piece, I believe we are excited by the virtuosity of execution at stake in seeing the small puppet unwrap the bandage from the head, so we are not only willing but eager to spend the time to watch this slow, deliberate process. We are, I think, equally captivated by the independent movement of the cloth as it unravels; we put our attention to that action and indulge in that moment, which is a poetic experience of its own. We might compare how this works to how an aria functions in an opera. An aria is a moment that doesn't necessarily move the plot forward but allows the performer and the audience to indulge in an emotion, and to do so through splendid music and singing. Listening to the vocal majesty of singers is the heart of opera. Musical, emotional indulgences are not unnecessary because they don't provide plot devices but are instead essential to bring us deeper into the intrinsic artistic experience of the form. In puppetry, we do not come to the theatre primarily to hear beautiful singing but to see animated matter, so it is fulfilling to watch a piece of cloth do its own dance with the laws of physics as it unravels to the ground. Spectators are willing to stop the world for a moment to watch this simple, poetic act. Boerwinkel brilliantly includes this event, understanding that it offers a moment in his drama when his audiences get to indulge in one of the pleasures particular to the art of puppetry. Puppeteers and dramaturgs working with puppeteers need to be sensitive to this aspect of puppetry as they structure a performance. We can think of a show like a road trip that has a defined route and an eventual destination, but part of the drive includes scenic lookouts and stops at historical or other sites of interest that we wouldn't want to miss out on, even if it means grabbing our coats and getting out of the car. In fact, these stops constitute a great part of the fun and the reason for taking the road trip at all. We might even need stops just to get something to eat or take a break from sitting. Practical divergences (the time required to change objects, set up a moment, etc.) may be as important as scenic ones.

 Much of the joy of puppetry lies in seeing and taking in objects as they display their physical presence and possibilities. The ways they may or may not be subject to physical laws can surprise and enchant. I once saw a theatre piece that included beautifully crafted, interestingly designed animal puppets brought into a world of human performance. These puppets came onstage and left so fast that, sadly, we never got to take them in, to apprehend fully how they could move and express their natures through their movements and physical presences, even though these figures had some ingenious moving parts. Although these puppet animals fulfilled a plot necessity in the storytelling, spectators were cheated of the full pleasure of the addition of puppets to the show. Allowing time for a puppet to establish its presence and its world, to show off its unique nature and build that into the structure of the performance, perhaps even using it for dramatic effect or to express an important moment in the story, is dramaturgically smart. It takes advantage of what spectators viscerally crave in watching puppets and uses it as part of the broader intentions of a piece.

Playing with expectations

We might compare putting performing objects onstage to playwright Anton Chekhov's famous advice to playwrights about putting a gun onstage: if a gun appears onstage, hung on a wall for example, at some point during the course of the action it should be shot. If not, for Chekhov, it constitutes a kind of false dramatic promise. Puppets and performing objects of all kinds are like these guns. If they have physical characteristics that are never revealed or exploited, we feel we have missed something or been misled by the setup of the puppet drama. Unless, of course, the production is intentionally playing with and then thwarting these expectations for a reason. Chekhov pointed to guns as objects within a human drama in a play, but in puppetry the objects *are* the drama, and all the aspects of them that can be and do and revealed are part of the scope of that drama.

What Chekhov is also pointing to in his note about guns is the role expectations play in theatre and to the artists' work in setting up and meeting or countering them. Dramas, whether with human actors or puppets, are built on the foundations of audience expectations. We all enter the theatre with a background of experiences that inform what we anticipate seeing and going through and how we might be taken along such journeys. At a basic level, we have deep, underlying notions of dramatic structures that help set up these expectations. Some come from the natural rhythms and patterns of life. The flow of seasons from the barren cold of winter to earth's renewal at springtime or from the parched heat of dry months to the monsoons of rainy seasons are cycles that impart visceral experiences of rhythm and patterns of change that form the outline of structural models. Built into them are anticipations and expectations. Rise and fall. Opening and closing. Beginning and ending. Birth, growth, maturity, death. These ideas shape an internal sense of structures that are at work, even if we decide to play with them: rise, fall, almost rise, greater fall, meteoric rise. Opening, closing, opening, closing, opening, opening, *grand opening*. Beyond these, we have been schooled in structure and other aspects of performance and storytelling by any performances or other artistic experiences with which we've engaged: novels we've read; theatre, film, and television shows we've seen; fairy tales we've heard; dances we've done; music we've listened to; etc. You don't have to have ever seen a puppet show to come to it with expectations and ideas about trajectories of events. Good artists understand these and can play with them, skillfully leading us to and away from expectations. And as the Boerwinkel example shows, objects and their relationships to physical laws set up their own intrinsic expectations.

What happens in the rest of Boerwinkel's piece? The little figure from above, having let the bandage fall from the rod, then uses the rod to remove the top dome of the large figure's head, as if lifting the cover off a pot, and, in a continuation of that visual metaphor, stirs the inside of the head with the rod as a figurative spoon. Here visual metaphor takes us from one action/image to the next. The stirring eventually leads to a smaller bandage-headed puppet emerging from within the head to look around and disappear again inside it. Eventually, the eyes of the large head open, as if being awakened or enlightened following a long sleep. A cluster of plump cactus-like leaves slowly grow out from the inside of the large puppet head, splaying forth in different directions as the piece, with the accompaniment of music, swells to its ending. The entire dramatic structure here has been traced by physical events and material transformations. Poetic, suggestive, metaphorical, and imagistic, the piece nonetheless has a clear trajectory and a sense of beginning, development, and conclusion.

Performance is always playing with our expectations, sometimes trumping them, sometimes fulfilling them. In a play with human actors, what is in operation is our sense of psychology, how humans will act, especially within the characterizations and circumstances developed through the performance. In an object performance, our expectations are also set up by our knowledge of the physical world, our sense of physics, and our experience interacting with objects. These create further parameters of what we believe to be possible and how we expect objects to work, function, or behave. In constructing drama from performing objects then, puppeteers are playing with our sense of what we can expect from the objects in front of us, sometimes, as with Boerwinkel's unwinding cloth, fulfilling that expectation at an appropriate juncture, where its lyrical quality fits in with the emotional tone of the moment. That moment might more accurately be understood as a mix of the unexpected—we don't expect a piece of unraveling cloth to take focus in a puppet show—and fulfillment of expectation—since we all know how a roll of cloth on a stick will respond to gravity. This play of expectation and surprise in material movement can be thought of as the equivalent of a plot twist in a human drama.

Of course, in theatre our sense of expectation doesn't only derive from our knowledge of how human beings act; it also comes from how a show is setting up its own set of conventions about how characters act within the world of the play, and each new scene retests how that expectation is or is not fulfilled. This is also true within puppetry, where artists create a world for a particular show that dictates the style and presence of objects within that world, how they will be manipulated, whether we read the puppeteers as present or absent, etc. Here again, surprise can come from playing with conventions set up within a particular production. Finally, our expectations of a play are also set up by other plays and forms of dramatic storytelling, genres, and tropes that have accumulated throughout the history of the art and have set parameters of expectation of what kinds of stories have been expressed onstage and how they usually progress. Within puppetry our guideposts are other puppet shows, well-known genres of puppetry, typical tropes within them, and, similarly, how a particular show does or does not draw on or fit into these previous models.

Abstraction and structure

Another example I like to turn to in illustrating how objects can express story, especially a more abstract notion of "story," is the music video for the song "Katachi," which means "shape" in Japanese, from the Japanese pop group Shugo Tokumaru.[5] The visuals in this video consist simply of the appearance of objects, which have been cut from paper plates, appearing one after another on a tabletop surface within the camera frame. In the introduction, the objects materialize in random locations within the frame. One might argue that these very flat figures are more images than objects, revealing a dichotomy between two-dimensional and three-dimensional elements that I will interrogate more fully in the following chapter. The rest of the video, however, shows each new figure placed directly in front of the previous one, giving the impression of images moving forward and building in time. Some of the cutouts represent very specific things, like a bird or a hammer, while others are merely colored, geometrical shapes. At different points in the video, a series of cutouts of a human form, each placed in front of the previous one, invites us to see a person walking forward or swimming.

Reading the lyrics in the original Japanese or even in translation[6] may or may not add to one's understanding of the object storytelling. But the objects, just from their appearance in sequence, are constructing a tale that we can follow, even though what they seem to tell is, for the most part, abstract and not distinctly defined. Specific actions, like a person walking, are followed by geometric objects changing shape. Yet there is a feeling of continuity and development. These sensibilities are, of course, supported by the structural aspects of the music, its rhythmic patterns, repetitions, and crescendos. The objects and the music work together to give us the sense of an emotional journey. Puppet and film artist Janie Geiser once said to me that, for her, puppetry was basically like cinema in being moving images accompanied by music, and this view is borne out in this video. Structural models and devices in music and poetry are important in devising formats for puppetry productions. What these arts allow for is a mix of abstract or imagistic elements, which might still have emotional feeling and impact, along with or existing without more figurative or straightforward delineated particulars and devices. The "*Katachi*" video is different for me from something like Oskar Fishinger's 1938 *Optical Poem*,[7] in that the objects in "*Katachi*" aren't illustrating the music or dancing to it. Their sequential appearance is expressing a deliberate trajectory of their own that the rhythmic motifs, musical builds, and other structural parts of the music underline or complement. However flat these cutout plate figures are and however much the sequential nature of them seems to mimic animation—moving images—I believe our minds find an additional or particular layer of interest in them in seeing and knowing that these are not just drawings but real, three-dimensional shapes that have been meticulously placed one next to another. This video underlines how the appearance of objects in sequence can lead our minds into story lines and structural pathways that might not be fully spelled out in the objects themselves, especially when supported by music.

Further important notions about how abstract artistic elements can express performance structures were clarified for me in my work as dramaturg on Stephen Earnhart's *Wind-Up Bird Chronicle*, a stage adaptation of Japanese author Haruki Murakami's novel of the same name, which premiered at the King's Theatre as part of the Edinburgh International Theatre Festival in 2011. The show combined human actors, visual projections, and puppet sequences in rendering Murakami's enigmatic tale. For the production, Murakami's six-hundred-page novel was trimmed into a two-hour stage show. Much of this work was done by playwright Greg Pierce, as well as others who worked on various drafts of the script. But the director and I, over the course of a series of workshops and presentations, continued to play with the arrangement of the show's various plots and subplots. These contained many compelling events taking place in various different realms—some set in a seemingly everyday reality, others taking place on a more psychic or mysterious plane. We worked out different ideas of how the scenes might be sequenced by taking colored index cards—using different colors to signify the particular plotlines or realms the scenes inhabited—and writing on each card the details of a particular scene or moment in the show. For example, blue cards might represent everything that happened in what we called "the hotel world," a mysterious realm of the collective unconscious that the main character reaches when he descends into an abandoned well behind his house and which appears to him as a strange hotel with numerous rooms. Another color might represent not a location or event sequence but a motif. For example, each of the main characters had a long monologue at a moment when they came to understand something deeply fundamental about themselves. These could all be written out on, say, yellow cards. Through our arrangement of index cards, we hoped to track where, when, and how these various visual storylines and themes expressed themselves over the course of the show. We sat for many days on the floor of the director's apartment arranging and rearranging a layout of colorful index cards in front of us representing different models of the flow of stage events, some of the many possible, multifaceted, overall structures the performance might take. Our goal was not just to see plot elements move in a chronological or even logical order but to create something that was more of a visual, even musical notation of themes and motifs across the whole production. The monologues, for example, could serve as a form of punctuation and so would be placed at careful intervals throughout the show, rather than bunched together at any one juncture. The hotel world might provide a continuous counterpoint to the story's everyday world during most of the show, until the end when that sphere of uncanny events eventually takes over and the climax of the drama resolves itself in this powerful, alternate realm. The leitmotif of a white dress (zipping his wife into her white dress is the last thing the main character remembers of her before she disappears, the catalyst that sets the story in motion) reappeared in different manifestations—on a film projection, as a manipulated object—and at significant intervals throughout, serving in its own way to propel the action forward. The colorful index cards spread across the floor charted these trajectories for us all at once, and we could play with rearranging them to try various options. Like the *kaavad* box, this process offered another way of visualizing and physicalizing dramatic structure.

If you take away nothing else from this book, perhaps you can at least hold on to the fact that using colored index cards is a very useful way of plotting out structure. What I loved about using the cards was that we could pick them up and rearrange them in their sequence on the floor at any time. It made the somewhat abstract idea of "structure" for performance tangible, palpable, an object. The director and I could also look at the ensemble of cards on the floor and see the variegated experience of the performance in the immediate presence and arrangement of blue, yellow, white, and pink. The colors represented not only changing emotions or plot points but the shifting textures of the performance, showing the different elements (human, puppet, digital) called into play at each moment.

What I want to emphasize in telling this story is that we weren't just looking at plot in a simple model of "and then and then" events but rather tracking several important aspects of the show, especially the powerful impact visual imagery was having onstage. At one point in the production process, as we were reworking the show for its international premiere after an initial run in New York, the director, hoping to give the piece its final shape, solicited input from everyone involved in the production, including the actors, about anything they felt might be needed to clarify the show. Some of the actors offered that scenes could be added to lay out plot elements and character development more clearly. While some clarifications were useful, the actors, immersed within the production and connected to the story through the motivations and actions of their characters, could only perceive some aspects of how the show was telling its unusual tale. They could not step out of the production to see the cumulative effect of the projections and visual motifs layered in throughout and how these were also telling the story on a more poetic, intuitive plane. The show's many means of storytelling, which included haunting projections, a variety of performing objects, music, and a dance sequence, worked to not just take us through events but to express the mood of the world and its sense of mystery, to delve into the characters' subconscious minds, and to evoke a realm of seemingly magical coincidences. They were doing their jobs in less straightforward but equally effective ways and having a cumulative effect. The show didn't use visual and technological features merely as design elements but also as foundational structural ones. This is, to my mind, also the way puppetry operates.

Wind-Up Bird Chronicle also included a puppet—a faceless, white, bunraku-style figure, designed by Tom Lee—as well as some shadow sequences. The bunraku-style puppet stood in as an incarnation of the main character—played by human actor James Yaegashi in the scenes in the everyday world—for those events that took place within the eerie hotel. An interest in using puppets was present from the very first workshops, but the final choices of what kind, how many, and how to use puppets emerged from a long process. An early workshop incorporated three types of puppets of different sizes and means of manipulation—bunraku-style figures, *kuruma ningyō* (or cart puppets), and shadow figures—all interesting and captivating in and of themselves. But stepping back, we had to think more clearly about what role these various puppets served and how they fit into the production. Why did the show need three different types of figures? What function was each type serving? What was each of these different choices communicating? These questions were on par with those we also asked about the use of both English and Japanese within the show. While the production was mostly in English and addressed primarily to English-speaking audiences, there were many reasons why bringing in Japanese at particular junctures was a powerful choice. But what did the switching of languages at specific moments signify or express? When, where, and why would a character speak at one point in English and at one point in Japanese? The uses of the visual languages of the puppets needed to be clarified just as those of the spoken languages of the actors. Puppets express their "language" in their aesthetic aspects, their visual qualities, how they are manipulated, and their sense of movement, and each type of performing object "speaks" in a different way. The visual languages of puppets onstage need to make sense and seem purposeful to be understood.

Material invitations

The excitement I conveyed previously at my ability to rearrange index cards easily on the floor might mistakenly lead people to think that I am imagining or advocating that elements of a production like *Wind-Up Bird Chronicle* are completely modular and not intrinsically linked one to the next. That is not wholly correct. Still, there are many ways to think about how events can be linked or move forward in a show. I would like to offer the idea of *invitation* here as one further model. We can ask, how might one set of stage circumstances, led by an interest in performing objects, *invite* a next moment? In *The Cenotaph of Dan Wa Moriri*, turning over the table could be seen as *inviting* further discoveries of what this new set of circumstances offers, engenders, proposes. Eric Bass of Sandglass Puppet Theatre expresses something similar when he writes,

> The relation between the physical and the visual is just this: the dramatic visual image, sustaining a special tension, contains the need for an object (or puppet or human) to physically move. Such an image seems to demand that the actors, puppets, or objects fulfill a task in which their identity is at stake. They contain a need to transform: the need to achieve balance, for example, or to hold themselves together or to transcend the material of their creation. (59)

Another example I can offer to explain the idea of *invitation* is from a show for children developed by Tom Lee called *Tomte*, featuring the Swedish folk figure of the same name, a sprite who protects farms and their animals while people slumber. Lee gave an informal presentation of this piece as a work-in-progress at Hunter College in June 2019, encouraging feedback from the small, invited audience. The show mixed projected shadow figures and digital images on the same large, white paper screen. In the story, one evening Tomte visits each of the animals on a farm, comforting each in its own unique animal language. He also passes by the sleeping children and wishes he could somehow connect with them in their unique way, as he does with the animals. Seeing a toy helicopter on the floor of their room, he hits on an idea. At this point, the screen projection shifts to present a grid of nine small frames, each showing one of the various tasks Tomte takes on in bringing his secret project to fruition: taking measurements, chopping wood, hammering nails, etc. Eventually, an actual blade comes through the center square of the projected image, cutting it away, revealing for the first time a three-dimensional, bunraku-style Tomte puppet, waving and smiling at his audience. This character then disappears to emerge from the side of the screen, flying in on a crazy helicopter-esque contraption he has built from scraps collected around the farm. Lee flies the puppet and his helicopter around the audience, giving as many spectators as possible a personal, up-close hello from Tomte.

The emergence of Tomte and his flying machine is a wonderful dramaturgical moment that makes a powerful shift from two-dimensional projected and shadow imagery, with no direct audience interaction, to three-dimensional objects and direct audience connection. And it does so while manifesting the story's important plot moment of the character achieving his ambition to connect with children. These are now no longer the children from the farm on the screen but the real children in the here and now of the audience. The shadow/projection tools give way to a real tool that actually cuts the screen. How powerful is that?!

In material object terms, the cut opening in the screen also seemed to me to offer a further *invitation*. It seemed to invite Tomte to not just appear in the opening to wave and then come out from the side but, ideally, to somehow fly *through* this opening that tore apart the integrity of the screen and the previous division it established between "in front" and "behind." Of course, at this point, practical considerations come into play as much as theoretical ones. How would one bring a puppet through the screen in a one-person show, with the puppeteer holding and manipulating the puppet from behind the screen? Is a mechanism or another performer required or desired? Etc. Puppetry is always a negotiation between vision and practicality. Through its further development, this piece took some very different directions overall than what I describe here and saw in this early work-in-progress presentation, but I bring out this early version as an example of what might be thought of as a material "invitation," not just for action but for a dramatic, structural, performed moment.

In conclusion, I would like to summarize some points about puppet/object dramaturgy, which might be useful takeaways. First of all, puppetry as a form lends itself to thinking about "dramatic" structure in concrete terms, captured in tangible, physical objects and their expression onstage. That structure doesn't need to be linear or simply plot-driven, but even a nonlinear, nonverbal, poetic piece needs some shape and some understanding of how the elements and moments onstage build a performance experience or emotional trajectory. In puppetry, we have the advantage and maybe even the obligation to express important moments of transition or progression through materiality. In any case, doing so, I believe, can lead to powerful choices. Indulgence in the animation of matter is the central pleasure of puppetry but not the full sum of a puppet piece. Some useful terms I have used here that can help to think about how a puppet performance might be structured include dramaturgical moment and invitation.

Finally, a good rule of thumb is that the dramaturgy—storytelling, emotional trajectory, meaning-making—in puppetry is in the object. Let objects lead in the progression of events and the telling of puppet tales.

Notes

1. Nina Sabnani is an artist, filmmaker, and now retired professor at the Industrial Design Center in Mumbai. She began her investigation of the form for her doctoral dissertation and has continued to work with the communities of craftsmen and storytellers, not only to document their tradition, but also to aid them in finding new ways of using their creative skills that honors their traditional talents, while bringing them renewed prominence in contemporary culture. Together they have created several animated films based on the *kaavad* stories that showcase these traditional artists' unique painting and storytelling styles. Her book, *Kaavad Traditions of Rajaasthan: A Portable Pilgrimage* (Niyogi Books, 2015), offers a comprehensive understanding of the various aspects of the tradition.
2. It is important to note, however, that the actual, traditional *kaavad* boxes contain many stories painted on them and that the storytellers each elaborate on the tales in their own way.
3. Written by Gerard Bester, Tony Miyambo, and William Harding; directed by Gerard Bester.
4. In 1996, Boerwinkel founded the Magisch Theatertje or Little Magic Theatre, in Maastricht with Charlotte Puijk-Joolen and continued his work there.
5. You can enjoy watching "*Katachi*" online here: "Shugo Tokumaru - Katachi [OFFICIAL MUSIC VIDEO]" *YouTube*, uploaded by Polyvinyl Records, 6, December 2013, https://www.youtube.com/watch?v=RpLBR38kVvY
6. You can see the original lyirics of "*Katachi*" and attempts at translating them at the following websites: FeelBritish_ru. [Japanese -> English] – Shugo Tokumaru, Katachi. *Reddit*, www.reddit.com/r/translator/comments/3suis2/japanese_english_shugo_tokumaru_katachi/. Accessed Date; and Pots, Ruben. "Shogu Takumaru." *Lyrics Translate*, 11 Nov. 2018, lyricstranslate.com/en/katachi-shape.html. Accessed Date.
7. You can watch *Optical Poem* here: "Oskar Fischinger: An optical poem (1938)" *Daily Motion*, uploaded by storiadelcinema, www.dailymotion.com/video/x6wte7p. Accessed Date.

Works Cited

Bass, Eric. "Visual Dramaturgy: Some Thoughts for Puppet Theatre-Makers." *The Routledge Companion to Puppetry and Material Performance*, edited by Dassia N. Posner, Claudia Orenstein, and John Bell, Routledge, 2014, pp. 54–60.

Blumenthal, Eileen. *Puppetry: A World History*. Harry N. Abrams, 2005.

Craig, Edward Gordon. "The Actor and the Übermarionette." *The Mask*, vol. 1, 1908, pp. 3b–16b.

Jurkowski, Henryk "Henk Boerwinkel." World Encyclopedia of Puppetry Arts. Translated by Steve Abrams, Union Internationale de la Marionette, 2015, wepa.unima.org/en/henk-boerwinkel/. Accessed Day Month Year.

Sabnani, Nina. *Kaavad Traditions of Rajasthan: A Portable Pilgrimage*. Niyogi Books, 2015.

3 The Image Aspect of the Puppet

In the previous chapter, I focused on the object as the central meaning-making tool on the puppet stage, as the locus for expression and storytelling. Puppetry is, as we have seen, primarily about the objects onstage. While the emphasis on the object in puppetry is essential, there is another highly visual and crafted aspect of puppetry that is also important but has not received as much critical attention, what I will call *the image*. By image I am referring to several things. On the one hand, there is the visuality of puppets, as opposed to their more three-dimensional and kinetic qualities. For example, we can look at several marionettes within a single performance or genre, and they may all have basically indistinguishable mechanisms for operation, crafting, and jointing, such that their kinetic aspects are relatively similar. Yet the various characters are distinguished by how they are painted and decorated. Of course, decorations like flowing hair or a cape will add to their expressive movements. But we react to their overall visual appearance as much as to their movements. The puppet's visual qualities are the first things to grab one's attention when seeing a figure, making an initial impact, whether one sees the object in a performance, a museum exhibit, or hanging inert backstage. The visual aspect of the puppet is our introduction to it. Advertisements for puppet shows judiciously exploit this attraction, pulling spectators in with impressive, eye-catching views. I know I am always at the mercy of gorgeous puppet photos tempting me to see productions. How a puppet is painted and decorated can, of course, give it a unique spirit and personality as much as how it's constructed. The visual design also distinguishes the styles of different puppeteer-builders. Anyone who has tried their hand at painting even a simple papier-mâché figure can understand the amount of work, care, and attention that go into painting an object in order to complete it. However, this aspect of puppetry rarely takes critical focus in discussions about the power of the puppet, which inevitably circle back to the importance of the kinetic object and the gesture of the inanimate made animate. Adding to our contemplation of the art, considerations about how the kinetic object and its visual image work in relation to each other can amplify an understanding of puppetry. For example, they might reinforce each other, complement each other, or be at odds with each other, purposefully or not.

In some puppet performance traditions, especially in Asian forms like Japanese *bunraku* and Burmese *yoke thay* marionettes, painting the eyes is the last thing an artist does to finish a puppet. These traditions understand completing the eyes as the act that gives the puppet its life and soul or awakens these in the object. The common saying that the eyes are the window to the soul captures the sense of how having eyes that appear alert and vivid offers a sense of inner depth to a figure. In these traditions, painting the puppet is the culminating act that brings life to the figure. Curiously, through this view we might understand that it is the painting of the puppet's eyes rather than its movement that makes the inanimate alive. If puppetry, as we have seen, is centered on inanimate matter becoming animate, in these cases the act of enlivenment is accomplished through painting, a key visual element of the puppet, as much as through its kinetic, moving, object qualities. This idea forms a curious contrast to what we have looked at previously, the general view that an object's movement is what gives it life. These two different perspectives are both pertinent to understanding the animation and life of the puppet.

In speaking about image, I am interested not just in the visual style of objects onstage but also those elements in puppetry that are flat, two-dimensional, or drawn—everything that we associate with the terms "image" or "picture." It is this idea of image which I see as having a growing presence in contemporary object performance and that I will explore more fully in this chapter. Two of the examples about performing objects in the previous chapter already introduced the centrality of images in puppetry, even while highlighting the importance of the object. Although I directed our attention to the dramaturgical ideas illustrated in the physical construction of the Indian *kaavad* box, the object's native purpose is to display and present its painted images that tell a story. In the example of Shotoku Maru's "*Katachi*" video, I said that the paper-plate cutouts are so flat as to beg the question of whether they should be considered objects or images. The question of when the two-dimensional image becomes or is appreciated as a three-dimensional object is an interesting one and something puppeteers often play with in using flat objects in performance. Whether, how, or why we might want to separate out the object from the image painted on it in how we think about a performance or how an artist creates one are also compelling questions. What do we understand by making distinctions between what we might see as an object and what we might interpret as a two-dimensional image? There are surely scientific and philosophical approaches to answering these questions, but I am more interested in the artistic and dramaturgical implications that the distinctions help us appreciate. Investigating the centrality of the visual and two-dimensional within an understanding of puppetry, its history, and its artistry can reveal how the image aspect of puppetry connects puppets to a further web of interrelated artistic fields—such as film animation—which are coming to be understood at least as sister arts to, if not fully encompassed within, puppetry. Since many contemporary performing object artists are delving into creations that capitalize on the use of images as much as objects, as well as the puppet's connection to animation and film, acknowledging and contemplating the use of images within puppetry has become more essential than ever. We can ask, "What happens when the object one brings onstage is an image or presents a

```
                        DOLLS/TOYS
                MASKS
                                STOP MOTION FIGURES
        ROBOTS
                    OBJECT      HAND PUPPETS
    DAILY OBJECTS
                                MARIONETTES
        RITUAL FIGURES
                                TOY THEATRE
                SHADOW PUPPETS
```

Figure 3.1 A diagram showing the many connected realms of object performance.

picture?" We might also explore the tipping point when image becomes object or vice versa. What is the dramatic excitement generated by moments like these, when our perceptions of object and image bump up against each other? How do we move between the two-dimensional and the three-dimensional in performance? Such questions lead us to further considerations: What is at work in fluctuations and distinctions between the arenas of drawing/writing/painting on the one hand and performance on the other, and what are ways of reading, apprehending, and enjoying them? How does puppetry bridge these realms?

When we think about objects as the center of puppet performance, we might consider all the kinds of performing and related things as forming constellations around the notion of "object," which is so central to thinking about puppetry. As Figure 3.1 expresses, dolls, daily objects, ritual figures, etc. are all objects related to the idea of puppet and which, on occasion, have been used in puppet performances. This image delineates some of the eclectic kinds of objects that form part of a contemporary view of what might count as or perform as a puppet.

However, rather than only acknowledging the object as central to puppetry, a center around which various related realms gather—such as masks, daily objects, stop-motion characters, ritual figures—bringing them all into the world of puppetry, we might instead see the iconic puppet—a marionette, for example, or hand puppet—as a center of two trajectories that go out in two directions, one toward a world of objects in ritual, art, performance, and other realms, and one toward a world of images, in the visual arts but also in moving images of animation and film. Maybe in the end these are not distinct trajectories but webs of connections between a variety of different arts, which articulate the wider realm of puppet performance that artists are currently exploring. Still, we can make an initial shift in our understanding of puppetry from the first model to this diagram (Figure 3.2):

This new model reveals how in pop-up books, shadow puppets, and toy theatre, for example, notions of object and image overlap and collide. Let's explore some of these connections further.

Puppets and picture storytelling

The early history of puppetry includes sculpted and crafted figures—idols, statues—thought to be embodied with spirit and used in religious contexts.

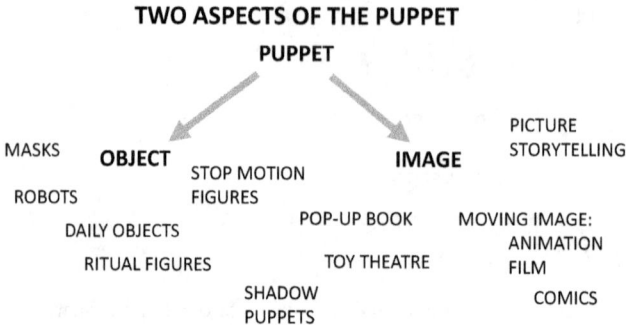

Figure 3.2 A diagram showing the connected artistic realms of both object and image.

Some may have had jointed elements to show their movement or, as mentioned in chapter 1, like the medieval statues Eileen Blumenthal alludes to, may have wept or been seen to speak, providing concrete evidence to believers of the spirits embodying them. But puppetry has another important ancestor in the two-dimensional spiritual realm in the art of picture storytelling. Many traditions have existed and continue today, especially in Asia, in which, as with the *kaavad*, a storyteller points to a series of images as illustrations for their tales while reciting the story. The *kaavad* is unique among these in being a constructed box. Such images were more often painted on scrolls that were easy to roll up or fold and carry. Victor H. Mair's *Painting and Performance: Chinese Picture Recitation and Its Indian Genesis* (University of Hawaii Press, 1988) offers a detailed early history of this subject in some of its prime and originary locations.

India is home to several of these traditions. It is significant that South Asia, which today continues to have such a profusion of puppetry forms,[1] is also home to several robust scroll storytelling practices. These forms inhabit a sphere of illustrated storytelling using constructed, painted objects that is comparable to puppetry. In the very same region of Rajasthan where the *kaavad* performers travel, there exists yet another picture storytelling tradition called *Pabuji ki phad*. The performers in this form are usually married couples, with the husband known as the *bhopa* and the wife as the *bhopi*. For their performance, they hang a large cloth covered with painted images out in the open air. Spectators in the desert villages they visit gather in front of the cloth for several nights in a row as the performers sing tales of the local hero Pabuji, known for his daring feats protecting cattle, of great importance in the region. The large square rectangular cloth scroll has many images painted on it. Some are used uniquely for a particular character or episode, while others are more generic—men on horses going into battle, for example—and might be used many times over, standing in for different characters and events throughout the tales. The *bhopa* sings an introduction to each episode and then points to the images that illustrate it while narrating the story. His wife holds a candle up to the pictures, illuminating them one at a time in the dark night for the audience to see. They perform folk songs between the narrative episodes. As with the *kaavad* boxes, the visual artists in this tradition come from a different town than that of the performers, in this case, Bhilwara. As with the *kaavad* carvers, the visual artists associated with the *Pabuji ki phad* tradition, like Kalyan Joshi, are able to exploit their skills to expand their business and sell artworks to collectors and tourists. Joshi has also diversified his artistic genres, adding line drawing, collage, montage, and animation to his oeuvre. He also offers workshops and art classes. Such options are largely unavailable to the singer-storytellers, tied as they are to the performative nature of their events and reliant on their language, familiar epic tales, and the patronage of remote spectator communities (Figure 3.3).

West Bengal is home to another important Indian scroll storytelling tradition called *pattachitra*. Artists in this form are multitaskers, as they compose both the music and poetic narratives of the tales they sing in addition to painting their own scrolls. These artists all share the same last name of their caste, Chitrakar, and most live in Naya, a village devoted to the *pattachitra* community in Midnapore. Unlike the *Pabuji ki phad* scrolls from Rajasthan, where the images are all visible at once, arrayed throughout the cloth's wide surface, these scrolls are long and relatively thin, with single-scene images painted along them from top to bottom and are meant to be displayed vertically in sequence, one after another. Instead of hanging up their scrolls as the Rajasthani *bhopa* does, revealing all the visuals at once and then illuminating specific parts of the canvas with a candle,

Figure 3.3 A performance of *Pabuji ki phad* by singer-storyteller Pappu Bhopa (and his wife Kamla Bhopi, not pictured) with a scroll painted over fifty years previously by the uncle of Kalyan Joshi, an artist from the last family painting in this tradition. Performance at Devena Singh's Art Inn Jaipur. Rajasthan, India, April 2014.

Photo: Claudia Orenstein.

the Chitrakars unroll their scrolls slowly as they sing, revealing one image at a time. Since crafting and selling artworks can be a more lucrative trade than performance, especially given the appeal of visual arts to tourists and art collectors, these singer-storytellers have, in recent years, invested more of their time and energy in painting scrolls for sale than in performing. Their works attract tourists and serious folk art collectors. Some of the artists, like husband-and-wife team Madha and Hazra Chitrakar, have even had gallery exhibitions of their visual art. The entire Chitrakar community has also taken up new, contemporary themes for their scrolls, especially those that appeal to foreign collectors. Scrolls depicting the 9/11 terrorist attacks in the United States, with Osama Bin Laden and then US president George W. Bush, represented in the art's traditional visual style, and the deadly 2004 Indian Ocean tsunami have proved particularly popular.

Because of their appeal as paintings, some scrolls, like the one made by Madha and Hazra Chitrakar about the tsunami, have abandoned the traditional compositional model of distinct, sequential pictures for a more free-flowing style and appear as a single image covering the full length of the unrolled canvas. Scrolls like these look and function more like wall hangings. Curiously, while the scrolls sell as examples of beautiful folk art, some of the unique cachet they possess for collectors continues to lie in the fact that they are not just paintings but are associated with this performing art, even if a specific scroll they purchase will never be used for performance. When selling the scrolls, the artists still usually sing for the patron a story-song they have composed to go with it. During my visit to Naya with researcher Atasi Nanda Goswami, who specializes in the folk traditions of West Bengal, Sayam Sundar Chitrakar, a senior artist, demonstrated for us how he performed in the past, carrying several scrolls rolled up in a bag hung across his shoulder. He would travel from one house to the next and, at each door, offer a performance of stories in exchange for food, cloth, or money. This itinerant model takes place rarely today, if at all. In the past, carrying a painted object, with its promise of sacred stories, lifted the itinerant artist slightly above the beggar class (Figure 3.4).

There exists a notable contrast between the older and more contemporary models of the *pattachitra* scrolls and their uses. On the one hand, we have the traditional use and nature of the scroll as an object, carried house to house in a bag and unfurled one image at a time, along with singing-storytelling. On the other hand, we have a similar scroll, now sometimes with the images splayed across the long canvas instead of parceled out in sequence, hung up in a museum or home as an art object, static and disconnected from the performance of sung tales. The *pattachitra* tradition, its changes and development, illustrate both the fine line and the great distance that exist between the image as performing object and as art object. There is a vast philosophical and cultural world to explore in these distinctions as well. The shift in the use of the scroll is exemplified in the change in composition we see in the tsunami scroll. In this example, the object in its kinetic expression remains ostensibly the same. The change in use is reflected primarily in the shift in the manner of painting—in the image, therefore, not the object.

In Japan, scroll storytelling or *emaki*, also has a long history. Ono Shunjo, the head priest at Dōjōji Temple in Wakayama, Japan, continues to perform a scroll

Figure 3.4 Left, Rani Chitrakar sings the story, unrolling one panel of her *pattachitra* scroll as her daughter, Shushana, points to the images, and her granddaughter, Shima, looks on. Right, Hazra Chitrakar displays her scroll on the theme of the destruction of the 2004 Indian Ocean tsunami. Here the image, not painted as discrete panels, spreads from top to bottom in the style of a painting or wall hanging. Naya, West Bengal, India, 2013.

Photos: Claudia Orenstein.

storytelling sermon that's been handed down in his temple for around five hundred years. Its history connects to even older practices of storytelling, going back to at least the eleventh century. Scroll storytelling was so popular in the region and throughout Japan at one time that it even engendered scroll storytelling competitions. The Dōjōji Temple scroll tells the tale of a young woman whose unrequited love leads her to transform into a serpent and destroy the young man, who is the object of her affection, along with the temple bell under which he hides trying to escape her wrath. This story is also the basis for famous plays from Japan's classical *noh*, *kabuki*, and *bunraku* traditions, under the title *Musume Dōjōji*. Performers from these arts seek blessings at Dōjōji Temple before embarking on their own performances of the tale and often follow up their debuts by sending the temple photographs from the events. These and other memorabilia connected to the many performative renditions of this famous story line the temple walls.

Ono[2] speaks of his events as sermons teaching about the value of compassion, but he is also aware of having to use performative techniques to capture the attention of his audiences—visitors who travel to the temple to hear the story and its teachings—and of needing to attend to the materiality of his performing object while recounting his tale. As he reads the text on the scroll, pointing out the images and explaining the events in his own words, Ono also adds in jokes and personal reflections. He speaks directly to spectators, inserting specific questions or references to them over the course of his narrative to engage them in brief exchanges. While the performance, he says, is roughly ninety percent the same each time he does it, he shifts his tone, some language choices, and examples he uses depending on the nature of his audience, such as their ages, genders, or nationalities. Ono remembers interesting responses he has received from spectators and interweaves them into subsequent renditions.

Ono is also acutely aware of the materiality and fragility of the two separate scrolls that he uses in his telling, one carrying the first and the other the second part of the story. He jokingly announces "intermission" and "commercial break" as he changes between them. While he doesn't perform with the oldest artifacts (the temple preserves several aged, retired scrolls that they only exhibit on special occasions), each new set is meant to support around a hundred years' worth of daily (often multiple times a day) performances. Some older versions show wear in particular spots where past performers had continually grabbed at the paper as they pulled it across. Precisely because of this, Ono says he studiously avoids touching the paper itself as he performs. The wooden handles on one side of each of his scrolls have been replaced with pieces of plastic piping, which are more durable but less attractive. The worn wooden ones were retired by Ono's father, who maintained the tradition before him. The plastic ones are on the stage left side of each scroll when the images face the audience, the side the storyteller continuously turns and pulls throughout the sermon.

The physical nature of the scrolls has had to be responsive to the tradition's changing audiences as well. In the 1920s, when the railroad found its way to Wakayama, larger crowds began coming to see and hear the tale. This increase in visitors was a drastic transformation from the occasional individuals and small groups of pilgrims who had arrived previously. Dōjōji commissioned new scrolls one hundred and fifty percent bigger than the previous ones to accommodate the larger audiences and allow all visitors to see the images easily.

The Dōjōji scrolls, which unroll horizontally, sit on a wooden podium for the recitation. As Ono stands stage left of it, he pulls it across to reveal sometimes a long length of images and at other times a shorter one, following what the visual revelations in collaboration with the storytelling moments dictate. He notes that he has two major ways he moves the scroll: one he calls *sue mawashi*, or "fixed rotation," a slow turning of the bolster the scroll is wrapped around, which shifts the images along at an unhurried and steady pace. He uses *sue mawashi*, for example, when he tells of the young woman walking to visit her father. He calls the other method *hiki*, "pull" or "stroke." This involves a longer pull of the scroll, making for a quicker journey of the paper that also displays more of its length and, thus, more images all at once. He uses this method, he says, when the woman is running to catch the man she has fallen in love with as he flees from her. With these two options, he makes his own movements of the scroll echo and represent the actions of the characters within the story and illustrated on the paper. Ono's grandfather was also a master of this tradition, handed down through three generations of the family, all temple priests.[3] When his grandfather was in his eighties, his hands shook from age. Instead of being a hindrance, this affliction, Ono says, added drama to the performance, as spectators felt they saw the serpent painted on the page come to life in the unintentional quivering of the paper as he unrolled it (Figure 3.5).

The Image Aspect of the Puppet 65

Figure 3.5 Ono Shunjo, head priest of Dōjōji Temple, Wakayama, Japan, performs his temple's famous scroll story. (He wears a mask as the photograph was taken during the worldwide COVID pandemic.) January 2022.

Photo: Claudia Orenstein.

Ono also embellishes his narration with his own performative actions. In the version of the story performed in the *noh* theatre, there is a spectacular moment when the main actor does a specific pattern of stomps while standing under a large bell prop, hung center stage, right before leaping up into the bell as it simultaneously descends around him. Ono has inserted what he calls "an homage" to this famous scene in his own telling of it by doing a similar stomp pattern himself when revealing the image that shows the young man hiding in the bell. He has also adopted some waves of his hands, trying to imitate flamenco finger motions as another homage, this to the time he did the sermon/performance at the University of Spain in Santiago de Compostela. He doesn't change things just from one experience, but he was inspired to think about flamenco when traveling to Spain. He says he also thinks about the rhythms of what he calls Korean gospel music, the rhythms of paid mourners who cry at Korean funerals, which have a distinct melody, as inspiration for speaking the young maid's similarly rhythmic language. In these examples, Ono's physical movements or vocal expressions lend performative qualities and even rhythmic timing to the static images. In so doing, he acts, one could say, like a puppeteer, bringing life to the inanimate images on the scroll.

The Dōjōji story is also done in the *bunraku* puppet theatre. The roots of Japanese scroll storytelling are, nonetheless, distinct from those of Japanese puppetry. Some picture recitation traditions, however, show a more direct link between their picture storytelling and puppetry forms. In Indonesia, it appears that *wayang beber*, a form of scroll storytelling in which the reciter narrates tales from the Hindu epics, the Ramayana and the Mahabharata, predates the currently more widespread and well-known *wayang kulit* shadow puppetry tradition. The visual style of the characters one finds on the *wayang beber* scrolls echoes that of the shadow puppets, as well as those in another tradition predating the animal-hide shadow puppets, one that uses flat wooden puppets called *wayang klitik*. The image aspect of the puppets—their carved shapes, profiles, internal details, and ornamental features that project as shadows on the screen—owe a strong visual debt to the painted scroll figures. One can imagine that the *wayang kulit* and *wayang klitik* puppets might have begun historically as painted images that then came off the page, so to speak, to stand up before their audiences and perform as these flat, figurative objects. As we have seen, the heart of puppetry is watching inanimate matter brought to life, becoming animate. In this case, however, we might say that instead of inanimate matter being brought to life, it is the two-dimensional image off the scroll that has been brought off the scroll and into a flat, but still more object-like, three dimensions in the shadow puppets and flat wooden puppets and has, in this way, been brought to life or given an added dimension of life. So, we might understand the image here as what is initially being brought to life rather than the material per se. It is worth remembering as well that when we watch a shadow show, what we are watching is not the object or the puppet but a projected shadow *image* of the puppet. In places like Indonesia, of course, spectators might choose to watch a *wayang kulit* show from behind the shadow screen rather than in front of it so they can appreciate the work of the *dalang* (puppeteer) and the gamelan musicians in action. On the other side of the screen, however, where most shadow audiences sit, is the shadow projection of the puppet's *image*. Moreover, in a long evening's performance of *wayang kulit*, which might go on for several hours or even all night, while there are certainly lively battle scenes, there are also long slow sequences during which most of the puppets remain static, their rods stuck in the banana log beneath the screen, forming a *tableau*. Maybe the *dalang* will move the arm of one character or another to indicate who is speaking, but these sequences reveal even more forcefully the roots of the tradition in scroll storytelling and the image aspect of the art.

Indonesia is also home to a tradition of round, wooden rod puppets known as *wayang golek*. Again, the iconography and visual style of these puppets is generally similar to that of the scroll images and both the shadow and flat wooden puppets. Interestingly, in 1918 in "The History of the Puppet," used "flat" versus "round" as a way of dividing and categorizing puppets (Kaplin, 29–30). Dimensionality as a design idea was understandably of interest to Craig, as it was in line with his explorations of new models of scenography and lighting and his desire to bring three-dimensional elements into stage sets to replace the flat, painted drops that were ubiquitous in Europe in the late nineteenth and early twentieth centuries. Three-dimensional set elements, in contrast to painted cloth drops, could harmonize with human performers onstage and allow light and shadow a greater visual role in design. With *wayang golek*, we see a more three-dimensional, fleshed-out, rounded-out version of the same characters that exist in *wayang kulit* and *wayang klitik*.

Wayang wong refers to dance-dramas done with human actors often wearing masks, which is also iconographically in line with the scroll imagery and the puppet figures. These dancers' physical movements, with their elbows angularly jutting out away from their bodies, resonate with the jointed features of the puppets derived from the scroll imagery. Many of their poses show the dancers attempting to exhibit the same flatness as the images on the painted page. It is an accepted view that, in Indonesia, puppetry developed before the human performance forms that mimic it. In Indonesian performance, then, we can see a trajectory that travels from painted scroll image to puppet to human performer. The flat profile characters and stances originating in the scroll paintings carry over to the puppets and then to human performers. The *image* has come to life, from scroll to puppet and finally to flesh-and-blood performers.

Another telling example of the close relationship that exists between pictorial images and puppet objects can be found in the large *nang yai* shadow puppets of Thailand, a form nearly identical to Cambodia's *sbek thom*. Both traditions relate tales of the Hindu Ramayana epic, known in Thailand as The Ramkien and in Cambodia as The Reamker, adding their own regional variants. These large shadow puppets are different from the *wayang kulit* figures, and from the smaller shadow traditions of each country—*nang thalong* and *sbek touch* respectively—in that they do not primarily represent individual characters with jointed arms but rather depict more complete visual scenes, often of single or multiple characters in a setting, with no jointed or independently moving parts. A single puppet might display the image of the demon King Ravana tearing apart his victims in battle or Rama heading through the forest mounted on his battle chariot. The puppeteers hold up their figures by grasping the puppets' bamboo poles and lifting the puppets above their heads, as they dance the objects both in front of and behind the shadow screen. In fact, in this tradition, the puppets and puppeteers spend more time in front of the screen than behind it. The physical stances and movements of the puppeteers echo those of the court dances from their regions, such as Thailand's *khon*. These shadow puppets feel less like articulated characters flattened and projected onto a screen than like full visual images (such as paintings) that the performers hold up and dance across the stage. They remind me of the anecdotes about the riotous soirées that Italian Futurists artists organized in the early twentieth century, in which they presented and promoted their new art movement not only with short, provocative plays and performed readings of their manifestos but also by having Futurist painters carry their artworks onto and across the stage. For the Futurists, this way of displaying artwork marked an avant-garde change from hanging paintings up to be viewed in galleries and supported their calls for more energy and dynamism within Italian art. They experimented with crafting art for the "modern" era that could revel in action and speed. During the soirées, these paintings became active performers as they were paraded onstage, even though they did eventually end up on museum walls. Thai shadow puppets are not part of this avant-garde world, of course, but the comparison I am drawing is in the way they can also feel like fully presented images, already containing their own characters and movement within them, which, in being carried onstage, are called on to perform.

It is not only the presentation of the puppets in *nang yai* that imparts movement and dramatic action to the stage. The flickering of the coconut shell oil lamps, which have traditionally lit up the screen, bring their own wavering actions to animate the shadows on the white cloth as they illuminate the performance and help cast the shadows. Some have even seen in these lively shadows the spirits themselves of the godly figures that are represented in the puppets manifest on the screen.

The puppets become livelier in battle scenes as the *nang yai* puppeteers swing their figures against each other to enact a fight. They smack their puppet objects into one another as they do battle. Sometimes one puppeteer will climb on the haunches of another who stands with bent legs, and both, holding their puppets aloft, will pose briefly, offering a momentary, static *tableau* that consists of the two puppet figures engaged in combat and their puppeteers entwined in their acrobatic stance. The actions in these examples seem to be as much, if not more, about the performers' movements and physicality than those of the puppets. In all these cases, movement is coming from something other than the object itself—the flame's quivering, the puppeteers' physical force and gymnastics—and is visited on the objects, not from any internal joints, mechanisms, or actions built into them. Of course, puppeteers always manipulate their objects, but here the objects resist to a degree, as they offer no internal devices or easily moveable parts. The performer must move the entire large figure at once. There are a few puppets in *nang yai* that are smaller and more easily manageable. These are figures drawn from *nang talung*, Thailand's small puppetry tradition (related to Indonesian and Malaysian *wayang kulit*) and less prevalent in the shows. Three important figures of this kind are used solely in rituals that take place before the show or on other special occasions. If an image is generally thought of as something static and a performing object as something kinetic or holding kinetic possibilities, contemplating where movement comes from in puppet action offers a useful approach for analyzing puppetry and the role of imagery within it.

There are today only three companies in Thailand that continue to perform these large shadow puppets, each at a different Buddhist temple that also cares for its own collection of puppets. The Wat Khanon temple troupe received a UNESCO grant to help support the tradition, which they used to create a museum display of older puppets that are no longer used in performance. In this museum, one can admire the carving and artistry of the visual designs of the enormous flat puppets in full, prolonged stasis, lit from behind in glass cases. Puppets in museum displays generally sit uncomfortably between their aspects as visual art imagery and performing objects. Displays present them as inactive objet d'art, but the kinetic qualities built into them can cry out to be performed. In the museum at Wat Khanon, *nang yai* shadow puppets get to show off their image aspect, even though, like all puppets, they beg to be put into action. But perhaps more than some other types of puppets, they are also well suited to the museum context, as each conjures its own dramatic scene (Figure 3.6).

The Image Aspect of the Puppet 69

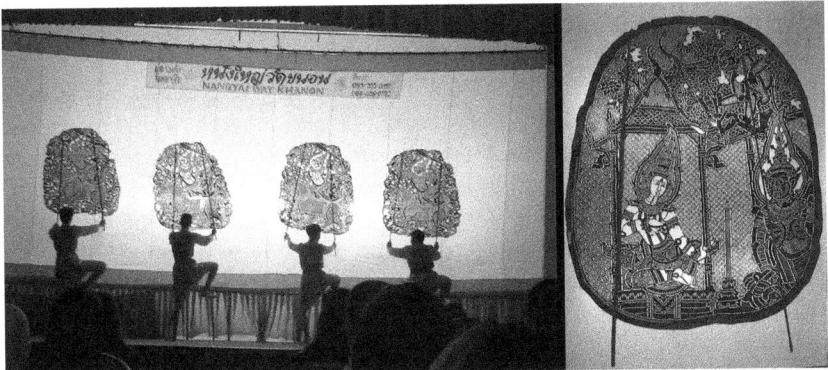

Figure 3.6 Left, performers at Wat Khanon temple in Thailand dance their *nang yai* puppets in front of the screen. Right, a *nang yai* shadow puppet displayed in the museum at Wat Khanon temple showing the Demon King of Lanka, Thotsakan (Ravana), and his captive, Nang Sida (Sita). Photharam, Ratchaburi, Thailand. January 2018.

Photos: Claudia Orenstein.

Performing Japanese screens

Japan offers yet another unique example of the performance of images or imagery in the *fusuma karkuri* moving screen enactments from an area that includes Tokushima Prefecture and Awaji Island in Hyōgo Prefecture. This territory can be considered as the cradle of the early Japanese puppetry forms that later birthed the now-well-known *bunraku* tradition based in Osaka. Tokushima also developed its own rich practice of *bunraku*-like puppetry done on *noson-butai*, rural, outdoor stages, plentiful in the area, many of which are still in use. In the past, during breaks between plays or scenes, the beautifully painted screens, or *fusuma*, used as stage sets for these puppet shows would be shifted, with musical accompaniment, in order to set up for the next presentation. Watching the lovely screens in motion became so captivating and popular in and of itself that the moving of scenery, *dogugaeshi*, eventually developed into its own elaborate performance form. I was able to catch a showing of this art on November 3, 2021; it rounded out a full program of puppet plays by Katsuura Puppet Theatre at Inukai, a rural puppet stage in Tokushima and, importantly, a space equipped with the many screens and built-in mechanisms necessary for this kind of presentation. The show was a roughly half-hour mesmerizing display of continually transforming imagery—sometimes abstract, decorative patterns, sometimes recognizable visuals (birds, flower vases, Mt Fuji)—done through an ongoing dance of changing sets of two or more panels moving in unison, entering, leaving, coming together, turning sideways, sometimes interweaving one image with another, always revealing yet further screens behind. All was accomplished to the constant, hypnotic musical strains of two shamisen, masterfully performed by Takemoto Tomowaka and her student. The screens decreased in size as the event continued and ever smaller panels were revealed behind others, all forming in the end a grand visual image of a deep tatami room; the floor pattern painted below, with its forced perspective lines, aiding in the creation of the illusion. Puppeteer Basil Twist famously re-created one of these performances within his own 2004 production, *Dogugaeshi*, a show that recounted the history, demise, and local memory of this tradition on Awaji (an island near Tokushima, also in Hyōgo Prefecture), even as it reconstructed and paid homage to the form.[4] In this traditional art, visual imagery and the movement of objects—here painted panels—create the performance. The impact of the show comes through the partnership of the continually unveiled, sumptuous images on the one hand and the dynamic actions of the moving screens on the other. Both set up expectations, establishing patterns and rhythms, while also offering surprises and novelties throughout. The extended length of the event is itself astonishing and seems to defy what one imagines to be possible within the constraints of the simple form at play. The music helps sustain the spectator's anticipation of evermore new visual immersions. No text, dialogue, or story is necessary. Our minds detect or build unarticulated, implicit stories or suggested connections between the images as they emerge.

Contemporary creative explorations

Hamid Rahmanian, an Iranian-born puppeteer based in the United States and trained in graphic design, is a contemporary artist whose work reflects a trajectory from visual graphic images to live-action puppet performances to humans acting like drawings or flat objects, echoing the developmental progression we saw in traditional Indonesian forms. His work has taken off in various directions, including cinema. In a series of projects based on Iranian epic tales, his artistry moves from page imagery to stage performance and his graphic images come to life, even as they incorporate human actors. *Shahnameh*, first published in 2013 by Quantuck Lane Press, is an illustrated version of the Persian Poet Ferdowsi's epic poem, written between the ninth and tenth centuries, and contains more than five hundred of Rahmanian's beautiful, detailed color images. With *Zahhak: The Legend of the Serpent King*, published in 2018, Rahmanian brought a select group of tales into three dimensions as a pop-up book. Through the pop-up book, his images shift from lying flat on the page to standing up and out of it. The two-dimensional renderings remain similar in concept, but in the *Zahhak* project, the paper on which they appear has been crafted to fold and stand. Is the excitement that we find in pop-up books about watching inanimate material (paper) come to life or about seeing drawings come to life, or at least start to make their journey into a three-dimensional world? In the stage production *Feathers of Fire*, Rahmanian then used his graphic imagery to create shadow puppets. These he blended onstage with animated backgrounds and the work of actors wearing headgear with designed cutout forms on them that allow the human performers, their silhouettes projected onto the screen, to fit stylistically into the overall visual shadow design of the performance. This production borrows techniques developed by US puppeteer and filmmaker Larry Reed (who also trained as an Indonesian *dalang*). Reed's live performances use cinematic techniques to create large-scale shadow shows that give the feeling of watching a movie being created in real time.

Books themselves are interesting objects that highlight the conundrum of distinguishing between flat and more dimensional objects. A book is made up of piles of thin, flat papers covered with writing and/or imagery. Layers of these pages make a book into a thick, palpable thing. Script on a page can have symbolic elements that read like drawings, and both drawings and writing in books can be read through as stories that come alive in the imagination. The pop-up book turns images that lie flat on the page into three-dimensional, tangible life. The simple act of folding and lifting a piece of paper puts it into the realm of the performing object. What it performs is the showing of an image as it also performs as an object itself.

Performances, as we explored previously, can engage us by playing with our expectations. Books, as objects, also incorporate horizons of expectation based on our experiences of them. We assume predictable limitations of how they function and occupy space. The pop-up book plays with these assumptions by suddenly transforming in unexpected ways and, in so doing, taking us from a realm in which we think of books as collections of flat pages, containing words and images apprehended in sequence through the turning of pages, to one in which pages can stand in unpredictable ways and may even have moving parts contained within them. What was once viewed as known and finite opens to reveal new ranges of possibilities.

Many contemporary artists have incorporated pop-up books as part of puppetry performances. I first witnessed this technique in Chicago's Redmoon Theatre's *Hunchback* (2007), based on Victor Hugo's 1831 novel *The Hunchback of Notre Dame*. The show used a large pop-up book center stage as a device to provide the backstory for Claude Frollo, its central character. The pop-up elements revealed the physical settings of his past, and small puppet figures ran through the architectural elements that emerged from the pages. A full-scale set and masked actors loomed behind the book, bringing the main plot to life in larger proportions. The metaphor of this production emerging from Hugo's novel was expressed concretely with the pop-up book. In the show's final scene, the Narrator stuffs a Quasimodo puppet into another book he has been carrying throughout the show, putting Quasimodo physically back into the story from which he emerged, a literalized staging of metaphor through materials.

A more recent example of using a pop-up book in puppetry comes from the French company Les Anges au Plafond's *Le Cri Quotidien*, or *The Daily Cry*, directed by Brice Berthoud. In this show, a woman (Camille Trouvé) sits reading her black-and-white print newspaper on a chair to the accompaniment of live cello music performed by a cellist (Sandrien Lefebvre). As she reads one of the articles, she tears at the newspaper page lying open on her kitchen table, and, in so doing, allows black-and-white print paper figures to pop out from inside the sheet. Simultaneously embodying her own stage character and manipulating the enlivened materials in front of her, she subtly jiggles each figure to hear what they have to say while speaking for them as puppeteer. Soon, a whole room full of government officials seems to have sprouted out of the newspaper to conduct their official business on her kitchen table, alongside her morning coffee. Each page she turns enacts a different news story through novel, creative manifestations, all constructed entirely out of paper. In one story about a fatal multicar collision, the pop-up displays a quiet country road. The actor/puppeteer pushes various paper cars across it. Her words, as she moves the cars, reflect snippets of the mundane discussions and activities taking place inside the vehicles before the tragedy. She enacts the crash by smashing the paper cars into each other, crumpling them in her hands, turning crafted paper objects into crumpled paper balls. On another page, a small town grows into an overcrowded city, as new buildings emerge next to initial pop-up ones. The performer then pulls further rising paper towers out of the buildings, turning them into skyscrapers. One resident's simple act of feeding chickens and collecting the eggs to sell from a cart also transforms before us with the city's growth, as a large paper edifice emerges for processing the chickens and their eggs. Within this paper building cluck rows of chicken heads, their paper mouths opening and closing, while paper eggs move along a paper conveyor belt. Before the introduction of the clucking chickens and conveyor belt, each action has come from an image popping out of the book or the performer pulling it out. The conveyor belt and clucking chickens, however, reveal something new and unexpected: paper objects with functional mechanisms inside them (Figure 3.7).

Figure 3.7 Les Anges au Plafond's *Le Cri Quotidien*. Political figures emerge from the morning newspaper.

Photo: Vincent Muteau.

Bringing the discussion of dramaturgical moments from chapter 2 to bear on these examples, we could say that revealing a book to be a pop-up book by turning pages that, instead of lying flat, rise in surprising, creative constructions, offers a dramaturgical moment, a moment that shifts the physical potentiality of the performance world. When a puppeteer then brings a small, manipulated figure or car onto a pop-up set and moves it through the landscape, we have another dramaturgical offering, or at least these are physical moments of shift, pregnant with new embodied story possibilities. Likewise, when a pop-up book structure reveals movement within it, some mechanism that a puppeteer puts into action, as with the egg conveyor belts and the clucking chickens, we again have what I have been calling a dramaturgical moment—and a powerful one. Each new revelation about the potential of the material or the way it can be used discloses further trajectories of action, of physical storytelling. Les Anges au Plafond used the disclosure of each new device within its show's newspaper world effectively to express the stories of each article and pace the progression of the show overall. Each dramatic event of the show was expressed through a physical shift or change in the material onstage. Each turn of a page is itself a piece of physicalized, rhythmic structure, showing a new juncture in the presentation, dividing one event—one news story—from another.

The very act of drawing has itself also been adopted within puppetry, highlighting the creation of imagery as a performative action and the relationship between visual and enacted materials onstage. Tortoise in a Nutshell's *Feral* (2012) is one example, and both the themes and the material enactments of the show play with ideas of creation and dissolution. The show tracks the journey of a small, friendly town's transformation and eventual blight following the establishment of a gaming arcade promoted for its economic benefits. All the set and character pieces in the show are made from white paper with simple line drawings, giving the impression of a child's drawing come to life. The public bus is a paper cutout depicting a bus that the performers pull along the front of the playing area. The buildings of the town are made from paper and constructed into three-dimensional forms with rectangular cutouts representing windows. The show also incorporates projected, live-feed imagery, both from cameras that follow the actions of the paper characters and of a series of drawings done in real time by a performer sitting in front of the tabletop stage. This performer initiates the show's action by drawing childlike images of the seaside town of their youth, which then come to life around them (Figure 3.8).

Toy theatre

Toy theatre is yet one more form absorbed today within the puppetry world that shows a direct link between the performance of animated material characters and the two-dimensional image. Following the growth of industrial printing in the nineteenth century, toy theatre emerged in Europe as a family pastime. Kits containing flat reproductions of the stages, sets, and characters from theatrical productions, along with their scripts, were printed for purchase, usually in the

74 The Image Aspect of the Puppet

Figure 3.8 Tortoise in a Nutshell's *Feral*, directed by Ross Mackay, set design by Amelia Bird, lighting by Simon Wilkinson, performed by Arran Howie, Ross MacKay, Alex Bird, Jim Harbourne, and Matthew Leonard. The scene shows the paper city set and three of the puppeteers, below, and a live feed projection of the main family of characters inside their house, above.

Photo Credit: Amy Downes.

form of a book with pages to cut up. People could snip out and assemble the different paper parts to set up their own small paperboard theatres at home and then enact the plays in their parlors, reading from the printed scripts while moving the paper actors across their model stage. You may have played with similar paper toy theatres yourself as a child. The original idea of toy theatre as home entertainment declined in general popularity with the rise of realism in theatre and further still with the advent of television and other home entertainments. But it reemerged at the end of the twentieth century as a form of public artistic performance. The company Great Small Works, whose members—John Bell, Trudi Cohen, Stephen Kaplin, Jenny Romaine, Roberto Rossi, and Mark Sussman—are all veteran performers from Peter Schumann's Bread and Puppet Theater, adopted and adapted the form, contributing to its renewed prominence, especially within New York puppetry circles. *Terror As Usual* is Great Small Works' ongoing series, featuring events drawn from the news and reflected on in creative ways within a tabletop, proscenium stage. Toy theatre work moved the troupe from Schumann's large-scale, processional puppetry model to a small-scale form. They have maintained Bread and Puppet's commitment to creating community around performance by offering their shows with a line-up of other entertainments at the Spaghetti Dinner events they curate, which also exchange Schumann's tradition of handing out homemade bread and aioli sauce to his audiences for a full pasta dinner. Great Small Works has promoted toy theatre in the many workshops they offer and at the ten editions of the Toy Theatre Festival they organized in New York from 1993 through 2013 and picked up again as an online festival during the COVID pandemic, with participation from artists across the globe. The song they sing to kick off each day of festival events, to the tune of "Head, Shoulders, Knees and Toes," describes the form's basic stipulations: "It has an arch, it's miniature, and it's flat," reminding us of the form's intersection between image and object. These stipulations have been much more adhered to in Europe, where performers might be berated for bringing round objects into a show. In the United States, by contrast, the term and the festival have allowed for a wide range of small-scale puppetry. Artists have taken toy theatre in numerous creative directions that go beyond the confines of the nineteenth-century parlor model. For example, in the short piece *Leyendes*, performed by Alejandro Benitez and Ana Martinez at Great Small Works' Eighth International Toy Theatre Festival in 2008,[5] a woman accused of being a witch languishes in prison. She is a flat cutout, but behind her cardboard prison bars is a film projection of a seemingly endless expanse of water, which eventually provides her escape. The addition here of video projections—moving images—adds a new element to toy theatre. Would the projection of a video in this case still qualify as "flat"? Figuratively speaking, it proposes more dimensional possibilities for the character's constrained life.

In toy theatre, the performers, who are generally visible alongside their small stages, have a stronger presence than might be the case in some other puppetry forms. They often serve as narrators of the events they show and even lend themselves as enactors to help amplify the expression of the flat figures in their charge. Flat puppets, with such limited ability for intricate actions themselves, allow for and may even require more accompanying language than other types of objects to enhance their performances. (I will speak more about the relationships of human actors and language to performing objects in chapter 5.) Suffice it to say that, despite being set up and moved in three dimensions, these flat objects still act very much like illustrations, and the role of the performer here often continues to be, in some part, that of a narrator/storyteller.

Banners and cranks

Clare Dolan, another Bread and Puppet Theatre company member, has created a further series of festivals for performances directly related to picture storytelling called Banners and Cranks. Bread and Puppet has used picture storytelling or, borrowing the Italian word for it, *cantastoria*, for many years. Their style employs cloth banners, painted with simple images—either a single visual image or several panels on each cloth—hung on a pole structure. The performer stands beside the setup and points to the images on the banners, flipping each cloth over the pole while narrating, to reveal the next image or set of images in a sequence.

"Cranks" refers to a cranky (or crankie), an unpretentious device that allows a performer to turn a spool wrapped with a stream of paper or cloth adorned with images so that these visuals pass before the audience's eyes one after another. It is a kind of mechanized version of the scroll turning done by hand by Ono at Dōjōji the temple? This device, as with the moving mechanisms of the chickens in *Cri Quotidien*, takes the display of images more forcefully into the realm of performing objects by putting the paper or cloth on which the visuals are painted into dynamic, mechanized action. The audience's interest is simultaneously drawn to the parade of images before them and the mechanism that moves them. Artists likewise can bring as much care and creativity to designing their crankies as to the imagery they display.

In the performance Dolan does to introduce the picture storytelling genre and its history at her Banners and Cranks festivals, she adds one more element that complicates the relatively clear-cut definitions of banners and cranks. Like the scroll-singers and others previously mentioned, Dolan sings and recites the history of picture storytelling by pointing to images, but these images are not on a banner or a cranky but painted on various parts of a costume she wears, a dress equipped with flaps that she lifts or opens to reveal additional hidden pictures. At some points in her presentation, she turns around to show images painted on the back of the dress; at these moments, she spins in place as she "la, la, las" a refrain between verses, displaying the whole shape and expanse of the outfit. As Dolan shows off the full dimensions and all the surfaces of her costume one portion at a time, she recites the complete history of the storytelling tradition painted on it. Unlike the pop-up book, the images here do not stand up to come to life. The living body of the actor makes them alive in an unexpected way. What is living, embodied, or moving here? Is a dress worn by an actor a performing object? The dress is not just a hanging banner nor is it a mechanized device. Its movement cannot be fully disassociated from the movement of the performer within it, her twirling and dancing between verses, or her displaying of the different parts of the garment and her animation of the material covering her. Image, object, and performer merge here in a new way. In some moments, that melding of elements has a particular force. For example, with each refrain of the song, Dolan reminds spectators about the birthplace of the art as she sings "in India, which is where the whole thing got started," and in doing so, points to a picture of the triangular-shaped Indian continent painted suggestively on the dress over the area of her own body from which new birth might take place. The performance also provides an interesting moment of doubling when we see Dolan pointing with her stick to a picture of a storyteller on her dress, who is himself pointing to a picture with his own stick (Figure 3.9).

The performance of the human body in this act, and its relationship to the object (dress) and the dress's presentation of images, adds a further element for analysis. We are here made aware not only of our expectations of images, as with the pop-up book, but also our knowledge of how a body moves and its possibilities and limitations. These thoughts guide our horizon of expectation in watching the performance. How many images can fit on this dress? How many flaps can be

The Image Aspect of the Puppet 77

Figure 3.9 Clare Dolan displays the full expanse of her picture storytelling dress. Before a performance at the Detroit Institute of Art, 2015.

Photo: Dave Buchen.

constructed into it? Will Dolan be able to reach and point to all parts of the garment, even on her back? Even with her stick? What physical dexterities or performance novelties might she have to invent to accomplish the task at hand of presenting an entire history? The act also offers a new artistic element to admire and think through, not just the painting of images and the singing of scroll texts, but the design and stitching of this unique costume with all its movable parts.

At the Banners and Cranks festivals, artists experiment with stretching or interrogating these forms. Some have used multiple crankies simultaneously to give overlapping different views of sung or narrated events, or to show complex, fragmented visual images; others have used three-dimensional objects in conjunction with crankies or banners, creating an interplay between two- and three-dimensional elements. Videos from the 2015 festival show a variety of examples. Dave Buchen's *Takes After His Father* uses three crankies concurrently within a single wooden frame configuration. On the left are two short ones set on top of each other—the top one scrolling from left to right, the bottom one scrolling from bottom to top—and on the right, one long crankie scrolling from top to bottom. Although these crankies don't always move at once, they work together to create tripartite images in which each visual informs the others in a combined expression of the story (Clare Dolan). Such displays of objects and their movements fall within the analytic models of performing objects.

To dissect the ways these visuals work together further, one might turn again to the critical insights provided by Scott McCloud's *Understanding Comics: The Invisible Art*, alluded to briefly in chapter 1. I consider McCloud's book a version of Aristotle's *Poetics* for comics. It is a comicbook that illustrates the ideas it describes. McCloud carefully identifies the different elements at work in comics and analyzes how each functions individually and in conjunction with others to express a story. The book deals with such topics as how comics, defined as "[j]uxtaposed pictorial and other images in deliberate sequence, intended to convey information and/or to produce an aesthetic response in the viewer" (9), manifest meaning, not only in their pictures but also in the gutters between pictures as readers use their own imaginations to link the images. As readers move from one image to the next, their minds fill in whatever events may have happened in between to create a continuous narrative. McCloud also deals with the relationship between language and visuals in comics, clarifying the different roles each can perform and showing the interesting juncture where what is word and what is visual symbol converge. He discusses how comic artists express time and movement, not only within a single frame but by juxtaposing frames, and many other fascinating aspects of the art. His book offers many useful insights for puppetry, especially for performances like the ones I have been discussing that include pictures. The layout of the three crankies within Buchen's single wooden frame creates a visual ensemble similar to what might be seen within the pages of a comic and functions to create meaning in ways comparable to what McCloud describes. However, Buchen's crankies add an extra dimension to McCloud's examples because of the mechanism that puts his images into motion. Rather than merely lying on the page, waiting for the reader's engagement to set image into action and to turn the pages of the comic, Buchen's performance does the turning, the moving forward for us. The pace and style of the movement and the process of revelation of the images are all additional interpretive elements.

In *The Macanuda*, puppeteer Deborah Hunt, who is originally from New Zealand but who has lived in Puerto Rico since 1990, uses the materiality of the picture scroll itself to reveal new dimensions of her story. In this performance, she unfurls a long horizontal scroll of painted scenes to tell her own mythic tale that starts with a naked woman being born out of an egg as the beginning of the world. At the end of the tale, the physical scroll itself, painted on its opposite side as a green snake, becomes the snake character in the story that devours the woman—a painted object attacking its own story images. Like the table in Tony Miyambo's show from chapter 2, the scroll here shifts from a position of background support to one of central actant. In Miyambo's show, the actants all live in the realm of three-dimensional objects. Here the story visuals or means of expression shift from images to objects as Hunt brings the snake to life. To do this, she puts her hand in a pocket at the front of the scroll that is painted with the viper's head and turns that part of the paper around toward the images splayed out along the rest of the scroll, now understood as the snake's body. We watch the snake devour itself while ostensibly attacking the woman. In *Towards an Aesthetic of the Puppet*, Steve Tillis outlines the idea of "double-vision" in puppetry (59–66) referring to the fact of seeing the puppet simultaneously as an object and as a living character. Here that double-vision is of the object as a character and as an image-displaying scroll.

Movement in image-imbued puppetry

Movement in puppetry not only indicates that something is alive but also contributes to or is itself the origin of action and drama. Identifying what is offering movement onstage—an object, an image, a performer, or any combination of these—helps in understanding where the drama is located. Playing with our expectations of where movement should come from also engages us in a performance by surprising us or asking us to question how this world operates or what we can anticipate. Consider this scene from Theodora Skipitares's 2003 show *Helen: Queen of Sparta*, part of a trilogy of puppet performances Skipitares did dealing with the Trojan War as a way of addressing the contemporaneous Iraq War. Skipitares developed these works inspired by the *pattachitra* performers she met during a research trip to India. In fact, she begins the show with a scroll-singing sequence about Helen and her infamous story, performed in the model of the *pattachitra* form with a scroll painted for her by *pattachitra* artist Dukhashyam Chitrakar. A later scene in the show enacts the Judgement of Paris, the event from Greek mythology in which Paris is enlisted to choose and then give a golden apple to the most beautiful of three goddesses: Aphrodite, Hera, and Athena. This episode famously forms a background to the story of the Trojan War, since Paris was persuaded to give Aphrodite the apple in return for having the beautiful Helen as his wife. In Skipitares's scene, the three goddesses are enacted by three Indian actresses whose filmed faces are each projected onto one of three strips of cloth that hang from the stage ceiling. At first, we see only the goddesses'/filmed actresses' eyes. These projections have some subtle movements in them from the live actors who were recorded, but for "moving images," they are relatively static. The cloth screens on which they are projected, by contrast, are full of movement. They flutter, rolling up and down, covering and uncovering the actresses' eyes to give the impression the goddesses are batting their eyes to flirt with Paris. It is captivating here that, counterintuitively, the movement comes primarily from the hanging cloths and not the images projected on them, despite the enormous possibilities for movement inherent within film. The fabrics here are more "alive" than the real, filmed human faces projected onto them.

Another useful example for thinking about where movement and action come from in a puppet production and how that relates to what images, objects, and puppeteers contribute to a performance can be found in *Paper Story* by the UK company Blind Summit. Blind Summit is widely known for their show *The Table*, in which a *bunraku*-style puppet, manipulated by three performers, in the process of trying to enact the story of Moses, educates the audience about *bunraku*-style puppetry and goes through an existential crisis regarding his own confinement on the table, his circumscribed puppet world. *Paper Story* (2011) is one of two short pieces Blind Summit has often performed with *The Table*. While *The Table* explores the nature of *bunraku*-style puppetry as a form through its enactment of a *bunraku*-style puppet, *Paper Story*, in less direct terms, simultaneously explores and manifests the enactment of the image in puppetry.

The piece begins with four puppeteers, dressed in black, standing nonchalantly over a table with a briefcase on it. One puppeteer opens the case. In swift, coordinated movements all four bend toward the briefcase together, reaching their hands in as each pulls out a sheet of white paper and, one by one, display the letters written on their papers to spell out Le Marionettisme Français, or French Puppetry. With another choreographed ensemble movement, they all wave their hands, letting their papers fall gently down onto the table. They dive into the briefcase again, this time emerging to stand in careless, ultra-cool poses, a cigarette dangling from each mouth, enacting a stereotypical vision of French avant-garde ennui. On the next round, they pull pages out of the briefcase, each taking theirs, one after the other, to reveal, bit by bit, the title "Her Diary Illustrated," then "The Year," "1968, "The Place," "Dorset." The puppeteer with the paper reading "Dorset" moves it slowly so that it lingers longer in the air than the others. This slow action visually extends the temporality of the reading of "Dorset," physically enacting what might otherwise be communicated through sound. Finally, to the dramatic music of Edward Elgar's *Introduction and Allegro for Strings*, they begin to pull out papers no longer with words on them but images. These consist of simple black cartoon line drawings on white paper. The first drawing is of a stick figure, followed by one of an arrow, which points the stick figure toward the following image, which is of a car. The puppeteer moves the paper with the car on it across the table, as if it were driving along. Another puppeteer then lifts above the briefcase the simple image of a sun—a black outline of a circle with lines jutting out representing rays—to enact the sunrise. Another image—a kite—is flown through the sky; a tree image is moved along as if passing by the car window. Then a rabbit image comes out and a puppeteer jumps the paper along the table, so we see the static picture of the bunny as hopping. The piece continues with this rhythmic pulling of papers out of the briefcase, each with an image or a word on it, to tell a dramatic tale: a fateful car crash; the police chase of the driver who runs from the scene; a dream sequence in which the driver imagines what will happen to his family if he is caught; and the driver's tragic suicide at the end. The visual aspects of the images, all simple black line drawings on ordinary sheets of white paper, draw on the tools and aesthetics of comics to convey the tale. But the actions of the puppeteers—the varying rhythms with which they pick up, display, and discard the pages; the position in relationship to other images, the briefcase, and the table, where they show their pictures or papers with words—all impart dramatic emphasis to the storytelling, often both enacting and humorously sending up the melodramatic nature of the tale. The show, in effect, brings a comic book to life. The transposition of elements that are common in comic books brought to the stage and performed through the choreographed pulling out, displaying, and discarding of images, moves these stick figures into a new realm, beyond the comic book. The enactment also constitutes a play or commentary on comic book imagery. In the chase scene, for example, a puppeteer shows an image of the stick figure running, placed upright on the table. Other images of the same figure running, in different poses, are pulled out from behind the first one to create a line of images that trace the character's flight until we see him hide behind a door with one page showing the door and another the word "SLAM." Movement and action are derived from a combination of the visuals on the papers and the actions of the puppeteers, enhanced by the swelling music that underscores the developments of the plot unfolding visually. The puppeteers are definitely manipulating objects, but those objects are sheets of paper whose visual images are also enacting the story through their own graphic lines.

Ukrainian Kseniya Simonova's sand-art performances are also, in essence, live comics in that they tell their stories through a series of sequential images, accompanied by music. The visual art here, however, is made in real time during performance through Simonova's adept drawing with and rearrangement of sand on a light table. Here the "gutters" between the images are filled in by the live creation of each new image Simonova paints out of the sand in front of her, often emerging directly from the previous picture. Instead of simply seeing one image followed by the next and doing the work of connecting them in our imagination, we wonder at each step of her process what she will change in the current picture, what new elements will appear, how her movement of or drawing in the sand will bring a new scene to emerge before our eyes. We can be amazed simultaneously by Simonova's artistic abilities, which we witness in action in front of us, and the ability of something as simple as sand to create complex visuals, with shading, perspective, and intricate details. Our attention can go as much to the act of creation in the moment, and everything involved in it, as to what the pictures themselves express. The movement of the sand, especially when Simonova adds more streams of fine grains to the table, letting them slip through her fingers, is itself engaging object performance. This show, as all puppetry, enchants with the physics of material, its movement and action. But the storytelling in this example is taking place more forcefully in the visual imagery than in the action and physical nature of the sand. We might be interested in the sand and its malleability, its shifting nature, and its thinness, but then equally amazed as this grainy substance crystalizes into an image. As in *Paper Story*, performance elements work in conjunction with displays of sequential visual images.

One last example points to yet a different kind of adaptation of comic imagery in contemporary puppetry. Canadian RustWerk Refinery's *Louis Riel: A Comic Book Stage Play*, adapted from Chester Brown's *Louis Riel: A Comic Strip Biography*, based on the life of nineteenth-century politician and Metis rights activist Louis Riel, is doing something quite different from *Paper Story* and Simonova's sand art in its use of visuals. The show does not rely on sequential images as its center. It does not show Riel's biographical story through a series of pictures but rather uses two-dimensional graphic imagery, taken directly from Chester Brown's work, to act out the story and impart a visual style that blends the performance of human actors and flat objects. Sometimes actors hold in front of their faces flat boards, masks bearing black-and-white drawings of the faces of the characters they perform. In this way, they bring the graphic novel's characters to life. At other times characters appear as flat drawn figures in the samestyle as the masks, but placed atop flat constructed torsos, basically making for large-scale, toy theatre–type figures. In other instances, actors perform with their own faces uncovered but carry props, such as rifles, that are, like the masks, flat boards with simplistic drawings of the objects in question upon them. Set elements also follow this general aesthetic as the artists play with a variety of ways of integrating the imagery from the book into performative representation and action.

In summary, all these examples show that, in puppetry, we are often not just dealing with performing objects but also with the performance of images. Understanding imagery and its interrelationship with objects and humans on the puppet stage helps clarify how puppetry is also in the family of other forms of visual storytelling, such as comics, animation, and film, and why these arts integrate easily within puppetry performances.

While objects may be at the center of puppetry, imagery, both in terms of the visual qualities of any puppet as well as actual images or pictures incorporated into the performance, deserves attention and theoretical understanding. Puppetry has a long historical link with picture storytelling and many contemporary puppeteers are playing creatively with bringing images and picture storytelling into their shows. For performing-object productions that actively engage with imagery, a theoretical understanding of how a picture and pictures in sequence are expressive needs to work in conjunction with views about how objects are acting and creating meaning on stage. There can be a fine line between what we perceive as and what acts like a two-dimensional image and what is a three-dimensional object. Objects and images can inform each other, even as each expresses content and structure in their own way. If movement expresses life onstage, images used within puppetry help us to ask and clarify where movement is coming from at any specific moment. Such questioning can lead us to a deeper understanding of how a sense of drama is created within a performing object production.

Notes

1 One could argue that India is the birthplace of puppetry itself as some of the oldest extant jointed figures, dating back to 2400 BCE, have been found in the Indus Valley near Pakistan,
2 The details about the Dōjōji scroll performance are based on seeing Ono do the presentation in both English and Japanese and an extended interview with him in January 2022 during my Fulbright Research Fellowship in Japan.

3 Ono likes to say he learned his Japanese as a child from listening to the scroll story.
4 A more complete account of Basil Twist's *Dogugaeshi* and my views of it can be found on pp 312-313 of the Performance in Perspective highlight box, "*Dogugaeshi*: Set Transformation As Performance," in the introductory theatre textbook, *The World of Theatre: Tradition and Innovation*, by Mira Felner and Claudia Orenstein (New York: Pearson; Allyn and Bacon, 2005).
5 My article "Thinking Inside the Box: Meditations on the Miniature at the Great Small Works Eighth International Toy Theatre Festival" (*Theater* 39.3 (2009): 144–155), delves into the topic and possibilities of toy theatre more fully and with many examples.

Works Cited

"Clare Dolan." Artsed4All, artsed4all.blog/tag/clare-dolan/. Accessed 15 July 2022.

Craig, Edward Gordon. "The History of Puppets." *The Marionette*, vol. 1, 1918, pp. 171–174.

Ferdowsi. *Shahnameh: The Epic of The Persian Kings*. Illustrated and designed by Hamid Rahmanian, translated and adapted by Ahmad Sadri, Quantuck Lane Press, 2013. Commas after Rahmanian, Sadri, and Press.

Kaplin, Stephen. "A Puppet Tree: A Model for the Field of Puppet Theatre." *TDR*, vol. 43, no. 3, 1999, pp. 28–35.

McCloud, Scott. *Understanding Comics: The Invisible Art*. Harper Perennial, 1993.

Rahmanian, Hamid, and Simon, Arizpe. *Zahhak: The Legend of the Serpent King*. Fantographic Books, 2018.

Tillis, Steve. *Toward an Aesthetics of the Puppet: Puppetry as a Theatrical Art*. Greenwood Press, 1992.

4 Humans and Objects

Pilgrimage puppets

It is perhaps fitting that I was never able to see in person the two puppets that most occupied my mind during the summer of 2021: Little Amal and Mocco. Little Amal at eleven feet tall is anything but "little." Created by artists from South Africa's Handspring Puppet Company for *The Walk* project from the UK organization Good Chance, Little Amal is a figure of a nine-year-old Syrian refugee child[1] that requires three puppeteers: one framed inside her, who operates her moving eyes and mouth and walks her legs with their own while on stilts, and two outside, one in charge of each arm controlled by a long rod. For particularly difficult terrain, an extra pole is fitted to her back and one more puppeteer is added to the crew. This giant puppet's four-month journey took her through nine countries across Europe, from Turkey to the Netherlands, with numerous stops along the route where local towns and organizations created their own festive, artistic events to greet her.[2] The overall narrative conceit of this enormous undertaking, which brought all the disparate events together within a single story-frame, was that Little Amal was a refugee child fleeing Syria, trying to be reunited with her mother. Her search ended in Manchester, "where – on the final night – she turned into a real little girl. Her mother became the people of Manchester" (B. Jones, personal communication, 7 Mar. 2022).

Mocco, built generally on the model of an upside-down marionette hung from an enormous crane at a height of thirty-two feet, was even larger than Amal and required thirty puppeteers pulling its strings from outside and below as they traveled along with it. Designed by picture book artist Arai Ryoji and Prague-based Japanese puppeteer Sawa Noriyuki, who were commissioned by the Tokyo Organizing Committee and Paralympic Games, Mocco was part of the events planned for Japan's run-up to the Tokyo 2021 Summer Olympics. With the intention of highlighting the rejuvenation and ongoing recovery of the Tohoku region, devastated by the 2011 earthquake and tsunami, Mocco traveled through three Tohoku prefectures—Iwate, Miyagi, and Fukushima—before arriving in Tokyo. The figure participated in events that highlighted local culture at major stops in each area. These events included Mocco's rendition of three local folk dances at each location. Mocco's very body reflected the rich natural

DOI: 10.4324/9781003096627-5

environment of Tohoku. Its design was based on drawings from children in the region affected by the disasters. They took their inspiration from readings of a short story by Matayoshi Naoki. Matayoshi's writing drew from northern Japanese legends of *yokai* or supernatural spirits, notably *Daidara-bocchi,* a gigantic mountain-like being whose movements and actions, the stories say, shaped Japan's northern landscape, creating lakes and other natural features as it passed by. Mooco's resin eyes incorporated paper cut-outs representing animals from Tohoku and flowers from the area ran throughout its body. On arrival in Tokyo, Mocco joined the Tohoku Kizuna festival at Shinjuku Gyoen Gardens, an annual event started in 2011 to commemorate those lost to that year's catastrophes. The festival incorporates elements from six major traditional Tohoku festivals.

The extraordinariness of these two enormous puppets, each at the center of larger cultural programming and directed at both local and international audiences, could not help but captivate my attention along with that of so many other puppet lovers around the world. Moreover, while both were taking place at other ends of the globe from my New York apartment, they were brought enticingly closer through a brush with the possibility of seeing each one live. Being asked by a scholarly journal if I might write a review of the Little Amal project sent my mind reeling into daydreams of following Amal across Europe (on my own dime). What would it take to meet Amal in Turkey and move with her from country to country? It was a tempting, and almost feasible, possibility. But family obligations, financial calculations, and basic prudence kept me home during the ever-morphing Covid pandemic. Seeing online that the United States State Department had three different Travel Advisories for US citizens contemplating trips to Turkey offered no encouragement. And so, for a further summer, after over a year of pandemic seclusion, like so many others, I stayed home, cautious of disease and world events, while Amal, created as a victim of unrest, traveled. The journeys of refugees are dangerous and foreboding. *The Walk,* however, taking place during the pandemic and enveloped in artistry and celebration, made the idea of walking and walking across new terrains, seeing something beyond the four walls of one's bedroom, desperately alluring. A vision of open vistas was inscribed in this large walking puppet figure, even as the project focused on issues of closed borders. Little Amal, with her innocent perspective from on high, could see far across the constructed barriers that keep people apart, over the heads of the border controls and into the landscapes beyond.

My desire to see Mocco was also frustrated on multiple occasions. I rose very early on the morning of July 23rd to watch the TV broadcast of the opening ceremonies of the Tokyo Summer Olympic Games, finally taking place after a year's postponement. Having caught glimpses of Mocco on the internet with blurbs referring to the "giant Olympic puppet" and a few short videos, I had convinced myself that it was constructed in order to make a grand entrance at the opening ceremonies. What better way to fill a large stadium than with a thirty-two-foot-tall colorful, dynamic figure? Other Olympic opening ceremonies had already proven the value and interest of including large puppets, as with those designed by puppet artist Michael Curry for the 2002 Winter Games in Salt Lake

Figure 4.1 Little Amal walks across the Brooklyn Bridge during her visit to New York City. October 2022.

Photo: Claudia Orenstein.

City. Why else would Mocco be traveling to Tokyo where the opening ceremonies would take place? To my dismay, I watched all the way through the telecast, but no Mocco in sight. Mocco coming to the opening ceremonies, it turns out, was never part of the plan, just an incarnation of my imagination. Nonetheless, I remain puzzled as to why ceremony organizers did not see this as the obvious way to end Mocco's journey and bring the recovery theme of the puppets' walk directly to Olympic events and international spectators, while adding a fitting dynamic visual element to the opening celebrations.

I was not alone in missing out on seeing Mocco in person. While crowds gathered at festivals throughout Europe to greet and occasionally protest Little Amal's arrival, people were prohibited from coming out to watch Mocco as a Covid-precaution. The Japanese government entreated people daily to stay home

Figure 4.2 The large Mocco puppet standing against the Tohoku landscape, with control apparatus and crew, alongside another puppet: a helmet Mocco wore that came off and transformed into a flying bird.

Photo courtesy of Rock'n Roll, Tokyo, Japan.

as the Covid situation worsened over the course of the summer, the very time the country was playing host to athletes from around the globe. Apart from the first event in Iwate, where spectators were allowed and a few showed up, and for the organizing officials supervising Mocco's travels, the world only saw this large puppet remotely, online. Again, the puppet traveled while people stayed home.

It looked as if I might be afforded another opportunity to encounter Mocco in person. In preparation for a fall 2021 Fulbright Fellowship in Japan, which the Fulbright organization somehow magically arranged to proceed in spite of travel bans, I contacted Sawa, who told me Mocco would be at another event in November. I put it on my calendar determined to go. Then, like all other public festivals in Japan that fall, this too was canceled as a precaution against the pandemic. One more opportunity seemed to arise for a sighting when I found out Sawa was planning something big with puppets in Hokkaido in February. Surely by February, gatherings could resume and Mocco would be present. But no. In mid-November, I discovered that not only was Mocco not meant to be part of that performance (which was subsequently canceled as well during Japan's February Omicron variant surge), but the puppet would not even be around to take part. By stipulation of the Olympic Committee, this grand, glorious puppet was to be fully dismantled before the new year to protect Olympic copyrighted materials from being used in other contexts. The destruction of the puppet was slated for the end of November. Several days of wild text exchanges and arrangements had me planning a five-hour plus ride from Tokyo to Iida City where Mocca was stored; someone in Iida City had offered to pick me up when I arrived and drive me to Mocca's location to catch a glimpse of this remarkable figure while it was at least somewhat intact. That trip, sadly, was also canceled when it became clear that the puppet would be fully dismantled before I ever arrived, some parts recycled, others sent to the trash. My friend in Iida, who had been involved in the project, reported that the puppeteers who had built Mocco had tears in their eyes as they dismantled their creation. The puppet that took two years to build was destroyed in less than a week. Mocco remained elusive. The full-life journey of this puppet, with its abrupt, untimely end, expressed to me a dourer metaphor than the symbol of rebirth from devastation the project intended. One could take comfort perhaps in the fact that Mocco's recycled parts might allow the puppet to have many future lives, enacting its own model of Buddhist reincarnation. Amal's continued story, by contrast, lies in her ongoing deployment in refugee awareness campaigns, codas to her original narrative. The Russian invasion of Ukraine, which began in February 2022, unfortunately called for a swift resumption of her activities. Another trip in October of 2022 brought Amal to New York, with its long history of receiving immigrant populations, for a two-and-a-half-week excursion. In New York, I did finally have not only one but several opportunities to see her and even participated in some of the planned performances that were part of these events.[3]

And yet, as I said at the start, it was perhaps fitting that I should miss seeing these two puppets in person at those times given the journeys I would have had to make to reach them. This is not because I am above making a long trip solely for the purpose of seeing a puppet. In fact, as you may have already discerned from reading this book, I kind of live for that. I have more than once enlisted friends for five-hour road trips to visit puppets in hard-to-reach locations, occasionally with no one in the party quite sure where we were headed. It is, rather, because I see these two puppets as what I have started to think of as *pilgrimage puppets*.

One of the things that made each of these puppets and puppet projects so unusual that summer was the fact that the puppets were doing the walking, putting their feet on the ground, one after another. They were not being carried aloft, as puppets are in so many protest marches, or on a cart, as is the case with Japan's festival *karakuri ningyō*, (automaton figures), mounted on *dashi* (festival floats). Instead, arrangements or mechanisms were created to allow the puppets to do, or at least to appear to do, the walking themselves.

A second set of remarkable features both projects shared was the extended lengths of the journeys the figures were undertaking and the vast terrains they would cover. In actuality, neither puppet walked their entire route. In each case, the puppet was, for the most part, driven in a truck from one location to another, where it made initial entrances and exits to participate in specific events. However, the characterization of each of the projects highlighted the idea of journey and travel, in essence, pilgrimage. These puppets were not simply processing down a street for a day of events, but traveling through, in Amal's case, different countries, in Mocco's, various regions, and both over several months. The disparate performance events for each were conceived within a larger storyline and framework. And each had a final destination as a culmination of their expedition, one that was full of emotion and metaphorical symbolism—for Amal the meeting with her mother in Manchester and for Mocco the Kizuna commemorative festival. Along their routes, Little Amal and Mocco both made many significant stops; they didn't simply walk by. Moreover, every stop affirmed the overall purpose and import of their undertakings. In contrast to the pilgrimages I would have had to undertake to see them, these puppets were each on a kind of pilgrimage of their own, coming to the people and the places, rather than the spectators traveling to them, at least in terms of the general conceptions of these projects. The fact that they journeyed at a time when so many people were prevented from traveling reinforced the ideas of displacement and excursion within their narratives.[4]

France's Royal de Luxe company has also been creating and performing huge, extraordinary puppets since *The Giant fallen from the sky* which took place in Le Havre, France in 1993. Like Mocco, Royal de Luxe's characters are operated as upside-down marionettes by a large company of performers journeying with them and controlling them by means of mechanisms hoisted on a kind of crane. Royal de Luxe's giant puppets also walk, or appear to walk, on the ground, and their actions are contained within a dramatic storyline. By contrast, however, Royal de Luxe's creations were born out of the company's "three days one city" concept, the desire to tell a story within a single city over the course of three days, something they first began with human actors in 1984 (History of the City). In shows like *Liverpool's Dream* (2018) in Liverpool, UK and *The Great Invitation* (2017) in Montreal, Canada, the company brought their puppets to a specific city and transformed it into a dramatic setting for the giant characters who then played out their tales within that city on a grand scale. People came to and gathered in the disparate locations within the city where performance events took place, sometimes moving with the characters to their next encounter. These large puppet events transform people's experiences of their urban spaces during the time of the spectacle and no doubt their relationships to those areas on into the future. However, traversing terrain, *journeying,* is not the main theme of these projects as it was for the two pilgrimage puppets, Amal and Mocco, in the summer of 2021.

Peter Schuman's Bread and Puppet Theatre, using a collective construction and performance model, has been integrating huge figures made of papier-mâché into the company's shows and protest marches since the 1960s and has influenced generations of artists, who have participated in puppet pageants at their home in Glover, Vermont as well as in their numerous national and international tours. In "Louder than Traffic: Bread and Puppet Parades," John Bell eloquently describes how these figures match the urban landscape. Schuman's figures tend to be iconic, archetypal, or emblematic, capturing large-scale ideas in their oversized forms. They are not attempting to be specific individuals with personal stories. Bread and Puppet's figures are workers, bureaucrats, the oppressed, bankers, The Devil, Mother Earth, etc. Mocco and Little Amal, by contrast, may point to greater issues—the resilience of the Tohoku region, the struggles of refugees—but these puppets are more specific in their characterization and in the humanity of the physical details crafted into them. Especially Amal, who has a personal story and a lively, human face. Her eyes can stare right into yours and her mouth can open in awe at the world around her. Mocco looks more like an anime figure in design. And it is a mythic creature but still seems to be more a unique character than an archetype or iconic idea. Bread and Puppet's creations may march or be carried in protests, but they are not fundamentally about travel and journeying.

Other models of encounter

The story of my interest in these two pilgrimage puppets serves as an introduction to further contemplations about the relationship of puppeteers and spectators to the objects of performance, the physical, phenomenological experience of human bodies in relation to objects, as well as the metaphorical and symbolic implications of those experiences and arrangements. A default metaphor of puppetry that those in politics frequently invoke is that of a hidden operator pulling the strings from behind the scenes to control a hapless figure. In today's diverse world of puppetry arts, the idea of a hidden puppeteer is only one of the innumerable kinds of relationships performers and objects can have, and each variant, each set of choices, evokes and expresses something different. While the style and thematic implications of hidden puppeteers are important, I will spend more time in this chapter discussing the many visible ones that are today ubiquitous on puppetry stages. Such relationships between humans and objects on stage shouldn't be taken as simple givens—these kinds of puppets are presented in this way—although it goes without saying that addressing practical concerns, learning tried-and-true methods from established puppeteers, and absorbing techniques from traditional forms are all invaluable. They can instead be considered as further opportunities to enlist all the elements of performance to their fullest potential of expression. Meaning is expressed in everything that is visible, physicalized, and apprehended on the puppet stage, and so the very essential choices about the relationships of humans—on stage and in the house—to performing objects should be made with thoughtful, critical care. While puppetry intentionally gives focus to performing objects, human stage presences and audience members are undeniably part of the full experience of a show. Artists, audiences, and critics can consider how a production takes these into account and makes the most of them.

Although the examples these examples are about my own journeys or lack of journeys to these giant puppets, they also express for me the relationships of these figures to their puppeteers and how the characters are presented and offered to spectators. Through my lens of thinking about these as pilgrimage puppets and the religious implications of that terminology, I can't help but then also think of them in contrast to other religious figures that are close relatives of the puppet.

For example, statues of deities housed in churches, temples, or shrines. Once, in northern Thailand, I had the experience of visiting a Buddhist temple that had a small museum of artifacts on its premises, and among them a life-size bronze statue of one of the important former head monks, long deceased, seated with legs crossed in a meditative position. The statue sat on a short platform. I can't fully explain what happened, but I had the distinct sense, as I walked into the upstairs gallery where it sat, that somehow it was inviting me to move toward it, to come and kneel in front as one might do in veneration or to receive a blessing. Although I can't fully explicate how that directive seemed to emanate from this powerful carved figure, I can ask how the relationship of someone coming to a statue and bowing in front of it—something religious people in many cultures do regularly[5]—differs from one in which the statue is, instead, like those of deities in places as disparate as Italy and Japan, processed through the streets at a festival, carried by throngs of devotees? The statue in the second case is displaced from its home to pass viewers, moving through or along in front of them, raised up, traveling on carts that are often balanced on the shoulders of the devout or pulled by devotees. What does it mean—physiologically, psychologically, metaphorically—to lift-up a god or a saint and carry them vs. kneeling in front of them? How are these experiences differently meaningful? Any particular culture may of course engage in a variety of these models in relating to figures of deities, but the experiences of these various phenomenological relationships can be experienced differently. These various embodied physical gestures in relation to objects are packed with significance that not only performers but spectators also apprehend, not just with their eyes in watching, but through the echo of these movements in their own bodies as they physically absorb these performed actions. Not everyone will have identical experiences, emotions, or references regarding such gestures, but they are still powerfully evocative. These arrangements are something to think about every time one picks up a puppet in performance or watches a performer doing so.

In these religious examples, the roles of performers and spectators can conflate as the devout become engaged enactors in relation to objects of reverence. The way their shifts in position relative to the objects changes their status within the event (from spectator to performer) is equally noteworthy. To hold up a statue, in physical contact with it, is to be more of a primary enactor, while to watch it go by is to be more of a spectator, even if such spectators participate in other ways (praying, cheering, etc.). What if the enactors holding up the statue look up at it? Now the nature of their enactment might shift as they also take on more of a spectator's orientation, simultaneously embodying multiple roles. Debra Hilborn's "Relating to the Cross: A Puppet Perspective on the Holy Week Ceremonies of the Regularis Concordia," does a wonderful job of unpacking how different gestures and words throughout this medieval ritual shift the roles of the participants in relation to the cross they carry and worship, simultaneously transforming how the object itself is seen variously as a cross or as an embodiment or even, at times, a stand in for Christ.

What then if this statue had some joints, at the shoulders for example, allowing the arms to swing forward and back and, thereby, invite one to move them? What now is the manipulator's relationship to this divinity as they grasp it and put it into action, animating it? In "Performing Death: A Medieval Puppet of Christ," Michelle Oing analyzes a 1510 jointed Christ figure from Stadtkirche St. Nicolai, Döbeln, Germany. From inspecting the object, she reconstructs how it may have been used at religious events and how the clerics involved in the performance would have interacted with it, both their physical dealings with the object and the roles they may have played alongside it as they dramatized the scenes of Christ's Passion.

What if someone then takes up a divine figure with jointed parts, maybe a small one, and lifts it up with their own arms, not on a cart, and moves it about in front of them? This figure is maybe now something more like what we commonly think of as a puppet. The performer might then take this puppet with them, outside of their abode, to other houses and show it to the people in them. Such actions are similar to those of the ritual *hakomawashi* puppeteers in Tokushima, Japan, as they go house to house to bless homes at New Year with puppets of the god Ebisu and three other figures that invoke the divine—Okina, Senzai, and Sanbaso. Nakauchi Masako, the main puppeteer currently upholding this long-established practice, moves her Ebisu puppet its head and arms and makes its legs swing back and forth so he appears to be walking as she brings him to each member of each of the roughly one thousand households she visits in January and February every year.[6] Ebisu pats the patrons with his hands in offering blessings. Here the puppet not only comes to the house, but to the individuals in it and touches them, his joyful face smiling directly at them. His full journey, along with the other three figures that accompany him, involves the puppeteer carrying him folded away in a box, on her shoulder or on her back, between houses and then unpacking him at every stop and taking up the control rods within his garments that allow her to animate his movements. Each of the *hakomawashi* puppet's initial actions at each stop take place facing the home altar. The unseen *kami* or god is the first, central audience for this event. The small Ebisu, with his moving hands, legs, and head, held up and carried about by a performer, is now physically active or alive in a different way from the enshrined statue, the paraded deity, or the jointed Christ. I am not making a contrast here between puppets and idols, but rather offering a way into thinking creatively about the different physical relationships performers and spectators can have with different kinds of figurative objects, in this case, all related in some way to religion or spirituality.

In these examples, rather than thinking about one object with more life or movement than another, we might think instead, as in our study of images, about the different places from which liveness, movement, or action emanates. With the large, processed statues mentioned previously, there is movement from the many porters of the shrines and sometimes from the rolling wheels of a cart. In Viterbo, Italy, the statue of Saint Rose is carried through the streets of her small town each fall. For this ritual, she stands atop a huge tower adorned with lights, weighing five tons, called La Macchina de Santa Rosa, or the Machine of Saint Rose, carried by a hundred devotees. The statue is without joints of any kind, yet she moves, swaying up on high as she is born aloft through the streets. By contrast, the Japanese *karakuri*

Figure 4.3 *Hakomawashi* performer Nakauchi Masako offering blessings with her puppet of the god Ebisu while Minami Kimiyo accompanies her playing a small drum. Nishinomiya, January 2022.

Photo: Claudia Orenstein.

ningyō, automaton puppets, paraded on floats, have mechanisms for movement of their own. Some even perform miraculous puppet transformations, manipulated by locals who are experts in pulling the strings that move the various parts of the puppets above as their operators remain hidden out of sight inside the float below. These puppet motions are additional to the overall movements of the floats that transport them through the town. Although these carts, unlike St. Rose's, have wheels, they still require throngs of locals to tug them through the often narrow streets of old cities like Takayama, which holds a large festival with its floats with puppets twice a year. In the case of the sitting monk statue I encountered in Thailand, the physical movement came from me toward the statue as I walked over to it and knelt. Its liveness was a kind of internal apprehension emanating from it or perceived as so by me. With the *hakomawashi*, there is no doubt that the puppet is in motion through the actions of the completely visible performer, who also carries her figures, packed away, from house to house.

These examples do not constitute any kind of evolutionary model of puppetry (from statue to moving figure) but set out one range of options of how enactors might be present in relationship to objects and how these configurations also organize how spectators encounter them. The fact that these examples are all drawn from ritual or religious contexts might help to highlight the different kinds of significance that can emerge from such relationships and emphasize how they are not to be taken for granted. Of course, we don't need to think of or treat every puppet as a god to bring the carefulness that might come in attending to ritual actions in our thinking about or staging of puppets in relation to human bodies.

Puppets to puppeteers

Let's now turn to examples of relationships between puppets and humans in non-ritual, performance events. Our discussion in this chapter began with giant puppets, and we might continue there with one of the biggest puppets to tread the commercial theatre stage. In November 2018, *King Kong*, a musical based on the classic 1933 film, opened on Broadway (after an earlier 2013 run in Melbourne). Pre-opening publicity and news items stressed the excitement of the 1.1 ton, nearly twenty-foot-tall animatronic creature at the center of the production, created by Melbourne's Sonny Tilders and the Creature Technology Company. The puppet required "14 performers, as well as 16 microprocessors to operate," and Michael Paulson of *the New York Times* described the work of the ten puppeteers on stage moving his limbs manually in this way: "They push, pull (via rigging ropes), and even use torque exerted by jumping off the beast's back to force his fists upward." He notes that there were three more operators,

> from a soundproof booth in the theater's balcony, manipulating Kong's hips, shoulders, neck, head and facial expressions using joysticks and pedals that operate motors and hydraulics inside his body. At the same time, an automation operator lifts and lowers the ape's entire body using winches

connected by steel cables to a giant gantry crane in the theater's fly space overhead. (Kong is too big to fit in a theater's wings, so he spends his offstage time hanging over the action …) (Paulson)

One of the backstage operators also provided Kong's voice, "digitally modulated—processed and mixed with sampled sounds — in real time to make it deeper and more animalistic" (Paulson).

The mix of artistic creativity, technological intelligence, and ensemble choreography that brought this enormous ape to life is, without a doubt, a major and impressive achievement. Having absorbed our astonishment at this feat of ingenuity and physical energy, and everything that has gone into it, and honored all the artists involved, we can start thinking dramaturgically. Now we can ask, how did Kong and his visible and invisible handlers appear in terms of the meaning they created onstage, not just as a huge element of spectacle and technological ingenuity, or even as a character, but as part of a drama? What kind of attention was being paid (by artists and spectators) to these various bodies on stage, and how did they all add up? I am not asking if the manipulation of the big puppet was excellently executed, but how the choices onstage for presenting the puppet vis-à-vis the puppeteers could be read or understood as part of the whole dramatic experience.

The videos included in the online *New York Times* article I quoted here show an impressive choreography of puppeteers moving in and around Kong as they operate him, their presences part of an intricate and vigorous gymnastic dance with object that is a show in and of itself. They are maneuvering him, but he also appears to sometimes act on his own in concert with them, as the viewer's eyes dart from one place to another attempting to take in the huge figure and all the actions of and around him at once. The article tells us the operators on stage were known as "the King's Company," a designation that alludes to Shakespeare's troupe of players, who held that title (Paulson). The name also seems to cast them as a cadre of retainers or soldiers guarding or going into battle alongside this formidable figure, his army if you will. A company of ten performers on stage is not negligible and all dressed in black, next to the large hairy black figure at their center, they stand both physically and metaphorically as the source of his power. How much more powerful is someone with ten supporters by their side, standing with them, than a person or ape standing alone? "*The New York Times*" article reveals that the production acknowledged the contributions of the visible puppeteers when Paulsen notes,

> Ms. Yalango-Grant is one of two women regularly in the King's Company. In the one previous production, in Melbourne in 2013, the group was all male; for Broadway Mr. McOnie suggested incorporating women, and they double as members of the ensemble when Kong is not on stage. ("In Melbourne it was clear Kong stood for man—masculine energy—and I wanted to change that," Mr. McOnie said.) (Paulson)

This is an important insight that shows the director's understanding that the audience reads not only the puppet, but the puppet along with its puppeteers as the character, and reveals how the presence of the puppeteers, their gender make-up and no doubt other elements as well, unconsciously impart personality and other qualities to the character. The puppeteers are not just puppet stagehands moving the big lug around. They are apprehended on some level as part of the character itself.

Despite all the creative energy, ingenuity, and hard work that went into both the production and the giant puppet, *King Kong* was not as successful a show as many would have hoped. In the *The New York Times* review, "'King Kong' Is the Mess That Roared" two major critics, Jesse Green and Ben Brentley, in conversation, both disparage the show for a variety of reasons. Notably, both felt the ape was the most interesting thing on the stage, although Green describes his movements as sluggish. Green sums up his views stating, "A car wreck of clichés like that simply can't put a feminist story across meaningfully. Or any story, really—and that's a bigger problem than the bad score and sluggish 20-foot marionette" (Green). I don't disagree with the critiques these formidable reviewers offer on the show's clichés or the music or even the sluggishness of the puppet. Nonetheless, I would like to suggest another view on how to consider the show's problems from a puppetry perspective. Brantley is thinking in the right direction when he notes,

> Yes, but as far as I can tell, the story—and the music and the gymnastic dancing—are basically just filler until Kong shows up again and looks noble and sorrowful and, occasionally (when Peter Mumford's lighting is really low), menacing. Didn't you sense the live performers knew they weren't the main attraction? (Green)

It is not simply that the human actors were being upstaged by a big puppet spectacle. This idea would imply that actors can't perform alongside puppets, which they can, and very successfully in fact. But rather, to my mind, it reveals how puppets are not successful when used primarily as stage spectacle or as crafted stand-ins for human characters. In bringing a puppet, and such a large one, into their stage world, *King Kong* entered what I want to call the *puppetverse*, the world of the puppet and puppetry, and needed to operate under its "laws." As we have already seen, in puppetry objects are at the center. Artists need to conceptualize all aspects of performance—storyline, human characters, etc.—in relation to them. Thinking about such a show should begin with the puppets and then build around them. It can be problematic to introduce a puppet into a world operating primarily on a traditional theatre paradigm that foregrounds the human actor. The entrance of the puppet changes the sensibilities and awareness of the audience, and the rest of the production must respond and adjust. Once spectators start paying attention to animated materiality onstage, I believe their attunement, their way of watching, shifts. Material in motion takes precedence and asserts itself, creating expectations of performance style.

For me, there were three extremely powerful moments in *King Kong*. Each was when the puppet's true strength onstage was fully expressed and the fact of having an enormous puppet at the center of the drama was most usefully employed. They offer views into ways the production successfully negotiated the puppetverse. The first is when Kong confronts one of the human characters who has invaded his haunt in the jungle. At this moment, the enormous puppet looks directly at the piddly human form in front of him, and all ten operators emerge simultaneously from different spots where they have been hidden or half-hidden on or around Kong and stare, along with Kong, in the direction of the human intruder. At this moment one can truly see Kong's enormous, daunting presence and, more importantly, the fact of needing and having ten performers on stage to make this object move becomes not a hindrance or a technical difficulty to be solved, but an asset, helping to physically express the strength of the figure in a way that even its own material immensity cannot. If the puppet itself is slow or sometimes a little awkward in its actions, at this juncture, the well-deployed presence of these ten performers more than compensates for any technological shortcomings. Moreover, Kong is allowed to express his power while standing still. The impact of this one moment reveals how the movements of the puppeteers might have been choreographed throughout not just to move the puppet, which surely they were, but to create an expressive meta-story or accompanying story for the show: an ongoing drama of the puppet's relationship to the beings that put it into action. Just as Basil Jones, as we saw in chapter 1, informs us that the puppet's striving to be alive is the ur-text or central story of every puppet show, a puppet's relationship to its operators, the source of its liveliness, especially when there are ten of these performers and they are visible on stage, is another accompanying story that spectators view and take in. Taking advantage of this fact offers further opportunities to deepen a show's expressive capacities.

No doubt it was difficult enough to get the puppet to move fluidly through the collaborative actions of fourteen hard-working puppeteers, a feat that deserves accolades. However, not being able to discern a physical meta-story that could add more depth of meaning to the main story feels like a missed opportunity when there is a huge puppet and a cadre of operators at the center of a musical. When one has entered the puppetverse, the language, customs, and habits of puppet objects should govern not only how one moves a single puppet object, but how one creates drama. This production seemed caught between its desire to be or the possibilities of being two kinds of shows: one, a familiar Broadway musical with a human love story at its center, acted out and sung between actors; and, the other, a puppet production in which the 1.1 ton gorilla in the room was the actual weighted center of the show around which all other elements defined themselves. The physical, material space alone that the puppet and puppeteers took up on stage necessarily made them the center of the drama. We could ask, how might *King Kong* have created a complete, physicalized, meta-storyline for the puppet and its relationship to its swinging, jumping puppeteers—the thing that the marketing team seemed to have sensed was the main attraction of the production—and then built the rest of the show around it?

98 Humans and Objects

The two other moments in the show I felt were powerful were these: one, when Kong, alone onstage, looks out and sees the audience. He moves forward, breaking the fourth wall, even crossing the proscenium, to come downstage toward the spectators, glaring. At this moment, the thin story of the musical is fully cast aside to deal with the reality of the performative event, an audience facing a huge puppet beast—miraculous, funny, foreboding, unpredictable; the audience has, as the kids say, "all the feels." What if, this moment says, this big beast came right at you? This one simple moment captured a pure encounter between animated object and spectator, one that enjoins audience members to watch each of the puppet's movements with rapt attention. One step forward or back could signal the enormous beast coming dangerously close to us or retreating again into the frame of its stage and constructed story. All the drama in the world is packed into this encounter. This moment was a powerful way of using the massive puppet at the center of the show. How might one build a drama around this, where such a moment is not a side note but a central element, integral to a throughline of the production's puppet-human relationships?

The third moment, or repeated moments really, that successfully exploited the large puppet were those showing Kong running through the streets of New York City. In these scenes, the puppet is animated by puppeteers who physicalize its running in place. In conjunction with the puppet's actions, screen projections, both behind and on either side of Kong, show New York streets speeding by. All the elements onstage work together to create the illusion that the ape is racing through the urban jungle. In these moments, the technological use of projections

Figure 4.4 King Kong on Broadway. One of the most powerful moments in the show, when the gorilla breaks the fourth wall and confronts the audience.

Photo: Sara Krulwich/The New York Times/Redux.

exists on par with the big puppet. The elements coordinate to create a single illusion that we can enjoy while also taking pleasure in *how* the montage of them—the in-place actions of the puppet and the moving images from the video—work together. One can appreciate watching not just the illusion itself but seeing how the elements come together to create that illusion. Montage, as we saw earlier, is something intrinsic to puppetry, so bringing projections and puppet actions together to create one combined effect is in line with the puppet's overall aesthetic model. This moment also offers another good example for thinking about where movement emanates from. Here there is the movement of the puppet by the performers on and offstage and then a different, additional sense of movement from the filmed projections—the streets whizzing by—which all combine to help spectators understand the object as moving through space.

You may be thinking that these examples seem to discard the singing actors essential to musical theatre and asking if puppets can successfully be part of a Broadway musical with human performers. They certainly can. One has only to think of Disney's *The Lion King* on Broadway and the multiple, brilliant ways director Julie Taymor and her creative team integrated human performers and performing objects throughout that show for evidence of how this partnership can work. Inspired by an animated film, *The Lion King* took visual and performing object storytelling, a kind of stage equivalent of film animation, as a central idea from the beginning and constructed characters and scenes from that governing perspective. Instead of placing human actors in contrast to puppets, the entire production lives in a world of expressive object-actor hybrids. While all the characters seem to have different relationships between human and object in their constructions or conceptualizations, the governing idea that nearly every character is a mix of human and object is visible throughout and helps put all the disparate figures into the same visual, imaginative world. For example, the character Timon, the meerkat who, with his pal the warthog Pumbaa, adopts and raises the lost lion cub Simba, is a full-fledged, independent figure, whose puppeteer stands behind it with his own feet connected to those of the puppet so that figure and operator walk together as one.[7] The puppeteer then uses one hand, usually the right, directly inside the head of the puppet to move both its head and torso while holding it upright. With their left arm, the puppeteer manipulates the puppet's left arm from a rod at the elbow. The design of this character further integrates puppet and puppeteer by having Timon's tail pop up behind the puppeteer who, dressed in green, provides a continual grassy scenic backdrop for the puppet figure's actions. With his own head visible over the Timon puppet, the puppeteer (Max Casella in the original cast), is also present as an actor, speaking for and echoing, amplifying, doubling, in short, adding in various ways to the puppet's expressivity. Pumbaa, like Timon, visually replicates the familiar character in the animated movie, but the stage version is a built figure hanging off of and around the body of the actor/puppeteer performing him,[8] whose own head protrudes from the top of the character and whose own legs serve as the warthog's front legs. A black wig, with hairs standing upright, further integrates the actor's head into the full image by evoking the warthog's mane. Again, the performer here acts in concert with the material figure he ports on and around his body, even as it also bears its own face. The theme of integration of human and object is echoed in all the lions—actors who sport beautifully styled lion heads atop their own. One of the few figures that is a completely constructed object, not visibly integrated with human performers, is the newborn lion cub, a doll-like figure with jointed limbs, held aloft on the savannah clifftop in the iconic moment of welcoming a new life into the world that occurs at both the beginning and the end of the show, symbolically encapsulating the continually renewing circle of life. The newborn is only a brief presence for these stage moments and may lead us to ask, what kind of object-human world has it been born into? How will it grow within it?

The show keeps the concept of portraying all of the natural world as a mix of object and human in its flora as well as fauna, beyond the example of Timon's green costume. The grasslands are presented as alive and moving, embodied in the grass sprouting boards carried on the heads of ensemble dancers dressed in white, their silhouettes reminiscent of African women carrying jugs for water or goods to market. Even the jungle plants are alive, vine dancers in green wriggling down from above, and others on stage, enwrapped in elaborate green leaves. Whether lions on the plains, plants in the jungle, or warthogs in the swamp, all the characters, no matter how differently designed, with their own distinct integrations of human and object and particular animating methods, live together in the same dramatic, aesthetic world, each providing its own imaginative take on the integrated object-human visual theme.

One might even look more closely at the balance of object and human presented in each of the characters and think through the expressive ideas contained in those equations. Rafiki, the wise shaman mandrill, performed originally by Tsidii Le Loka, is the one human character not presented as a blend of human and constructed elements, except for some extensions on the performer's fingers. Rafiki's only other object is more of a prop, a magic stick held in hand. Colorful make-up and costuming place this performer in the same visual world of an imagined African plain as the others. But Rafiki's position as someone in touch with forces beyond the daily struggles of the savannah, liberated from that physical world and connected to larger, cosmic realms, is manifest in the design concept for this character, with nearly no puppet or object elements. Does the amount of materiality in each blended human-object character express something about how earth-bound they are? Does this idea play out through the entire cast? Do Rafiki, played by a human actor, and the newborn lion, a doll-like figure with no human incorporation, form two poles of a continuum? I leave it to you to investigate the answers to these questions but propose this conceptual framework as one way of seeing an object interpretive logic within the constructed object/human performer choices in this production. What is clear, however, is that Taymor and her design team were not satisfied with a limited view of what a performed object on stage could be, or do, or mean. Instead, the production shows careful reflection on each character, and how its design could recall the beloved figure from the animated film while allowing for a thoughtful, integrated stage performance of object and actor. *The Lion King*'s varied, expressive integrations of human and material are a central means of its theatrical storytelling.

It would be correct to point out that there are no *human* characters in *The Lion King*. One task of the production was to craft a stage world of animals living on a half-mythical African plain. *King Kong*, on the other hand, is specifically about a strange mythical creature that appears within a more familiar human world and does not fit in. How could the puppetry qualities of this misfit in the human world continue to be highlighted and emphasized not just through a storyline, but *physically* to bring home that point while also attending to the injunctions of the puppetverse? What could happen at each moment to stress this idea? How could the operators become part of that idea? The conceptual idea of what the puppet character's situation is, an ill-fitting outsider in a human world, might somehow become a concrete metaphor and a further entry point into the physicality and staging of the object and its relationship to human performers.

Puppeteer and scholar Stephen Kaplin, in "A Puppet Tree: A Model for the Field of Puppet Theatre," offers an important conceptual model for how to understand puppets on a continuum of human performers, masked actors, and puppets of all kinds. His model helps explain the aesthetic continuity that can exist in a production like *The Lion King* within all the diverse material-human incarnations it offers. In his model, actors and puppeteers are all understood as doing the job of projecting character. Actors do it through their bodies, voices, and actions, aided by the material elements of costumes and props. An actor who dons a mask is still projecting character through their body, but now does so in concert with the crafted object of the mask that obscures their face and, in so doing, forces them to draw on other means and skills for expressivity. The performance of character through materiality becomes more forceful with objects that are not directly linked to a performer's body—different kinds of puppets. The further detached these are from the artist's direct touch, the more low or high-tech means a puppeteer needs to operate them—strings, rods, animatronics, etc. Another continuum Kaplin proposes, on a different axis of the chart he offers, describes the relationship between the number of puppeteers to the number of objects in performance. A single puppeteer can perform a full cast of characters, as Indonesian *dalang* do, or a group of many performers can manipulate a single, huge figure, as in Bread and Puppet Theatre's large, outdoor pageants. In Bread and Puppet's *Domestic Resurrection Circus* festivals, a whole community of artists manipulates a single large-scale figure as it moves across an expansive outdoor stage. As *The Lion King* shows, even within these basic equations of performers to objects, a wide variety of possibilities exist. The continuum that links human actors to those using masks and then to performing objects is significant to acknowledge and understand. One might also ask what might constitute the tipping points at which human/material balances shift, and how to understand these and their implications for production. For example, even the organic presence of the bodies of masked performers can seem startling after long stretches of watching only crafted figures.

Diverse puppet and human interconnections in puppetry traditions

The Lion King's unusual integrations of human performers and objects seem to be entirely innovative, contemporary creations. Yet traditional puppetry around the world also reveals puppeteers experimenting with various ways of positioning themselves in relation to their performing objects to achieve a range of practical and artistic goals. Julie Taymor's work is, in fact, inspired by her travels in Asia, where diverse puppetry traditions abound. Many of the forms from which she borrows involve visible manipulators, and spectators in these traditions it seems must, on some level, take in the presence of the puppeteers along with the actions of their figures. Even if the habit of seeing such shows and their accepted conventions render the performers, if not invisible, at least generally unremarkable to audiences who focus instead on the liveliness, beauty, and drama of figurative objects, the presence of puppeteers is still an undeniable aspect of the experience. The relationships of objects to performers, therefore, are always part of the full dramatic equation. Different physical arrangements of human bodies and materiality by which performers set objects into action propose disparate conceptual frameworks for thinking about meaning expressed through human-material configurations.

Japanese traditional puppetry offers a good terrain of examples in that it holds a variety of models of how puppeteers connect to performing objects that use similar types of puppets in different visible puppeteer-puppet configurations. The Japanese *bunraku* tradition, mentioned previously, has become world renowned for the truly unique technique it developed that requires three manipulators on a single puppet. This model has been adopted and adapted by puppeteers around the world (in what is often called *bunraku*-style), for how it allows intricately articulated movements of full, complex figures. *Bunraku* puppets, some of which can be up to four feet tall, have detailed faces, heads that can turn, jointed limbs, and hands that can open and close. Some have eyes and eyebrows that move or faces that can transform instantaneously, say from a beautiful woman into a horned demon, just by the puppeteer pushing one or more small levers on the handle descending from the puppet's head. The head and neck piece, or *kashira*, is the most prized and carefully crafted part of *bunraku* puppets. Their torsos, by contrast, under their generally lavish costumes, are minimal in substance, almost non-existent, except for a structural frame and some strategically placed padding. The wooden carved legs and arms, with mechanisms for opening and closing hands, are attached to the torsos by tied strings and, like the heads, are potentially interchangeable between figures. Female figures don't have legs or feet at all, the presence of these is invoked by a puppeteer's simulation of them in moving the bottom of the puppet's kimono. This construction helps to make bunraku puppets flexible and lighter than they might otherwise be given their size and the heavy layers of kimono or armor characters wear. In this tradition, a lead performer operates the puppet's head and right arm while a second one controls the left arm and a third the feet. Lead puppeteers spend years mastering the other performance positions before moving on to the head. Knowing the work of each manipulator enables them to cue and direct the team during performance so that all three performers can work together as a tight-knit ensemble, moving their figure in unison to present a physically and psychologically integrated character. The interconnected movements of the puppeteers with each other are as important as any of the puppet's own actions.

What interpretive ideas might this arrangement and the presence of the three puppeteers looming behind their highly expressive figures invite? Jane Marie Law, a scholar of Japanese religion, suggests that *bunraku* puppeteers can be read as embodiments of greater forces, the Shinto gods and Buddhist karma at work in shaping the lives and unfortunate fates of *bunraku*'s often doomed characters (Law). Many *bunraku* plays follow individuals who, within the tightly configured social structures of the late Edo period, when much of the repertoire was established, find themselves desperately caught between, on the one hand, their social duties and obligations (*giri*) and, on the other hand, their personal feelings and attachments (*ninjō*). As such, they suffer the constraints of circumstances not fully within their control. Audiences might unconsciously apprehend these larger fateful forces at work in the presence of the human operators directing the puppets' actions. The idea of constructed figures interacting with invisible energies hews close to Shinto practices in which dolls or other human-shaped forms, called *hitogata*, are employed to mediate with spiritual elements in various ways. These can include carrying off illness and pollution or attracting and embodying spirits. Law suggests, therefore, that in Japan the experience of the physical relationship between *bunraku* performers and puppets onstage is informed by this broader cultural lens.

While the *bunraku*'s three-person manipulation model continues to be mesmerizing, practical and other considerations have led to the development of further performance techniques in Japan that use puppets similar to those in *bunraku*, even to perform the same plays, but with different human-object arrangements. These different configurations may also express or, when borrowed outside of their traditional repertoires, be consciously used to express different interpretive resonances.

During the nineteenth century, *bunraku*'s popularity diminished and having three highly trained performers for each puppet became a practical and financial liability for many companies. In response, in 1874, Nishikawa Koryū developed a new way to manipulate large, fully articulated figures, similar to those used in *bunraku*, with only one puppeteer. The form that emerged, *kuruma ningyō* or cart puppetry, is still practiced today, primarily by the Hachioji Kuruma Ningyō company, under the direction of Nishikawa Koryū V. The *kuruma ningyō* puppeteer sits on a small, wheeled box or cart. These puppets have wooden pegs jutting out the bottoms of their feet, which the puppeteer grasps with their own toes. The puppeteer can then walk themselves and their puppet forward or backward while propelling and directing the cart on which they sit. The puppeteer manipulates their figure's right arm with their own right hand while their left-hand works the character's head. The puppet's left arm is set into action in two ways: a looped string on the puppet's left arm hooks around the puppeteer's right upper arm allowing for lateral movement. For vertical movement, the performer moves the figure's left arm with the thumb of their right hand. Instead of working as an ensemble with other puppeteers, as in *bunraku*, the *kuruma ningyō* performer is linked to the puppet and the cart, wheeling themselves and their figure through the space while moving the character's limbs and head. The process requires full engagement of all the puppeteer's extremities at once. In contrast to *bunraku*'s three-person technique, in which the puppets float in the air, allowing the foot puppeteer, crouching down, to get underneath the character, *kuruma ningyō* figures touch, walk on, and stomp directly on the floor. These figures have a strong, visceral connection to the earth.

Stomping is an important aspect of Japanese performance that harkens back to the legendary, sacred roots of Japanese dance. Ancient chronicles describe a first performance taking place outside the cave where the sun goddess, Amaterasu, had sequestered herself after a fight with her brother, the storm god, Susanoo. Her seclusion drew all light and fecundity from the earth. To lure her out, the other gods and goddesses assembled and watched Ame-no-Uzume, goddess of the dawn, do a stomping dance atop an overturned bucket. She finished her dance by lifting her dress to reveal her genitals, provoking joyful laughter from the holy crowd. The noise brought Amaterasu from the cave, restoring life to the earth. The act of stomping is therefore culturally associated with the jubilant celebration of life and a powerful awakening of the gods. Stomping is also connected with the actions of planting rice, another Japanese life-sustaining essential.

Figure 4.5 Hachioji *Kuruma Ningyō* performer Nishikawa Koryū V with his Sanbasō puppet. The photo shows the unique manipulation method of this tradition and the master puppeteer's evocative facial expression.

Photo: Beto Freitas.

Kuruma ningyō's stomping feature has been put to good use by today's company in a puppet dance the troupe created outside of their traditional repertoire, which features a female flamenco dancer puppet, in a long dress, with the traditional tiers of ruffles that highlight this dance form's forceful footwork. The puppeteer who sits behind the figure also physically embodies the bravado attitude flamenco dancers carry, lending their own demeanor to the puppet, thereby enhancing the overall image. Generally, *bunraku* and *kuruma ningyō*'s puppeteers wear black hoods to cover their faces, which helps keep the audience's focus on their puppets. Master performers in these traditions who have reached a high level of expertise and public recognition, however, perform with visages uncovered, allowing audiences to recognize and admire these stars. To perform this way requires full control of one's facial gestures so as not to distract from the puppet character. In the *kuruma ningyō*'s flamenco dance, the artist works unmasked to add themselves and their emotional presence to their puppet.

Bunraku and *kuruma ningyō* figures relate to the performance space in contrasting ways. The action of *bunraku* is staged on a generally horizontal plane, across the front of the proscenium stage. This arrangement facilitates keeping the many puppeteers behind and out of the way of the puppets so as not to block the audience's view of the figures. The possibilities for movement offered by the *kuruma ningyō* cart, however, encourage the puppeteers to wheel their figures throughout the stage, into the depth of the playing area, opening up the playing space. *Kuruma ningyō*'s flamenco dance takes advantage of this aspect of the form; the puppet dancer strides and pivots throughout the wide expanse of the stage. From the audience's point of view, the relationship between the puppeteer and their object can feel more direct and intimate in *kuruma ningyō*, with a single performer so closely connected to the character right in front of them as the two wheel together through the space. That intimate connection of puppeteer to puppet can be apprehended and sensed by spectators and translated into their own close connection to the character.

A further *bunraku*-related form developed in Japan in the 1920s and 30s, a time when the presence of women on stage had become a draw for audiences following the end of a long historical ban on female performers and in response to influence from Western theatre. *Otome bunraku*, or young girl's *bunraku*, also adapted puppets similar to those used in *bunraku*, and required only a single performer per puppet. For this form, the figures were adjusted to allow young women, who could be slight in frame, to support and manipulate the large figures while showing off their own beauty. One aim here was not to hide the puppeteers but to keep them visible behind their puppets. The main structure and weight of the puppet is, in the earliest model, held up by attachments on the performer's upper arms, and, in a later version, by a device connected to the puppeteer's torso that the puppet hooks onto. The puppet's legs, or for female characters parts of the kimono, are then connected to an attachment tied on to the puppeteer's knees so she can move her figure's feet as she lifts her own legs. Strings connected to the puppet's head link to attachments on either side of the performer's own, allowing her to manipulate the figure's head with her own head movements. The puppeteer's hands are then free to activate the puppet's arms with their movement mechanisms by holding them through the character's kimono sleeves. *Otome bunraku* puppeteers don't cover their faces, a practice stemming from the original motivation of featuring the attractiveness of young female artists. Additionally, the attachment that links the head of the performer to the puppet would complicate donning a hood. The *otome bunraku* performer's face is always visible, close behind her puppet, and her limbs move in unison with those of her character. She provides a constant, visual echo of the puppet's actions, dancing along with and behind it. What an array of metaphorical possibilities this arrangement and its simultaneous presence of puppeteer and figure offer, especially to artists outside the tradition who might wish to borrow, adapt, or be inspired by this manipulation method; a constructed and human figure pair, dancing as one, twining their movements and actions.

The complications of describing and picturing the various arrangements of puppets and humans in the examples above—which can sound like a 1970s game of *Twister* for those of us old enough to remember that—underline the complex object/human interrelationships that exist in these traditional forms. In each case, the puppets are almost identical in size and visual qualities, with just slight differences to facilitate manipulation. And yet the set-ups of the actors to the objects, fulfilling practical needs, also create novel phenomenological experiences of the stage performance and might simultaneously present new interpretive ideas that could be mined for the meanings they impart. Scholars and critics writing about *bunraku* often say that the puppeteers, with faces covered or not, eventually become invisible to spectators who acclimate to the convention as they immerse themselves in the puppet dramas. But even as one concentrates on the captivating actions of *bunraku* dolls, the puppeteers in all these forms are always present to the spectator. Audiences take them in, their facial and physical gestures, and, on some conscious or unconscious level, think about them. In taking inspiration from such techniques or other models with visible puppeteers, making a conscious choice about what those presences and relationships express or represent is a powerful directorial tool. While the long histories of these traditional Japanese arts have already prescribed the configurations of performers and objects that will take place on their stages, when creating or witnessing new productions, the significance and impact of actor-object relationships are opportunities for offering deeper meaning to a performance. If we are not ignoring them, then how do we see them, understand them, use them?

Visibilities and presence

Through these examples we can understand that a simple division between hidden and visible puppeteers is inadequate for capturing the full extent of the presence and connected positioning of puppeteers and objects. While hidden performers may conjure the concept of an invisible actant, maybe a god, pulling the strings (or lifting the rods) from behind the scenes, as the saying often goes, visible puppeteers can be present in innumerable ways. It is important to not just clarify if puppeteers are visible or not but to ask, visible *how*? In what way? To what use or effect? How might a production be taking advantage of their presence and visibility? And how might the show be teaching spectators how to understand the presence of its puppeteers, how to read them, through the course of the production?

Sometimes, as we have seen with all the examples described here, different visibilities involve complicated intertwinings of limbs and matter. But choices can also be simpler and still powerful. Puppeteers generally look at their puppets while performing, not only to keep track of what the figures are doing as they enliven them but to bring the audience's focus to the objects instead of to themselves. So, when a puppeteer, present on stage alongside their puppet, chooses to look in a deliberate way out at the audience or at another puppet instead of at the figure they are performing, there is an instant moment of disengagement between object and performer, and in that moment an opening for the puppeteer to transform from an unacknowledged but present presence into another character within the drama. A puppeteer can also shift *how* they look at their puppet, the quality of energy and presence they express, to suddenly become a character now interacting with the object they are performing rather than a supposedly invisible figure, primarily present to animate the object. Puppet productions can experiment with different ways to signal desired interpretations of object-human relationships to spectators. In Dan Hurlin's *Disfarmer* (2009), a show about Mike Disfarmer, the reclusive Arkansas photographer, an ensemble of puppeteers in black manipulate their bunraku-style figure and the rolling platforms and other set pieces that create the barren, rural world through which the solo character moves. At one moment, one of the puppeteers places a counter, representing a grocery shop, on one of the platforms; Disfarmer walks up and leans his own elbow nonchalantly across it, instantly transforming himself from puppeteer into shop clerk, another character suddenly present to interact with the lone puppet. At a later moment, another puppeteer lifts a small car above his head, and then he and one more performer fiddle with it from underneath, becoming the mechanics tending to the automobile, one even prompting the Disfarmer puppet to hand him a tool. Through simple gestures and changes in attitude and energy, the small company of performers in this show move in and out of their roles as both puppeteers and fellow actors, reinforcing the piece's emphasis on Disfarmer's isolated life.

Developing the skill to continually give one's own focus and thereby that of the audience to a performing object rather than pulling it to oneself can be tricky as can letting the object-character express the emotions and situation rather than doing it with one's own facial gestures. These performance techniques are sometimes challenging for actors used to embodying characters themselves. But they allow a puppeteer who is present onstage to remain, more or less, unimplicated in the dramatic action. Breaking those conventions and intentionally bringing one's own presence as puppeteer into the audience's consciousness therefore can be a simple but powerful dramatic device. Puppet artists can be masters of these techniques, switching back and forth quickly and frequently within a production.

108 *Humans and Objects*

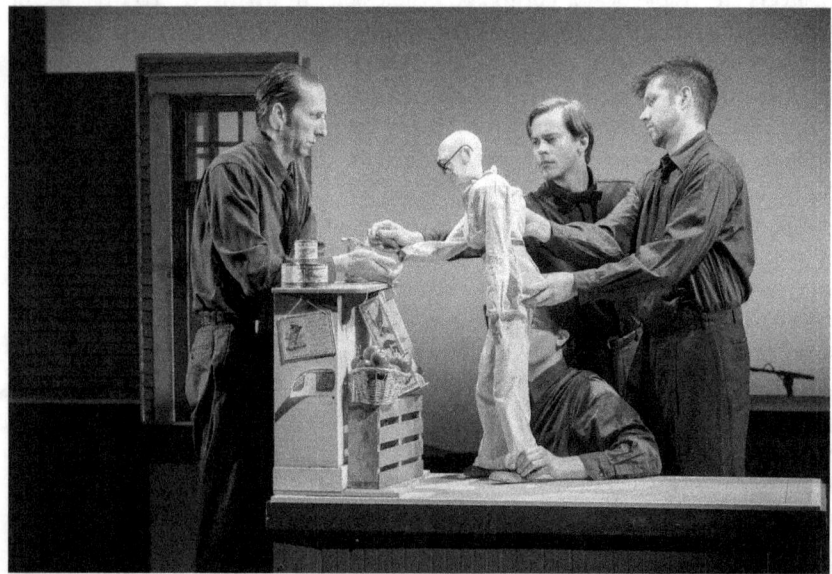

Figure 4.6 Disfarmer. The puppet of Disfarmer pays for his purchases by handing money to a puppeteer, who now acts as a character. Conceived, directed, and designed by Dan Hurlin; music by Dan Moses Schreier; text by Sally Oswald; presented by St. Ann's Warehouse; Brooklyn, NY. Photographed Monday, January 26, 2009.

Photo: ©2009 Richard Termine.

Dress provides another means by which human performers can be implicated in or cast in a role in the dramas of their performing objects. Standard dress for puppeteers tends to be black clothes, again, to keep from drawing focus away from the performing objects. Even when black dress does not fully hide puppeteers under low lighting, it reads as dramatically neutral. Therefore, making a choice of dress other than simple black already opens up the doors to interpretive ideas. *Peter and Wendy* (1996), Mabou Mines' take on the story of Peter Pan, is set in a Victorian children's bedroom out of which the tale of the lost boys and their leader, the eternally young Peter, and his nemesis, the pirate Captain Hook, emerges. The puppeteers, like the human actor who narrates the tale on stage amidst them, all wear long, white, Victorian dresses. The puppeteers' faces are concealed by beekeeper-like white netting descending from their white hats. These ensemble outfits add to the placement of the events of the show in their historical setting and within the fantasy play world of a children's nursery. They also support the production's conceit of its tale being told by a narrator as a kind of bedtime story. In Dan Hurlin's *Demolishing Everything with Amazing Speed* (2016), based on a short play by Italian Futurist Fortunato Depero, the puppeteers manipulate the show's colorful figures—these puppet's faces are collages of brightly colored, abstract geometrical shapes—with machine-like precision across dynamic platforms while wearing identical white jumpsuits reminiscent of factory worker uniforms and evoking the Futurist movement's love of industrialization.

Puppeteers might also dress identically to their puppets. In such cases, the viewer sees a set of doppelgängers onstage, a human and a crafted figure visually echoing each other. In Myanmar, there is a common performance in which a marionette and a human performer, wearing similar costumes, execute the same dance moves, almost as a competition between human and object. In *Anne Frank: Within and Without* (2006), directed by Bobby Box for Atlanta's Center for Puppetry Arts, the two women who move the doll-like figures representing Anne and her family hiding from the Nazis in their attic shelter, and who are both introduced as Anne, are "pin-curled and identically costumed in prim knee-length gray wool skirts, white blouses, gray cardigans and Mary Janes" (Goodman). This costuming, Brenda Goodman writes, makes the actors "seem to be personifications of Anne's memory or different aspects of her personality. Sometimes they seem like ghostly grown-up versions of an Anne Frank who has been allowed, in death, to age and return to tell her story" (Goodman). A puppeteer, as we saw with Timon in *The Lion King*, might also dress to represent the environment in which the puppets find themselves, providing a living, visual background for their characters.

Different kinds of puppets require different amounts of activity from their human performers, just to set the figures in motion, in some cases leading the puppeteers to be more physically visible to audiences than in others. A hand puppeteer with a small puppet on each hand might easily raise their arms above their head as they perform and maintain a measure of inconspicuousness, even if not hidden inside a puppet booth. By contrast, we have already seen with *King Kong* how the ten puppeteers for the gorilla needed to engage in sometimes acrobatic actions to move the limbs and torso of their giant figure. The physical requirements for putting this puppet into action do not easily allow these performers to pretend to invisibility. Jumping and swinging while pulling huge ropes can draw attention even from a colossal gorilla. As stated earlier, this necessary activity that draws the eyes of spectators offers opportunities, if not the requirement, for artists to make interpretive choices about how this stage action should be read as part of the drama, or of the metadrama of the puppet's life taking place alongside the main plot.

Racial and other identities on the puppet stage

A puppeteer's own personal identity can also be intentionally or unintentionally meaningful, especially in situations where age, race, ethnicity, gender, disability, or other factors may be significant to both the social context of performance and a show's themes. The strong racial divisions brutally enforced in South Africa under the apartheid system, and that lingered after, contributed to Handspring Puppet Company's choice, in many of their shows, to have figures that require two puppeteers to be performed by both a white and a black performer working together. In *Ubu and the Truth Commission* (1997), Handspring's adaptation of Alfred Jarry's absurdist 1898 play, which playwright Jane Taylor set in South Africa during the post-apartheid Truth Commission hearings, puppets representing black South

Africans who testified to the commission about the atrocities they and their loved ones suffered under the inhuman system appear to spectators flanked by the white and black faces of their two visible puppeteers. These performers observe and listen to the stories of the struggles their character endured. In both the contemporary social world of South Africa and that of the play, race is not inconsequential, so thinking critically about the implications of the racial presence of puppeteers next to their puppets is essential. Here the cooperative performance of the puppeteers models a more egalitarian society while also showing the performers bearing joint witness to the testimonies.

South Africa offers another interesting example of racial identity playing an important role in the interpretation of a puppeteer and puppet partnership in the work of white ventriloquist Conrad Koch and his latex puppet, originally a black character, called Chester Missing. Ventriloquist acts, in which a puppeteer interacts with a puppet that they also manipulate, speaking for them without moving their own lips, have historically cultivated a trope in which comedy derives from the puppet or dummy mocking, critiquing, and generally showing-up their human partner. In his stand-up act with Chester, Koch borrows this trope, letting Chester voice social and political critiques of South Africa's political system, the continued social oppression of Black people, and privileged whites, often with Koch himself serving as the butt of the satirical jokes. The racial differences between puppet and ventriloquist in these early stand-up routines offered a theatrical dynamic that allowed racial issues to be aired through comedy. Moving beyond the stand-up stage, Chester became a media celebrity in South Africa, taking on the surprising role of news analyst and reporter, appearing both as a correspondent on real news programs and later hosting his own television talk show. He gained renown for his questioning of South Africa's top politicians, chasing them down on the fly at political events as well as inviting them as guests on his show where they have willingly sat and allowed Chester to ask them about the most critical, controversial issues of the day, often in crude, straightforward terms. As a comic puppet, Chester takes license to be more direct and provocative than a human performer could be in his place. His interviewees find it difficult to negotiate taking the high ground while also being aggressively dismissive of a puppet. Chester's work in forcing politicians to respond publicly to social problems garnered him the Ahmed Kathrada Foundation's Anti-Racism Award, and his harsh Twitter comments about singer Steve Hofmeyr's white supremacist views earned him a restraining order, which required a court case to revoke. While the black Chester puppet had been a champion against racism and was popular with black audiences, in 2019, Koch became more aware of the problems of himself as a white performer having the cultural platform, through his black puppet, to serve as a critical spokesperson for the black community. His act could also be taken as a kind of blackface, especially as Chester spoke with a distinctly black dialect, something other white South African comics had appropriated for their own comic purposes. Koch first responded to this concern by having a black performer do Chester's voice on his television show. He subsequently transformed Chester into a white character, with only slight changes to the puppet itself. The pair continue to raise social issues but in a model that now takes their puppet/puppeteer dynamic in a new direction in accord with the new racial representation in the act. In their television show, *White Noise*, originally ironically entitled *How to End Racism*, Chester, in trying to figure out if he himself, as a white South African, is racist, forces Koch, as the puppeteer who created him, to question his own racist habits and white privilege. In the process, the duo exposes the greater social and structural systems that perpetuate a racially divided society.

In the United States as well, larger cultural and political dynamics concerning race, ethnicity, gender, and disability frame how audiences perceive and interpret the relationships of performers to their stage objects. It would be an obfuscation to imagine that puppeteers and their own identities in terms of race, gender, sexual orientation, disability, or other factors, however a puppeteer might identify or define themselves, are fully absent or inconsequential to spectators. Just as the human theatrical world, in response to the Black Lives Matter movement and pressure from other organizations and campaigns representing various disenfranchised communities, has finally been pushed to confront, more forcefully than before, important questions about who can and should play what types of roles and to consider how people of various diversities are represented on and off stage within the theatrical world, so too has the puppetry community had to face similar questions. Such issues can seem obscured in puppetry where a figure can be built to present any type of character—any racial or ethnic background, any gender, or with any set of different abilities or other identifications—and their human puppeteers, whatever their own identities, hidden from the audience. In this way, the facts of the bodies of human performers in puppetry, and how they present characters, might seem notably different from those in the human actor theatre. Moreover, a solo puppeteer doing their own show might perform numerous characters, possibly a very diverse cast. The concerns, however, are not only about what kinds of characters appear visibly on stage but also more generally about the greater inclusion of a diversity of people within the puppetry community, both on and offstage, and making sure a wider scope of individuals from various backgrounds have opportunities to develop their artistry, perform, share their stories, and be recognized and welcomed as part of the puppetry world. At the panel "Puppetry, Race, Gender, Identity," at the Puppets in the Green Mountains Festival in Brattleboro, Vermont, in September 2018, African American artist and scholar Paulette Richards recounted attending a puppetry building workshop at which the teacher unthinkingly only offered participants paint colors for and directions on how to create Caucasian skin tones for painting their figures. Richards, through her scholarly research and forthcoming book, *Object Performance in the Black Atlantic: The United States* (Routledge, 2023), is disclosing a rich fabric of black artistry related to preforming objects and critical perspectives addressing it. She has also stressed in public talks and her own artistic practice that, while *Sesame Street*'s multicolored monsters have been a handy way for the show to present characters disconnected from specific racial or ethnic identities, given the dominance of images of white in US popular culture, it is important for children's shows to present puppet characters that specifically represent people of color, characters with which children of color can identify. African-American puppeteer and teacher Edna Bland has, in recent years, changed the way she does her performances, from staying hidden behind her puppet stage to standing out in front so her young spectators, who are often children of color, can view her as a role model and see in her the possibility of pursuing an artistic path. Puppeteer Tarish "Jegheto" Pipkins, whose work includes *Just Another Lynching: An American Horror Story*, regularly performs with his son, Taryn, who has developed his own passion for the art. In conversation with me and at other public events, he has shared how spectators have expressed to him how moved they are to see this positive parenting model in performance, especially given concerns over absentee fathers within the black community. Artists who identify as black, indigenous, or people of color (BIPOC), in encouraging members of their own communities to embrace puppetry as spectators, expand and diversify the audience for puppetry performance along with the types of stories told. New York City's Teatro SEA, for example, founded and directed by Manuel Moran, who hails originally from Puerto Rico, creates bilingual productions that draw in New York's Latinx community, while also sharing Latinx culture and perspectives with the population at large. The troupe's version of the Pinocchio story, *Viva Pinochio! A Mexican Pinochio!*, for example, recasts the iconic puppet character as an unauthorized immigrant who's yearning to be a "real boy" translates into his desire to attain United States citizenship. These artists prioritize bringing the stories relevant to their communities to audiences of all backgrounds while also standing as role models for future puppeteers. The same can hold true for artists representing other minority or marginalized communities that have been the target of discrimination.

Object and subject

In the human actor theatre, people are subjects, with agency, desires, emotions, and goals. They matter. The material objects that surround them—props, set elements—only have importance in terms of their relationships to the humans in the stories. The set of pistols that appear in Henrik Ibsen's play *Hedda Gabler*, for example, draw their significance first from having belonged to Hedda's father, General Gabler, then from how Hedda herself uses them to exert her influence over others and ultimately to commit suicide. In puppetry, however, objects demonstrate their own agency, desires, and emotions. Objects become subjects. The metaphorical idea of objects becoming subjects and its inverse, subjects becoming or being treated like objects, are embedded within puppetry and ripe with implications for stories that deal with the very notions of agency and power. At the end of *Anne Frank: Within and Without*, for example, when the Nazis discover the family's hidden attic, the puppeteers place the doll-like figures of Anne and the other captured residents in a cart attached to the wooden toy train that will carry them off to the concentration camps where most of them will perish. The words from Anne's diary, read out during the show, famously express her personal feelings, her surprising faith in humanity even while growing up under oppressive circumstances, in short, her subjectivity. But piled in the cart, the stiff doll figures that represent Anne and her family are treated like and revert to inanimate objects, their agency and liveliness stripped from them, just as the Jews of Europe were divested of their agency—their rights, their freedoms, and their lives. Six million Jews were murdered by the Nazis. Death is the ultimate transformation of subject into object, human beings into lifeless materials.

Japanese playwright-director Oriza Hirata's *Sayonara* (in the version performed at the Japan Society, 2013), features a female android, controlled remotely by a human backstage, alongside a human actress. In the first part of the show, the human character, who has a terminal illness, converses with the very human-looking android bought for her by her family to have as a companion in her final days. The android comforts her by reciting passages of poetry, appearing to express its own emotional sensibilities and responding to the woman like another human. In the second part of the play, after the human character has passed away, the android sits alone, repeating the same few lines of poetry over and over. The figure now reads to spectators like a dysfunctional machine rather than a human-like presence. When a man enters, he again addresses the android like an independent agent as he asks if it would be willing to recite prayers for the dead at the site of the Fukushima power plant disaster. Humans, he says, cannot take on the task because of the dangerous radiation levels. When the android agrees, again displaying an apparent personal agency, the man gives it a very long respectful bow, as he would to an honored person. In stark contrast to this gesture, however, immediately afterward he slaps a mailing label on the android and hoists its rigid, machine-like body over his shoulder to carry it off, treating it like any random package. Androids and robots, especially ones like this one, operated in real time by hidden performers, are a kind of technologically sophisticated puppet. Their attempts to rival human capabilities mean they often occupy a position between our views of machines and of sentient beings. Hirata's production plays on this aspect of the android, highlighting its dual nature. In so doing, the show forces the question of where the line between subject and object resides.

A short show by Henk Boerwinkel plays with both the subject/object and visible/invisible puppeteer divide as well as the relationship between these. In this vignette, a marionette suddenly looks up and sees the strings that govern his movements and the hands of the puppeteer who, godlike, manipulates him from above. This recognition of the puppeteer by the puppet is not an unfamiliar trope. Here the puppet tries to climb up the strings to reach his creator, but, each time, the puppeteer pushes him back down to his tabletop. The puppet's actions of seeing the strings and climbing them bring the visible hand of the puppeteer into the show as a character. Boerwinkel makes his hand movements exaggerated and clear to deliberately underscore their newfound role. He eventually drops the strings and the control—the crossed wooden sticks from which the strings hang—onto the small stage and the puppet, predictably, falls lifeless to the ground. Or so it seems. In an unexpected twist, after a moment, the puppet begins to move again and eventually stands up, coming back to life seemingly of its own accord, now without any string manipulation. Once an object at the mercy of a puppeteer's actions, it now acts as if of its own volition. It picks up the control and hoists it over its shoulder, as if bearing a cross, and walks off. This resurrection of the puppet alerts spectators to the unmistakable presence of another invisible puppeteer manipulating the character by different means from below. This second performer is now acknowledged in the minds of viewers, even though absent from the stage, since the puppet, of course, remains an animated object that can never be a truly independent agent. At the end of the piece, the puppet has been thwarted in its quest to know its god, left in an existential world, unassisted by any heavenly presence, carrying its own burdens. And yet, there remains, unbeknownst to the figure, another "godlike" authority governing its actions.

Puppetry is not simply the choice to use expressive materials onstage *instead* of humans. Whether visible or not, present or absent from the stage, humans are always involved. Puppet shows are, after all, artistic creations by humans for other humans, so human beings are always part of the equation and shows are ultimately about the relationships of people to materiality. Puppetry, in fact, offers the perfect artistic form for addressing and commenting on this essential association. At the current historical moment, when we see the planet awash in human-made material objects and apprehend the threat these cause to the natural environment, and therefore human survival, these crucial interactions between humans and objects deserve as much attention as we can give them. Puppetry is always offering us opportunities to think about how we place ourselves vis-à-vis the things around us, those that we make and with which we create, and those that we find in nature. It also gives us the means to express our perspectives on those interactions. Such chances should not be overlooked but mined for their artistic uses as well as for the larger ideas they can express about the place of human beings in both the physical and metaphysical world.

Notes

1 An event in London during *The Walk* celebrated her birthday, so now she is said to be ten years old.
2 The full list of events for *The Walk* can be found at "Future Events." *Walk With Amal*, www.walkwithamal.org/events. 25 May, 2023.
3 My full account of this close-up experience of Amal, "Little Amal's New York Journey: Reflections on the Big Puppet in the Big Apple," can be found in the January 2023 issue of *Performing Arts Journal*.
4 Jane Taylor also echoes the ritual nature of Amal's pilgrimage in a discussion with Handspring Puppet Company's Adrian Koehler, who designed Amal. She notes that although Amal's image and travels were covered by "… a global community who attached themselves to her progress via social media …" that "[t]he extensive prefiguring and anticipation seem *not* to have diminished the impact of her arrival. One has here something of the texture and phenomenon of a sacred event, always more than its actual component parts." (Koehler, 14)
5 Once on a trip to the town of Sarnath, in Utter Pradesh, India, I visited the archaeological site of Gautama Buddha's early monastic community. It turned out the Dalai Lama was in town that day, drawing many of his followers to the town and the site. At the local museum that housed archeological finds from the area, including numerous statues of deities, visitors wearing Tibetan dress kissed and venerated the museum statues, as they would the figures of these deities in a temple, much to the dismay of museum guards who tried to enforce rules for not touching the artifacts, treating them instead as museum objects.

6 For more on the *hakomawashi* tradition, "see Orenstein, Claudia. "Class, Gender, and Ritual Puppetry: Negotiating Revival for the *Hakomawashi* Puppeteers of Tokushima, Japan." *Women and Puppetry: Critical and Historical Investigations*, edited by Alissa Mello, Claudia Orenstein, and Cariad Astles, Routledge, 2019, pp. 101–14." In addition, see Orenstein, Claudia and Tim Cusack, editors. *Puppet and Spirit: Ritual, Religion, and Performing Objects*. Routledge, 2023. 2 vols. Vol. 1 contains an interview with Nakauchi and her performance partner Minami Kimiyo from Kobayashi Tomoe and Simon Moers.
7 Timon's style of operation is somewhat similar to what the Japanese Kitabara company of Nakatsu, Fukuoka, uses for some of their puppets, which they call *hisezukai*.
8 Tom Alan Robbins played the role in the original Broadway cast.

Works Cited

Bell, John. "Louder than Traffic: Bread and Puppet Parades." *Radical Street Performance: An International Anthology*, edited by Jan Cohen-Cruz, Routledge, 1998, pp. 271–281.
Goodman, Brenda. "Puppet Show with Dark Tale to Tell: Anne Frank's." *The New York Times*, 25 Jan 2006, https://www.nytimes.com/2006/01/25/theater/newsandfeatures/puppet-show-with-dark-tale-to-tell-anne-franks.html.
Green, Jesse, and Ben Brantley. "Review: 'King Kong' Is the Mess That Roared." *The New York Times*, 8 Nov. 2018, www.nytimes.com/2018/11/08/theater/king-kong-review.html.
Hilborn, Debra. "Relating to the Cross: A Puppet Perspective on the Holy Week Ceremonies of the Regularis Concordia." *The Routledge Companion to Puppetry and Material Performance*, edited by Dassia N. Posner, Claudia Orenstein, and John Bell, Routledge, 2014, pp. 164–175.
"History of the Company." Royal de Luxe, www.royal-de-luxe.com/en/compagny/history-of-the-comany/. Accessed 13 Dec. 2001.
Kaplin, Stephen. "A Puppet Tree: A Model for the Field of Puppet Theatre." *TDR*, vol. 43, 1999, pp. 28–35.
Kohler, Adrian, and Jane Taylor. "The Walk: A Talk Between Puppet Maker Adrian Kohler and Jane Taylor." *Puppetry International*, vol. 51, 2022, pp. 14–17.
Law, Jane Marie. "Puppet Think: The Implications of Japanese Puppetry For Thinking Through Puppetry Performances." *The Routledge Companion to Puppetry and Material Performance*, edited by Dassia N. Posner, Claudia Orenstein, and John Bell, Routledge, 2014, pp. 154–163.
Oing, Michelle. "Performing Death: A Medieval Puppet of Christ." *Puppet and Spirit: Ritual, Religion, and Performing Objects*, edited by Claudia Orenstein and Tim Cusack, *Routledge*, forthcoming 2023.
Orenstein, Claudia. "Little Amal's New York Journey: The Big Puppet in the Big Apple." *Performing Arts Journal*, vol. 133, Jan. 2023.
Paulson, Michael. "Broadway's Biggest Debut: King Kong: You've Never Seen a Puppet Like This Before." *The New York Times*, 11 Sept. 2018, www.nytimes.com/2018/09/11/theater/king-kong-broadway-musical.html.
Tanner, Rich. "Disfarmer." *The New York Times*, 1 Feb. 2009, www.nytimes.com/video/multimedia/1231546487330/disfarmer.html.

5 Notes on Sounds and Words

The better part of this book reflects on how puppetry, such a visual art form, appeals to the spectator's eye. But we shouldn't ignore how it also engages the ear, and how aural elements help structure or express story, as touched on previously with the example of the *Katachi* video in chapter 2. The fabric of puppetry might be thought of as a kinetic visual sequence accompanied by a soundscape. The sounds of puppetry are often not language or dialogue, but more frequently music, sound effects, or even silence. When language is present, it might be sung or chanted. Even when rendered as dialogue, it may still foreground physical action by being stripped down or its rhythmic qualities highlighted. Words may even be distorted or incomprehensible, as with the use of the swazzle, a reed with metal sides that Punch and Judy performers, and those in related traditions around the world, place in their mouths to garble their main character's voice. Whether rendered as music or dialogue, the musicality or aural elements of puppetry's accompaniment tend to take precedence over literal communication. The focus on physicality in puppetry is perhaps more often in line with dance than with dramatic theatre in its demand for some kind of musical or rhythmic partner.

If you were to take a beginning puppetry performance workshop today, it is more than likely you would be asked at first to not use any language or words at all. As you moved through exercises, you might later be allowed to make sounds for your puppet's expression and, after further work, introduce some language. Yet you still might be instructed to speak only when you feel it is absolutely necessary. In this way, such workshops help sensitize participants to the enormous communicative capacities that objects have through their materiality. Playwrights, for whom language and dialogue are their main stocks in trade, and who are considering writing for puppetry, might feel stymied or frustrated by the art's emphasis on material expression over language until they can see how to embrace it and fit their craft into its framework. Liqing Xu, a playwright who took my puppetry class while in the MFA Playwriting program at Hunter College, initially struggled with the different modes of creation for actor and puppet theatre. However, things fell into place for her once she picked up the objects, in this case Barbie dolls, that she intended as the main characters for her play, *Bad Mom*,[1]

DOI: 10.4324/9781003096627-6

and started working with them. In a paper for the course describing her creative process, Xu says,

> For the project, I wrote a script, but then I found that I quickly had to throw out the entire thing. I hadn't written for the toy theatre[2] medium and I realized that I couldn't make it so dialogue-heavy. Things needed to be clear, concise, simple, and above all visual. I ended up actually just playing with the dolls and improvising and that is how I came up with the script.

By seeing what her objects/characters could do and how they communicated physically, Xu was able to provide language that could work in concert with their movements and material expression, enhancing and supporting these or filling in when needed.

In considering the aural aspects of puppetry, we can turn again to the centrality of the object. Sounds emerge first in the noises that objects themselves make in performance as they jiggle, shift, maybe hit against each other or the stage floor, or as their built-in mechanisms are set into action. These natural expressions of the object are available to be mined for their communicative potential. In Chapter 2, we saw in the example of Henk Boerwinkel's performance how a band of cloth falling off a baton and doing so of its own accord as it obeyed the laws of physics, exemplified the way enjoyment in puppetry can become heightened when watching objects create dramatic moments through their own natural kinetic actions. Likewise, things making their own noises, expressing themselves audially through their unique materiality and construction, purposefully employed, can captivate. When sounds emanate from the material of the puppet itself in action, rather than coming from a puppeteer, the figure seems even more alive, as if working on its own as an independent agent. A wooden string puppet of a horse and rider that I own, carved by Rajasthani carpenter Dwarka Prasad Jangid, makes clip-clop sounds as the rider rocks back and forth on his mount. The sound comes from the wood of the rider hitting against that of the horse at the point where the character is inserted into his mount, with some room to spare. The sound emerges as the rider falls forward and backward when one sways the puppet's strings. The correlation of sound, movement, and character suggests that the noise has been intentionally and cleverly built into the figure to render it animate, to make a sound that matches and complements the figure's motion, completing a full apprehension of the scene. This interconnection of elements simultaneously points us to admire the builder's ingenuity.[3] Such sounds can not only describe a character and its movements but suggest, manifest, and enhance dramatic action—the rider racing into battle or retreating in fear. A puppet's intrinsic sounds can be deployed for surprise, transformation, or punctuation; they can underscore or provide a dramaturgical moment or shift, perhaps as an object reveals a sound it can make that we hadn't anticipated or one that we had anticipated but hadn't previously had the opportunity to hear. The suspense of waiting for a violin or horn, for example, to play the music we know it has within it provides its own dramatic arc. An object's

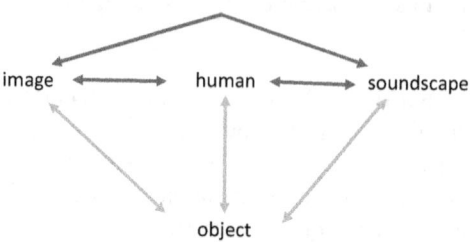

Figure 5.1 Diagram of the many interconnected realms of puppet performance.

sounds can be used as its character's natural language, replacing words spoken by a puppeteer with the figure's own embodied aural expression.

As we consider sound in puppetry, this diagram, in Figure 5.1, building on our previous ones, can help visualize the various interrelationships that exist on stage between all the elements we have looked at together, each interacting with and informing the others. I have placed the object on a separate level as it continues to take primary focus even as it engages with these other artistic aspects of performance.

Sounds can provide both dramatic punctuations as well as rhythm to a scene or a sequence either for its own effect or with a specific intention. The traditional Italian Pulcinella hand puppet show performed within a small puppet booth capitalizes on the wooden head of its central character during rhythmic sequences when Pulcinella sings while flipping backward and forward, from one side of the stage to the other and, at specific intervals, bangs his wooden head against the playing board or booth, punctuating the tempo of his dance. This technique might also be used within fight sequences along with the claps of a slapstick, another active wooden object that Pulcinella often carries.

Puppetry's focus on physical expression invites musical accompaniment just like dance. We already saw in the *Katachi* example in chapter 2 how music can lend its own structural and dynamic elements to the shaping and dramatic sensibility of the performance of objects. Many traditional forms of puppetry are accompanied by the music of a single instrument or by a live ensemble, like the *hsaing waing* orchestra that underscores the dances of the *yoke thay*, Burmese marionettes in shows that also include singing. Jan Mrazek, in discussing music in Javanese *wayang kulit* shadow puppetry, offers a robust and detailed analysis of how the sounds and rhythms of the accompanying *gamelan* orchestra function dramaturgically. He sums up his examination by saying his examples,

> demonstrate how musical structure and sound effects are actively used by the performers for narrative, representational purposes; to affect, to enhance, in an essential way, representation. The way that the dhalang relates the movements to music, and the drummer supports them, is an important aspect of narrative technique: for instance, it is made clear, or clearer, which character is more powerful (one is made to feel it), where events lead to (where are the climaxes), and so on. Thus, on this level, too, music "interprets" the narrative

and thus brings it forth. The interplay between music and puppet movements enriches the narrative, it articulates its sensations, and the tendencies of the narrative movement. (256)

Puppets can also perform in complete or near, often mesmerizing, silence, with spectators gripped observing the micro-movements of the figures before them in action. In *Chiflón: The Silence of Coal* by the Chilean puppet company Silencio Blanco, the puppets don't act in complete quiet, but perform without language and only occasional moments of music. Their primary aural accompaniment is a sound score consisting predominantly of usually unobtrusive, everyday noises that help delineate the daily lives and struggles of coal miners and their families. These sounds include footsteps walking across an old wooden floor, splashes from water while washing clothes, and creaks from elevator cables and pulleys while descending into the mine. The lack of language or full musical accompaniment, each being devices that might pull spectators through or structure dramatic action, here help draw the audience's focus to the most minute motions of routine activities, the quotidian work that absorbs and sometimes threatens the characters' lives, given their meager living conditions and the hazards of mining. The absence of the voices of real miners within the greater political and economic spheres that frame their circumstances is thematized in the near silence of this production.

Language, of course, is not always absent from puppetry and can be a powerful element. Different types of objects can support divergent amounts of language depending on their material natures and how they are made and used. Toy theatre, introduced in chapter 3, for example, in contrast to some other kinds of puppetry, often includes both lengthy and dense text, narrative as well as dialogue. The characters that appear in these productions are flat, made of paper or paperboard, generally with no joints or moving parts. Their possibilities for physical expression being extremely limited, language offers them further eloquence. They stand, as we saw, almost as illustrations come to life. The print model of heavy text accompanied by visual illustrations carries over to this new context, even as the images become performative, and the language is spoken instead of written. The necessity of further means of storytelling to fill out what flat, paper figures cannot express, allows for, maybe even demands language to take on a larger role. Toy theatre audiences, eager to see small paper characters reach their greatest dramatic potential, both for their own entertainment and perhaps from some empathetic impulse toward such small beings, appreciate the extra interventions from their narrator-partners that round out the performance world. At the end of the final festive wedding scene in *The Giant's Tale*, performed at the Eighth International Toy Theatre Festival in Dumbo, Brooklyn in 2008, puppeteer Peter Schauerter-Lüke raised his own arms while proclaiming a loud "Hoorah!," helping his small charges voice their joy at full-scale.

By contrast, both the large figures Little Amal and Mocco that we looked at in chapter 4 do not speak and, although events surrounding them included music, poetry, or other acts, these additions were not from narrators describing the characters' actions or emotions or acting as if speaking for the figures.[4] Such large beings, especially performing outdoors, invite us to apprehend them on their own terms as we gaze up to take in their expanded movements and awesome physical manifestations dwarfing our own. If they could speak, the sounds of their words might be greater than we could catch and clearly identify with our small ears and might even cause the earth to rumble beneath us. Such sounds might incongruously induce fear even coming from characters meant as benevolent. And what narration could complement the experience of a figure already requiring all our energy to take it in from our own comparatively insignificant perspectives? The phenomenological experiences of these large puppets in the framework of their traversing open landscapes discourage the addition of their own spoken texts.

It is not only small, insubstantial, unjointed beings, however, that can support extensive language in performance. The Japanese *bunraku* puppet theatre, which has, as we have seen, some of the most fully articulated, sophisticated, and detailed puppets in the world, also boasts a repertoire of expansive, poetic, dramatic plays. The plays of Chikamatsu Monzaemon, the *bunraku* theatre's most famous playwright, include historical as well as domestic dramas valued for their eloquent language and heightened dramatic situations. Notably, *bunraku*'s history lies in the coming together of three independent arts: the performance of puppets, originally simple figures; epic storytelling by traveling bards, who were generally blind singers; and the playing of the *shamisen*, a three-stringed instrument imported into Japan from China. Japan's independent evolution of ballad storytelling before its encounter with puppetry surely contributes to the richness of the textual material in this form and its continued importance. But these narrations have also, over time, been married so successfully to their material performance as to become interdependent arts. The *bunraku* storyteller, or *gidayū*, enacts the dialogue of all the characters as well as the descriptive, narrative passages that outline their situations and deep emotional experiences. This storytelling, accompanied by the strains of *shamisen*, is both a companion to the puppet performances, woven into them, and stands as its own prized art. Many aficionados come to the puppet theatre primarily to listen to the chanters, who often have their own distinguished reputations. Listening to chanters was a popular pastime in the Edo period (1603–1868) and, in the twentieth century, they performed frequently on the radio, and so necessarily without puppet accompaniment. Amateurs who train as *gidayū* today regularly give recitals unaccompanied by puppets. Perhaps the music and chanting in these cases also evokes the familiar puppets and their actions. The mix of the chanter's words, delivered in the form's carefully crafted traditional vocal renditions, and the strains of the *shamisen*, all in the distinctive *jōruri* style, create a lush, textured soundscape for the presentations as they each render the story's emotional moments through their own aesthetics. In fact, the appropriate term for this art form is *ningyō jōruri*, or the performance of puppets, *ningyō*, with *jōruri* style music and narration. Notably, *bunraku* puppets, that, by means of their three operators, perform all kinds of intricate, emotive, and life-like gestures, never pretend to speak. Any mechanism a *bunraku* puppet may have to move its mouth is generally built to enact a transformation, as with some women characters who, in a single transformative instant, become demonic, their mouths gaping open to reveal pointy teeth while horns simultaneously sprout from their heads. The *bunraku* puppets' actions on stage stand as continuous visual imagery and enactment played in conjunction with the constant soundscape of language and music. Both tell the story in different but interconnected ways, in their own aesthetic terms, as complementary intertwined arts.

A mix of narrative and music with puppets is not uncommon, especially in traditional puppetry forms throughout Asia. Music and poetic language fit the extra-ordinary (beyond the ordinary) nature of the performing figures, who often represent gods, demons, or epic heroes, and keep all elements of the art united in a single artistic sphere lifted out of the mundane.

Spoken text in puppetry doesn't need to replicate what the language of the puppet itself expresses but can, in various ways, complement it and contribute whatever its own distinct art can offer. Scott McCloud's analysis of the relationship between language and imagery in comics, and the roles each plays or ought to play, emphasizes that these arts should not simply be redundant, conveying the same aspects of the story, but supplement each other, each taking on a unique task. The same is true for puppetry, whose merger of arts and emphasis on montage can exploit the combined values and contributions of each technique when they work in concert. McCloud's view, of course, applies equally to any written language brought into puppet performance as we saw, for example, in chapter 3 with Blind Summit's *Paper Story*; the word "Slam," written on a piece of white paper, punctuated the end of a chase sequence, accompanying the image of a door behind which the fleeing protagonist sought refuge.

Puppets with mouths that move, like Jim Henson's Muppets, are made for dialogue. These are surely the types of puppets with which people are most familiar and that most closely arouse expectations drawn from human actor theatre and playwriting. Even in these cases, however, dialogue is made to fit the physical nature of the puppet and allow ample manifestation of its visual expressive potential. In "from Elements of Style" playwright Suzan-Lori Parks advises playwrights for the human actor theatre that,

> Language is a physical act. It's something that involves your entire body – not just your head. Words are spells which an actor consumes and digests – and through digesting creates a performance on stage. Each word is configured to give the actor a clue to their physical life. (11–12)

The puppet's physical life, by contrast, is crafted into its construction.

A human actor speaking on stage draws on controlled breath resonating in their corporeal frame to produce words that reach out to impact spectators. The physical experience of this linguistic effort of the performer supports, shapes, and enhances the meaning of the language itself. To find and form powerful language for actors, Parks advises playwrights to,

> *dance*
> If you're one who writes sitting down, once before
> you die try dancing around as you write. It's the old
> world way of getting to the deep shit. (15)

A playwright may need to engage in a fully embodied experience to understand their characters and dramatic situations; they may need to put their whole bodies into creating in order to bring out the texts for their performances. In puppetry, the expression of language is displaced from the character/object meant to be speaking since it necessarily emanates instead from a puppeteer or narrator. The resonances of text do not affect the puppet's own body through utterance; the physical impact of language is disconnected from the material performer. To write for puppets and performing objects then, artists may need to translate the process Parks suggests for playwrights in the human actor theatre to the world of performing objects and find ways to comprehend the embodied experiences of the bodies of constructed, found, or hybrid beings. As Xu discovered, playing with dolls, puppets, and figures of all kinds can help reveal the full complexity of such characters and how they communicate physically in performance. In so doing, they disclose the roles that language can play.

This brief meditation on language and sound in puppetry is not meant to discourage playwrights from working for the puppet theatre, but to signal to them how they might reorient their craft to take in the primacy of objects and what material storytelling offers performance. It bears remembering that the "wright" part of "playwright," (rather than "write"), is the same "wright" we find in words like "wheelwright" or "shipwright," old words we don't generally get to use much anymore, but that describe someone who is shaping, crafting, making, building an object, a wheel or a ship. While playwrights may put their text down as words on a page and create dialogue for characters, what they are doing above all is shaping dramas, with characters and events, delineating structures that will become living, breathing performances on stage. They are making the kinds of dramaturgical structures we investigated in chapter 1. In puppetry, the central characters are objects and other materials animated into apparently living, breathing beings requiring appropriate adjustments to the roles and uses of spoken text.

Notes

1 Xu has shared her performance of the play with dolls online: Xu, Liqing. Bad Mom. YouTube, uploaded by SX, 17 Dec. 2020, https://www.youtube.com/watch?v=zloOq PQWCqQ&t=1s.
2 Xu is not using the term "toy theatre" in the way it is employed within puppetry, as described in chapter 3, but referring here simply to using toys to make theatre.

3 Rajasthani string puppetry is usually accompanied by music and singing and often performed outdoors, so such sounds would not readily be heard. Moreover, most of these figures are not made by carpenters and are mostly cloth rather than wooden, except for their heads. But this particular puppet offers an excellent example of sound coming from the object. I do not know if this clip-clop sound was intentionally built into it.
4 In Amal's case, speakers may have relayed information supposedly coming from her, first visibly whispered to them by the character.

Works Cited

McCloud, Scott. *Understanding Comics: The Invisible Art.* Harper Perennial, 1993.

Mrázek, Jan. *Phenomenology of a Puppet Theatre: Contemplations on the Art of Javanese Wayang Kulit.* KITLV, 2005.

Parks, Suzan-Lori. "From Elements of Style." *The American Play and Other Works.* Theatre Communications Group, 1995, pp. 6–18.

Conclusion
Choices We Made

As I have stressed throughout the book, I am more a scholar, dramaturg, and critic than a puppeteer, and have here shared perspectives from that point of view hoping they might contribute something useful to students, academics, and critics, as well as artists and future artists, in a variety of fields who are interested in puppetry. However, I have also done my fair share of acting, hold a degree in directing, and have tried my hand at puppetry in numerous workshops and some performances. I have additionally—surprising now even to myself—toured schools in Vietnam giving puppet workshops and presentations to children of all ages. Still, I have too much respect for the skills and the full dedication of real puppeteers to their profession to call myself a puppeteer. Nonetheless, by way of conclusion, I thought I would revisit a few of the puppetry projects I worked on with my students at Hunter College and walk through some of our thinking and the choices we made. What I have set down in the previous chapters was never meant to add up to a how-to manual or specific model for directing or creating puppet performances; the essays should stand more as collections of observations, ponderings, and pathways of critical thinking that have occupied me over the years. Artists, as they continue to question and reinvent the form, inevitably astonish with unique, imaginative solutions, visionary ideas, and surprising decisions—pushing any established dramaturgical concepts out the window or in exciting new directions. Every production takes its own artistic shape, fulfilling its own goals and revealing its creators' originality in the process. Additionally, as artists know, when one arrives in the rehearsal room or construction shop, even ideas that are tidier and more clear-cut than those that I have put down can become muddled or be redefined when confronted with the complex realities that attend any performance project. Making performance always relies on a strong measure of inspired improvisation, especially when original plans don't pan out as expected or when new, exciting ideas present themselves. What follows, therefore, is not an account of an artistic team applying tried and true methods of puppetry creation like rigid equations leading to inevitable brilliant outcomes (if only). Instead, what you will get is a further taste of my own interest in and excitement about puppetry and a view into how, with my students, I leaned into these in bringing some object performances to fruition. It is only fitting, after all, that after so many pages of critical discussion, I should step up with a few street creds in the puppetry production department.

Eugene O'Neill's *The Hairy Ape*

The first project I worked on with students was a puppetry version of the first two scenes of Eugene O'Neill's expressionist play *The Hairy Ape* (1922). Interestingly, all the projects I will discuss here began, in contrast to many puppet shows, with a dramatic or poetic text. Puppeteers might start creating with a story they want to tell; a fairytale or newspaper item; a subject, incident, or situation they want to explore; a puppet or set of puppets or objects they want to use; or visual design ideas they want to pursue. Some do take a text, of course, even a play text written, like this one, with human actors in mind. Shakespeare's plays have been the basis for many puppet productions, as have numerous operas. Yet it is by no means de rigueur or even the most common point of departure for puppet productions to begin with a play script, as it still is generally in the human-actor theatre. Throughout the book, I have pointed out important differences between the human-actor theatre and puppetry and the disparate roles text plays in each, which further puts into question the choice of staging a theatrical script with puppets. However, *The Hairy Ape*, an expressionist play—one I have taught often in my play analysis classes—is, unusually for a dramatic text, full of long, visually rich descriptions, not only of settings but also of characters, placing them all forcefully outside the realm of psychological realism. The play is not meant to present a photographic depiction of everyday life. Descriptions, like the following one for scene 1, challenge directors and designers to figure out how to realize their visual invocations while tasking actors to present metaphorical imagery.

> *The treatment of this scene, or of any other scene in the play, should by no means be naturalistic. The effect sought after is a cramped space in the bowels of a ship, imprisoned by white steel. The lines of bunks, the uprights supporting them, cross each other like the steel framework of a cage. The ceiling crushes down upon the men's heads. They cannot stand upright. This accentuates the natural stooping posture which shoveling coal and the resultant over-development of back and shoulder muscles have given them. The men themselves should resemble those pictures in which the appearance of Neanderthal Man is guessed at. All are hairy-chested, with long arms of tremendous power, and low, receding brows above their small, fierce, resentful eyes. All the civilized white races are represented, but except for the slight differentiation in color of hair, skin, eyes, all these men are alike.* (scene 1)

As with some other expressionist plays, *The Hairy Ape*, whose subtitle is *A Comedy of Ancient and Modern Life in Eight Scenes*, draws on the model of medieval morality plays in which an everyman undertakes a physical and moral journey. Nearly every scene occurs in a completely distinct location with its own specific, exaggerated emotional mood. In these ways, *The Hairy Ape*, although written for human performers, begs to be staged in a highly stylized manner, both in acting and design, something which is more akin to and easily accomplished with puppets. In fact, I came to this project because I had been thinking about a professional theatre production of *The Hairy Ape* that had received widespread critical acclaim for acting and design a few months before I embarked on my own rendition. In contrast to the adulation of the critics, my reaction to the show had been something more like "how much further a production could go with all these surprising visual choices if it were done with puppets." So when a colleague in charge of a departmental fund told me, a week before the summer session began, that there was money that needed to be spent for some extracurricular summer activity involving students and invited me to take up the task, appealing to "all that puppet stuff you do," despite the short notice, a puppet version of *The Hairy Ape* sprang fully-blown into my head.

I brought on board as my designer and primary collaborator Bonni Benton, a brilliant Hunter student and talented artist, who had been in my puppetry class, served as a design apprentice on departmental productions, and spent several semesters interning at Puppet Kitchen, a puppet building shop in New York. Together we devised a project plan to fit the peripatetic lives of our students, their need to take summer jobs, and the fact that no grades would be given to secure their consistent cooperation. We set hours throughout the summer when we would build together in the space that became our puppet shop and when anyone who wanted could stop by and be offered projects to work on with both specific directives and parameters and opportunities for adding their own creativity. The more time a person gave to the production, the more they could contribute practically and artistically. Before the start of fall classes, we sent out a further call seeking students who could commit to some rehearsals and perform the show at the beginning of the semester. There were no auditions or class registrations; anyone who wanted to make time could take part. Some students also volunteered to help with publicity and stage management. We decided to focus solely on the first two scenes of the play, which already promised many ways to experiment with puppetry ideas that would require a lot of building. Students who have taken my puppetry class have come to realize how much time building eats from a production schedule, sometimes leaving them under-rehearsed for final presentations. Focusing on just two scenes allowed us to experiment without the pressure to complete something beyond what we could manage capably. The flexible setup was a comfort to me as I embarked on directing my first puppet performance project.

We trimmed down O'Neill's text, preserving his language, major moments, ideas, and plot elements but allowing the visual imagery onstage to take precedence. Bonni went far beyond the call of duty for any undergraduate, not only fashioning amazing designs based on my outlandish ideas, but sourcing materials and guiding participants in building throughout the summer, always finding opportunities for them to bring in their own imagination; and she did it all with incomparable patience and good spirit. I should add that Tim Cusack, alumna of our Theatre MA program, and Holly Hepp-Galván, a graduate of our Playwriting MFA program, both with a lot of professional theatre experience and who had each taken on adjunct teaching duties in our department, were mainstays throughout the process, donating time and expertise. One of the joyful aspects of all the puppet projects I have done at Hunter has been the time spent in collective building when all who show up, of whatever rank or status, chat together in a non-pressured environment while painting, cutting, papier-mâché-ing, and generally getting to know each other outside of class. Hunter is an urban campus in the middle of Manhattan's Upper East Side, so our students, all commuters, value these sometimes rare opportunities for informal socializing. To do so while participating in a creative project and learning new skills or contributing well-honed ones is a further bonus. For my part, discovering students' talents for sewing, drawing, construction, etc., and devising ways to use them in the shows has been another side benefit of the projects, as well as bringing undergraduates, graduate students, adjuncts, and senior auditors together. Participants from all of these groups stopped by our puppetry workshops at one point or another.

The Hairy Ape centers on the character Yank, who works in the stokehold at the bottom of a cruise ship as part of the crew that shovels coal to fire up the luxury liner's engines as it travels. He begins the play as king of the sweltering, claustrophobic ship's forecastle, admired by his peers, but his self-assurance is shaken when a rich, young woman named Mildred, to the consternation of her chaperone Aunt, leaves the clean, open air of the upper passenger deck in her pristine white dress to visit the workers in the stokehold. On descending into the ship's bowels, she sees Yank and, crying out "Oh, the filthy beast!," faints. Seeing himself now through Mildred's scornful eyes, Yank no longer feels at home in his realm or at peace with himself. Anger and self-doubt launch him on a journey to destroy those who disdain him. Away from the ship, however, he confronts an inhuman society that either ignores or punishes him, landing him first in prison and then in a cage at the zoo, where he is killed by a real hairy ape. The play ends with a final stage direction that is almost a question: "*And, perhaps, the Hairy Ape at last belongs*" (O'Neil, scene VIII). Although Yank identifies with the industrialized world that relies on his labor, the work he does deforms him, and society spurns him.

The first scene introduces the men in the stokehold as described in the long stage direction quoted earlier. A group of them, under the collective designation "Voices," act as a kind of chorus, a unified contingent laughing and singing together and providing commentary on what takes place. Standing out from the pack are three distinct figures, Yank, Paddy, and Long, each representing a different perspective on the working crew's life expressed in a lengthy speech. Yank, their leader, thrives on the rough, sweaty labor of shoveling coal into the steamship's fires, taking pride not only in making the engine run, but in feeling himself to be part of the machine itself and a lynchpin of industry. In his revealing speech, written in the unique dialect O'Neill gives him, he proclaims,

Everyting else dat makes de woild move, somep'n makes it move. It can't move witout somep'n else, see? Den yuh get down to me. I'm at de bottom, get me! Dere ain't nothin' foither. I'm de end! I'm de start! I start somep'n and de woild moves! It—dat's me!—de new dat's moiderin' de old! I'm de ting in coal dat makes it boin; I'm steam and oil for de engines; I'm de ting in noise dat makes yuh hear it; I'm smoke and express trains and steamers and factory whistles; I'm de ting in gold dat makes it money! And I'm what makes iron into steel! Steel, dat stands for de whole ting! And I'm steel—steel—steel! I'm de muscles in steel, de punch behind it!. (scene 1)

Fellow crewman Paddy, by contrast, represents the sailor's life prior to industrialization, before steam replaced wind power and sails. His language and its rhythms are more lyrical and poetic than Yank's when he reminisces nostalgically about the old days and ways:

Oh, to be scudding south again wid the power of the Trade Wind driving her on steady through the nights and the days! Full sail on her! Nights and days! Nights when the foam of the wake would be flaming wid fire, when the sky'd be blazing and winking wid stars. Or the full of the moon maybe. Then you'd see her driving through the gray night, her sails stretching aloft all silver and white, not a sound on the deck, the lot of us dreaming dreams, till you'd believe 'twas no real ship at all you was on but a ghost ship like the Flying Dutchman they say does be roaming the seas forevermore widout touching a port. And there was the days, too. A warm sun on the clean decks. Sun warming the blood of you, and wind over the miles of shiny green ocean like strong drink to your lungs. (scene 1)

The sailors of Paddy's memory are intricately connected to nature rather than technology and the heat they encounter is warmth from the sun not blazing fires from burning coal.

One more crewman offers a final perspective. Long, expressing socialist views, critiques Yank's passion for the workers' position within industrialized society, characterizing it instead as one of oppression. He says,

Listen 'ere, Comrades! Yank 'ere is right. 'E says this 'ere stinkin' ship is our 'ome. And 'e says as 'ome is 'ell. And 'e's right! This is 'ell. We lives in 'ell, Comrades—and right enough we'll die in it. [*Raging.*] And who's ter blame, I arsks yer? We ain't. We wasn't born this rotten way. All men is born free and ekal. That's in the bleedin' Bible, maties. But what d'they care for the Bible—them lazy, bloated swine what travels first cabin? Them's the ones. They dragged us down 'til we're on'y wage slaves in the bowels of a bloody ship, sweatin', burnin' up, eatin' coal dust! Hit's them's ter blame—the damned capitalist clarss!. (scene 1)

For our production, we decided to use cardboard as the central building material for scene I. Cardboard's low-cost and the ease of working with it made it ideal for our group of inexperienced, sporadic builders. This rough, simple material could also reflect the lower-class position of the stokehold characters. I sent Bonni to look at paintings by early twentieth-century German expressionist artists, like Edvard Munch and George Grosz, as well as US artist Red Grooms' stylized imagery of frenzied city life, as visual inspiration for the distorted, hellish stokehold. Reflecting the seamen's group identity as a chorus of Voices, we built them and their bunks as a single unit, a standing panel with characters painted on it whose heads and arms, beer bottles in tow, were additional pieces constructed onto the panel that puppeteers could move up and down in unison by pulling coordinated strings from behind. We painted the seamen bursting out of their cramped confines, their skin eerily discolored in purple, orange, and green. Their mocking laughter was meant to turn more ominous as their heads shook back and forth together.

Yank's style of construction was comparable to that of his brethren; he was also made from cardboard with green painted skin, but stood apart, an independent object manned by his own puppeteer. Importantly, his top—torso, moveable head, and jointed arms—could detach from his legs to be manipulated independent from the rest of him. In his long speech, he wouldn't just proclaim "I'm steam and oil for de engines," but become part of the machine itself. We asked the students to research or imagine different kinds of machine parts and make simple cardboard versions of them that incorporated some moving elements. In performance, as Yank's puppeteer, Chris Wilson, carried his top half across the stage, other puppeteers came in and out with various machine segments that moved around Yank and interlocked with him, sometimes connecting with him as another gear in the works or occupying the position where his legs would be with spinning wheels or moving pistons. Made of the same materials as the machine pieces that joined to him, Yank became a hybrid industrial-human mechanism. The ideas in Yank's speech took concrete form in unusual, shifting puppet constructions (Figure 6.1).

Paddy's speech, by contrast, shows him immersed in memories that present an idyllic vision of the past. He was among the seamen built on the communal panel, but made slightly more conspicuous than others. As he begins to speak, a puppeteer slowly pulls a rolled-up stream of deep blue cloth from his open mouth. The folded material, when fully extended, eventually unfurls to provide the blue field that serves as the sea on top of which a small model of a sailing ship (made of cardboard and white cotton cloth) rides the waves. A puppeteer, holding up the opposite end of the cloth, turns to blow at the little vessel, personifying the wind, a godlike presence whose breath pushes the small ship back and forth on the swells. As Paddy's memories deepen, the lights dim, and the cloth now becomes a dreamy, blue-tinted shadow screen on which his recollections play out in silhouette. A shadow wheel with Victorian illustration-style depictions of the moon, sun, wind, and stars spins round and round expressing the cyclical passing of days and nights on the open seas. Accompanying Paddy's speech, the other puppeteers sing *Roll the Old Chariot Along*, a sea shanty, to live guitar and fiddle music. The illuminated blue cloth, its dark silhouettes, and the rich musical folk strains place Paddy's tales in a charmed environment, far from the inhospitable stokehold.

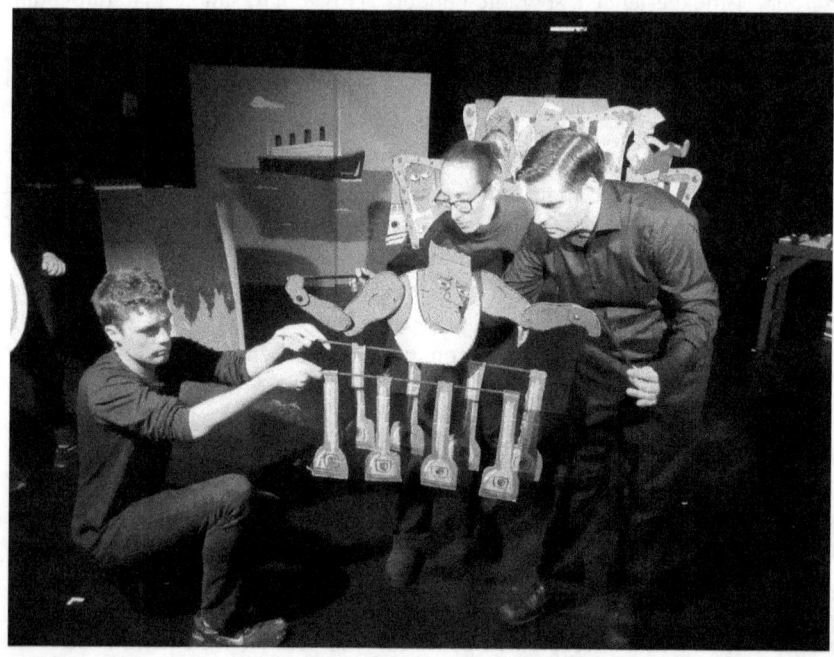

Figure 6.1 Hairy Ape. The puppet of Yank's torso (operated by Diana Benigno and Chris Wilson) combines with machine parts (operated by Nick Beach) during Yank's long speech in praise of technology. Hunter College, New York City, August 29, 2017.

Photo: Robert René Galván.

When Yank's gruff words break the spell, bringing the action back to the present, Paddy's past vanishes instantaneously, the shadow screen and all its marvels pulled briskly out of sight.

In the case of Long, his very being embodied his socialist polemics. Like Yank, Long was a solo figure, independent of the chorus panel. Reflecting his name, he elongated as his discourse became more and more heated. Raising Long's shoulders simultaneously unfolded painted panels, pleated into his torso, that revealed red, white, and black imagery inspired by early twentieth-century Russian constructivist posters. Long's growth in size also expressed his swelling sense of power in his embrace of socialist ideals; Long's puppeteer, Tim Cusack, panned the figure's accordion form from one side to the other, as the character tried to dominate the full expanse of the puppet stage along with his crewmate's ideological views. One further transmutation made Long an even more complete embodiment of his role as political propagandist: when his flat cardboard head bent forward, a small, constructed megaphone popped up to replace it. This metamorphosis of human into object took inspiration from visual tropes of morphing characters found in early animated films. Long's puppeteer then opened the front panel of a box constructed as part of the puppet's lower torso, which we had filled with mini pamphlets, and threw the leaflets about the stage. Every aspect of the puppet's transformations expressed his role in disseminating socialist ideas to his mates. When the chorus of Voices yells at Long to "Turn it off! Shut up! Sit down!" the puppeteer folded Long's body back up, returning him to his previous, silenced, subordinated state.

Scene 2, set on the deck of the ship, against the open sky and sea, forms a stark contrast to Scene I. Mildred and her Aunt, lounging on their deck chairs, may not have "*the appearance of Neanderthal Man*" suggested for Yank and his cohorts, but they are deformed in their own ways. O'Neill describes Mildred as "*bored by her own anemia*" and her Aunt as "*a gray lump of dough touched up with rouge.*"

For the Aunt, we decided to take O'Neill at his word and make the descriptive literal, forming her from a large ball of dough. Bonni devised a special formula for the dough that could hold up under the lights and remain fresh and malleable over several repeated uses. The need for a full set change between the two scenes and for the dough to be shaped anew at each performance, along with the fact that much of the show was staged on a tabletop, led to a transitional sequence that drew on associative ideas linking dough and tables with dining. In clearing objects from scene I and bringing on new ones on for scene II, puppeteers walked deliberately across the stage, napkins hanging over their arms like waiters at a restaurant preparing for evening service as some stereotypical Italian Restaurant-style music played in the background. They set out the cloth, with its painted treatment for the ship's deck floor, onto the tabletop as if laying a tablecloth across a dining table and put the railing, lounge chairs, and other constructed elements that set the scene on the ship's deck, on top of the painted cloth as if placing down tableware. Holly, who played the Aunt, took up the large lump of dough set on a wooden cutting board on the tabletop and tossed it from hand to hand as if getting ready to knead it into bread. Instead, however, setting it down, she took time to shape into it the Aunt's simple facial features—nose, eyes, mouth—and then, one by one, added accoutrements—wig, pillbox hat, necklace, scarf. Finally, to complete the image, she placed white gloves on her own hands, picked up a small lorgnette in one and a fan in the other, and positioned her hands on either side of the dough head to stand in for the hands of the character. The process of constructing this unusual figure—a montage of puppeteers' hands, shaped dough, and accessories—invited spectators to wonder and try to guess at what was happening as they witnessed the character take shape in front of them. It engaged spectators in an active way while foregrounding material performance as an artistic medium (Figure 6.2).

Mildred and the Second Engineer, the crew member she convinces to bring her down to the stokehold, were both small rod puppets. Mildred's pale white painted face with eerie blue tints captured her excessively anemic disposition while the Second Engineer, a functionary whom Mildred sees only as a means for her own ends and whom O'Neill gives no name, referring to him only by his position, had no face at all. He was a pair of pants, a jacket, and a hat, held in place by strings, with empty space where his head and hands should be. Both Mildred's elegant white dress and the crewman's formal, blue wool uniform were the meticulous handiwork of student Sandra May Flowers, a consummate seamstress.

132 Conclusion

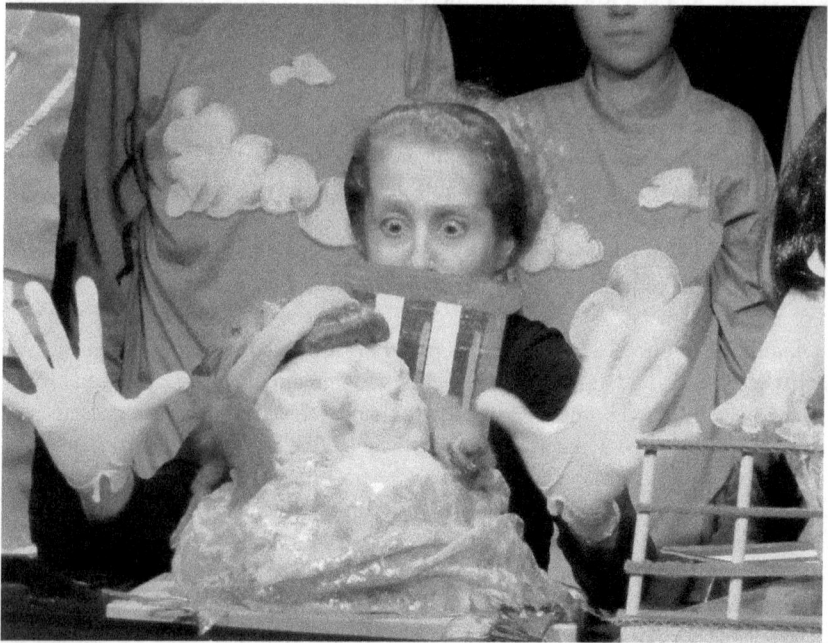

Figure 6.2 Hairy Ape. The Aunt, made from dough and dressed up, performed by Holly Hepp-Galván.

Photo: Robert René Galván.

Although scene II takes place out in the open air on a beautiful day, the vessel's burning coal sends forth plumes of smoke that darken the sky. Puppeteers wearing long-sleeved, light blue turtleneck shirts, painted with white fluffy clouds, took on the job of being the sky as they stood behind the characters; during the scene, they gradually pulled a length of black cloth out from the ship and across themselves to stage industrial pollution in action.

In these two scenes from *The Hairy Ape*, my students, other collaborators, and I experimented with numerous ideas that we hoped not only presented O'Neill's expressionist characters and story but demonstrated unique ways performing objects could embody the play. Although we concentrated on only two scenes, I held a vision for staging the whole play, should the opportunity arise. Notably, the important moment at the end of scene 3 that changes Yank's life, when he sees Mildred seeing him, when "*He glares into her eyes, turned to stone,*" and "*she looks at his gorilla face, as his eyes bore into hers,*" would be done with an animated film in which disembodied sets of eyes appeared, disappeared, blinked, stared, and moved in various ways within a black void. In this way, eyes could be isolated and enlarged, taking full focus to emphasize the themes of seeing and being seen that dominate the moment. Dynamic moving images could also temporally draw out the single instance of locked glances, accentuating its significance. For the final moment of the play, after Yank is strangled by the ape in the zoo and he "*slips in a heap on the floor and dies,*" a human actor, naked, would fall out from the cage to lie prone across the downstage floor. After an abundance of visual manifestations of grotesque, distorted, industrialized society, presented via material constructions, the audience would suddenly encounter the jarring presence of an organic, human form, offered as some discarded byproduct, spat out by the modern world.

Alfred Jarry's *Ubu Roi*

The following two projects I worked on with students were for different iterations of Gretchen Van Lente and her Drama of Works puppet company's Punch Kamikaze programs, presented at Dixon Place in New York City. Van Lente's concept for what she calls Punch Kamikaze involves her picking a play, movie, book, or other well-known work and inviting puppetry artists throughout the city to take one scene or part of it and stage it using any form or style of puppetry they want. All participants then perform the full work for an audience on a single night, with each company taking roughly ten minutes of stage time to do their section, in their own way, all scenes presented one after another in the sequence of the original work. These presentations add up to a fun evening of imaginative puppetry that offers both a unified theme and an enormous diversity of artistic styles and interpretations. Van Lente's low-stakes set-up, inviting playful experimentation, was a perfect match for the puppetry creation model we had started. The first Punch Kamikaze in which we participated took nineteenth-century French playwright Alfred Jarry's *Ubu Roi*—translated in English variously as *King Ubu* or *Ubu Rex*—as its subject. We volunteered for the top of the show, scenes 1–3. Although this undertaking took place during the semester rather than over summer break, we maintained a production model similar to the one we had used for *The Hairy Ape*: construction and rehearsals were extra-curricular; anyone who wanted to make time could take part; Bonni and I were again at the helm in our respective roles as designer and director; and we set hours for building when participants could stop by.

Ubu Roi is notorious in the history of theatre for its opening night in 1896 at Théâtre de L'Oeuvre, one of Paris' first avant-garde venues, when it purportedly drew riotous responses from the audience from its very first word, "*Merdre!*," a kind of ridiculously glorified version of the curse word *merde*, meaning shit. In consulting translations by David Copelin, Patrick Whittaker, and Cyril Connelly and Simon Watson-Taylor for our pastiche version, we settled on the translation "shit-eth." *Ubu Roi*'s main characters, Pa Ubu and Ma Ubu, are repulsive petit bourgeois versions of Shakespeare's Macbeth and Lady Macbeth who go about nonchalantly killing the Polish King, his family, and others in their hunger for power. Van Lente's solicitation also invited participants to consider the play and its distasteful despot in relation to President Donald Trump and his administration, in the White House at the time. *Ubu Roi* has frequently been adapted to characterize political regimes and figures, another example being Handspring Puppet Company's *Ubu and the Truth Commission*, which I refer to in chapter 4. New Yorkers by and large stood firmly on the opposite side of the cultural divide from Trump's supporters.

Given that we were presenting the play's initial scenes, we decided to stage the idea of Trump emerging from Jarry's protagonist in literal terms. Jarry's own drawing of Pa Ubu, with a conical head and red circular spiral on his corpulent stomach, has, over the years, become iconic for the famous character and his puppet-like qualities. We based the Pa Ubu figure we introduced at the start of our piece on Jarry's image, creating a large, papier-mâché head and arms attached to a big, pillow-like, stuffed, fabric torso, painted with the familiar red spiral. To make him even more eerie and repugnant, his eyes were painted onto separate panels that could each be pulled away, from the inside, to create openings where a puppeteer could place and look out with their own human eye. The mix of grotesque, cartoonish papier-maché figure and organic, human eye was disturbing. Pa Ubu's painted mouth had a similar device and, at one point in the show, a puppeteer's arm reached out of that opening to pull in streams of spaghetti-like yarn from a bowl as gluttonous Pa Ubu stuffed his face. The birth of Ubu's Trump-esque progeny involved the large head unzipping across the front, splitting in two, like a cracked egg, out of which emerged a small, yellow-haired face. I was happily surprised that Bonni's designs literalized my own casual metaphor describing this birth as the head's "unzipping" by the placement of an actual, functional zipper into the papier-mâché (Figure 6.3). The puppeteer of the small Ubu figure, Diana Benigno, strapped the Trumpian head, a half sphere, onto her forearm, already clothed in a long black glove with mini versions of a tie and pair of blue pants strategically placed on it to suggest the character's clothed body. Her middle and index fingers poised on the tabletop became the puppet's feet, while her other hand, bare, worked as the character's hand. Our Melania-esque Ma Ubu was of similar construction and assembly but wore a string of pearls, helping her puppeteer's black glove to appear as a slinky, elegant evening gown. The Ma Ubu puppet that partnered with our first Pa Ubu character was a large figure with jointed arms and a cloth body built around a pop-up laundry bin set on a long, wooden pole and required two puppeteers and the tabletop to support it. This Ma Ubu towered over Pa Ubu, who was more of a sedentary lump, as she prompted him to nefarious actions. Echoing her partner's conical hat, and making them an undeniable pair, Ma Ubu had two conical rolls of bright orange hair popping up on either side of her head. Her small avatar sported the same hairdo. The puppeteers, who ended up being a company of long-haired women, chose to echo this image as well, each rolling her hair into dual buns on the top of her head.

Having, myself, a French father and having attended French schools as a child, as well as having in our company a French graduate student and a Hungarian undergraduate who had lived in France and was fluent in French, we decided to begin our portion of the presentation in the play's original French, so audiences could hear a bit of Jarry's language, especially the play's famous first word. This choice could also provide a further transition between Jarry's original world and the Trumpian one elaborated on throughout the evening. We integrated English translations for the few lines we did in French within the performing object aesthetic, painting them in expressive lettering on a large scroll that two puppeteers unrolled as necessary. The scroll was also in keeping with the

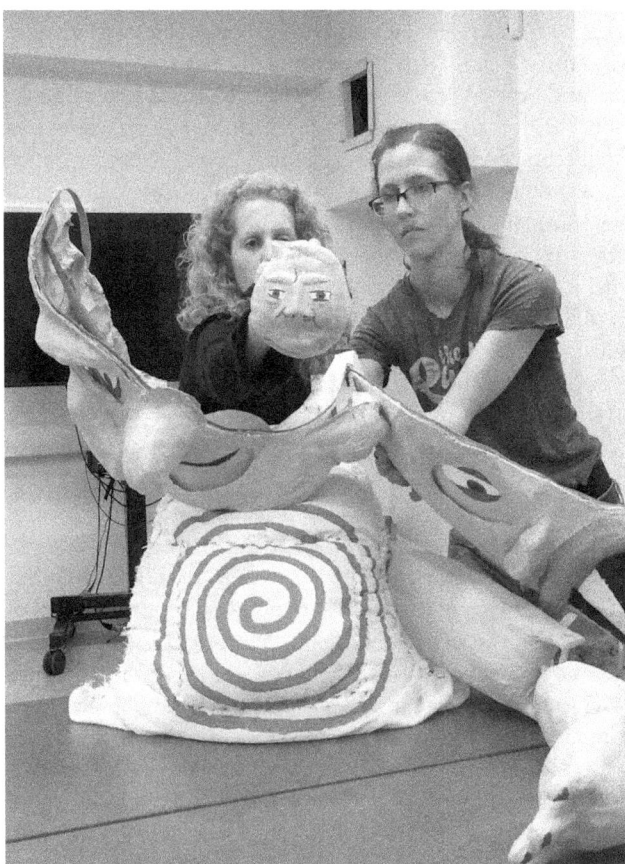

Figure 6.3 Ubu Roi. Designer Bonni Benton and performer Holly Hepp-Galván demonstrate how the small Trump version of Ubu emerges from the unzipped head of the larger figure.

Photo: Claudia Orenstein.

pseudo-arcane setting of the play. With the help of dancer and Hunter alumna Jillian Stevens, we also incorporated a big dance number for the puppeteers, with one holding a constructed upper and bottom set of lips and teeth to make a large, chomping, papier-mâché mouth. The mouth attempted to devour the dancers as they presented the various dishes the Ubus served to their guests.

Dante's *Inferno*

The last Punch Kamikaze program we participated in called for staging *Inferno*, the first part of Dante Alighieri's fourteenth-century epic poem *The Divine Comedy*. We took responsibility for the ninth, bottom-most circle of Hell, described in canto 34, where Dante comes face to face with the Devil himself. The poem depicts its ultimate incarnation of evil as trapped in ice that has frozen around him from the winds generated by his own enormous flapping wings. The theme of this ring is treachery, and the devil's three heads each devour one famous traitorous figure: Judas, who betrayed Jesus, and Brutus and Cassius, who both betrayed Julius Caesar. The drama of this section lies in Dante, a character in his own poem, seeing and gradually taking in the full scope and dimensions of Satan, in all his horror. Since our presentation would be the final act of the night and would depict the culmination of Dante's journey through Hell along with the underworld's most infamous figure, we knew we needed to do something spectacular.

To parallel this canto's step-by-step description of Dante's apprehension of Satan, we offered three different versions of the Devil in a connected sequence, each larger and more fearsome than the one before and growing materially out of its predecessor. Jacqueline Wade, an MFA student in Integrated Media Arts, who also performed here and in *Ubu Roi*, provided an eerie background soundscape for our Hell pit. We began with the tamest version we could imagine: a toy theatre scene that drew from Gustave Doré's 1870 engravings illustrating the poem. A simple black and white paper cut-out version of Doré's Devil, with jointed wings that a puppeteer moved up and down from above by strings attached to a stick, sat in the center of a small proscenium stage decorated with front pillars of similar artistic style. On the tabletop, outside the toy theatre frame, stood cut-out figures of Dante and Virgil (Dante's guide through Hell), again taken from Doré's images, looking on in amazement at the great, evil figure filling the toy stage. The puppeteers, standing alongside the table, spoke the poem's lines and roared together to impart some imposing dimension to their paper Devil. We enjoyed beginning our sequence with this modest, almost anti-climactic rendition (Figure 6.4).

But as Dante's words, performed by his puppeteer, Tim Cusack, describe more of what he sees, the stage imagery also transformed to present a visually closer, and more striking, view of our evil celebrity. The proscenium frame flipped down to reveal a larger version of the icy peaks entrapping Satan, jagged white and blue painted ice mountains cut from foam core. The pillars that had appeared to hold up the roof of the toy stage now hung down to appear as the larger Devil's legs. A blue torso rose from behind the table in the space where the toy theatre previously stood. Puppeteers on either side of it, in long-sleeved, blue shirts, each lent one of their own arms to act as a devil arm. A sizable, constructed, round head, with two long horns jutting out from on top and a bright red tongue hanging from its open mouth, completed the figure by taking its place atop the torso. The puppeteer who held the head from a wooden bar inside its hollow center swayed it back and forth in rhythm with the rest of the figure's undulating arms and body as it growled.

This second stage Devil was more ominous than the first, but we were not done. The final manifestation of the Devil required our whole company of nine puppeteers. The round head turned to reveal another, larger and longer one constructed behind it, jaw hanging down, a small togaed figure being gnashed between its pointy teeth. That head rose to make room for two more of similar design, connected to one another, that moved in underneath the first to complete the trio. Two more

Figure 6.4 Dante's *Inferno*. Designer Bonni Benton demonstrates the small, toy theatre version of the Devil puppet.

Photo: Claudia Orenstein.

puppeteers entered, each carrying one of the final Devil's arms. These were blue like the rest of him, made of tubing and a simple mechanism that allowed the arms to stretch and elongate as the claws on the hands, reaching out toward the audience and Dante—now played by Tim himself in a mask and laurel wreath—opened and closed. Two more puppeteers held aloft the Devil's wings (one on each side), made from flows of dark purple and black patterned cloth scraps sourced from the costume shop, sewn together, and attached to hinged wooden sticks. The wings, batlike, could spread wide to open and then refold. A final puppeteer joined the crew, twirling a long length of rope with an arrow-shaped point at its end: the Devil's tale. The tale danced and swung around both in unison with and independent of the rest of the looming figure. Spreading itself in all directions across the Dixon Place stage, this was not only the largest puppet of our section, but of the whole evening, and served as a fitting, climactic ending to the show (Figure 6.5).

In creating all three projects, my collaborators and I sought ways for the materiality of objects on stage to express character, mood, and plot, while also educating ourselves and our audiences about the dramatic possibilities inherent in puppetry, within a broad understanding of the form. As we devised our puppet creations, we let our minds roam freely across visual, metaphorical, and associative

138 Conclusion

Figure 6.5 Dante's Inferno. The final image of the large three-headed Devil, featuring the full company of puppeteers. Dixon Place, May 9, 2018.

Photo: Claudia Orenstein.

propositions, with any material or design style theoretically open to us, barring the practical limitations of cost and our novice building skills. We could, therefore, pick what we wanted to bring to the stage for its dramaturgical value. Doing puppetry didn't confine us to a particular kind of figure or material. Design and dramaturgical ideas could lead our creativity and unify apparently disparate performance elements into a cohesive stage world. While our constructions may not have always lived up to our grand ideas, material choices captured our intentions.

Most, if not all, the students and others who participated in these puppet projects, as well as those who have taken my puppetry classes, whether coming from backgrounds in theatre, film, the visual arts, or other areas, whether harboring ambitions to be actors, directors, playwrights, filmmakers, visual artists, or something else, have had their artistic sensibilities and directions notably transformed or enhanced by these experiences. Many have continued pursuing puppetry in their own diverse ways. Once we move ourselves out of the way and put materiality in the center of our thoughts and creativity, to see what materiality itself can express, new realms of artistic possibilities open up. We live in a world overrun with *stuff*. Puppetry can help us make sense of that world and transform our art.

Conclusion 139

Production Credits

The Hairy Ape. Eugene O'Neill. Scenes I and II.
Hunter College, Goldberg Studio. August 29–30, 2017
Supported by the Patty and Jay Baker Fund

Director: Claudia Orenstein, Designer: Bonni Benton, Assistant Directors: Tim Cusack, Holly Hepp-Galván, Puppet Costumer: Sandra May Flowers, Puppet Wig Styling: Gieselle Blair. Graphic and Additional Design: Devyn Cox, Additional Design: Diana Benigno, Lighting and Sound: Conrado Falco, Music: Taylor Carman and Sophie Carman, Technical Support: Michael (P.J.) Collins. **Performing Company:** Nick Beach, Diana Benigno, Bonni Benton, Sophie Carman, Taylor Carman, Devyn Cox, Tim Cusack, Sandra May Flowers, Gina Galván, Holly Hepp-Galván, Joshwald Martínez, Claudia Orenstein, Chris Wilson. **Building Crew, in order of time devoted to the Project** Bonni Benton, Claudia Orenstein, Tim Cusack, Devyn Cox, Holly Hepp-Galván, Sandra May Flowers, Diana Benigno, De Andre Brye, Jacob Scherer, Nick Beach, Ricky Charriez, Nicolle Marquez, Joshwald Martínez, Conrado Falco, Stephanie Re. **Additional contributors:** Elizabeth Amato, Perla Espinoza. **Special Thanks** to Michael (P.J.) Collins, David Bean, Ian Calderon, Brad Krumholz.

Drama of Works. Punch Kamikaze: *Ubu Roi.* Dixon Place; May 9, 2018
Act I, Scenes i-iii

Trade Winds Theatre: Director: Claudia Orenstein; Designer: Bonni Benton; Dramaturg: Samantha Grassian Choreographer: Jillian Stevens; Sound Technician: Cynthia Bajor **Building Crew:** Diana Benigno, Bonni Benton, Devin Cox, Holly Hepp-Galván, Samantha Grassian, Lois Horowitz, Zsofia Kozma, Claudia Orenstein, Ana Paredes, Natalie Rosolowski, Carl Stevens, Jillian Stevens, Jacqueline Wade, Talia Weingarten. **Performers:** Diana Benigno, Bonni Benton, Holly Hepp-Galván, Samantha Grassian, Zsofia Kozma, Jacqueline Wade. Thanks to support from a Hunter College Undergraduate Research Fellowship and Hunter College Theatre Department.

Drama of Works. Punch Kamikaze. *Inferno* by Dante Alighieri.
Dixon Place, April 9, 2019.
Canto 34: The Emperor of the Kingdom of Despair

Trade Winds Theatre: Director: Claudia Orenstein; Designer: Bonni Benton; Sound Design: Jacqueline Wade **Building Crew/Performers:** Tim Cusack (as Dante), Bonni Benton, Sandra May Flowers, Yanniv Frank, Tianding He, Angel Iparraguirre, Leonard Jacques, Brianna Jenkins, Zsófia Kozma, Rebecca McClain, Claudia Orenstein, Shaotong Pan, Christine Renee Snyder, Jacqueline Wade, Liebe Weinstein. **Special thanks to:** Hunter College Theatre Department, Louisa Thompson Pregerson, Tom Lee, and Bart Roccoberton.

Works Cited

Alighieri, Dante. "Canto XXXIV." *The Divine Comedy: Inferno. AmericanLiterature.com.* Translated by Henry Wadsworth Longfellow, americanliterature.com/author/dante/book/the-divine-comedy/inferno-canto-xxxiv.

Jarry, Alfred. *Ubu Rex.* Translated by David Copelin, illustrated by Chuck Carlson, Pulp Press, 1977.

Jarry, Alfred. *King Ubu.* Translated by Patrick Whittaker, https://www.patrickwhittaker.co.uk/ubu-roi.

Jarry, Alfred. *The Ubu Plays: Ubu Rex, Ubu Cuckolded, Ubu Enchained.* Translated by Cyril Connelly and Simon Watson-Taylor, Methuen, 1987.

O'Neill, Eugene. The Hairy Ape. Project Gutenberg, 4 Jun. 2009, www.gutenberg.org/files/4015/4015-h/4015-h.htm.

A Selective and Selectively Annotated Puppetry Bibliography

The bibliography does not profess to be comprehensive, although it is fairly robust. It also reflects, like the rest of this book, idiosyncrasies of my own ways into and interests in the art of puppetry. Much of what I have listed here follows what sits on my own shelves. These include books and articles I will pull out and recommend to students coming to my office. Following the overall bent of this project, I have included a section on resources that are not about puppetry, per se, but that are helpful for thinking about puppetry, providing insights from other disciplines.

Because of my own years of engagement with puppetry in Asia, and since Asian performance can often seem like a specialized field that people don't always know how to enter, I have included a fairly extensive list of resources with distinct sections on Chinese, Japanese, South Asian, and Southeast Asian puppetry. I have also included a section I call Punch and His Cohorts, derived from work I did early on in this area related to my book *Festive Revolutions: The Politics of Popular Theatre and the San Francisco Mime Troupe*. In short, I have tried to provide resources in areas where I can be most helpful, having already covered the field in my own research. By contrast, I have few resources, for example, on Czech puppetry or African puppetry, and include the ones I do offer in the section on General Puppetry. This section weighs heavily toward theoretical texts and puppet history, subjects akin to those emphasized in the book, although I do also include a few how-to books that I happen to find helpful or inspiring. I have also tried to include new publications as they appear although, happily, it is becoming difficult to keep up with the many new books coming out on the topic. Book reviews in the magazine *Puppetry International* offer a good way to stay abreast of new publications in the field. I have also included entries for magazines, journals, and publishers that specialize in puppetry. Most of the resources here are in English, although I have included a few foreign language works that have come to my attention for one reason or another and in languages I read. The resources on puppetry arts in languages other than English are no doubt extensive and deserve their own bibliographies.

I have taken the liberty of annotating the entries only where I feel I have something useful to add or want to make a specific statement, as I might do were I to hand you the book in person. If a resource is a favorite or particularly helpful, I have likely mentioned it in the previous chapters as well, where I have probably said a bit

DOI: 10.4324/9781003096627-8

more about it. I have also gone old-school by sticking fairly closely to things published as books or articles, although I realize that there are many other forms of media—web pages, online videos—with useful resources now available. Again, I can personally be most helpful as a guide to publications. The fact that something is not annotated here does not imply any negative view of the text; it only indicates that perhaps it hasn't been the most salient resource on my own radar.

Whether you are new to puppetry or have been involved with puppetry for years, if you are a person who wants to read and think more about this art but maybe hasn't known where to begin or how to proceed further to find new resources or to go more deeply into the topic, I think this bibliography should give you a good place to start, and maybe even keep you occupied for a long while.

General Puppetry

Arnoldi, Mary Jo. *Playing with Time: Art and Performance in Central Mali*, Indiana University Press, 1995.

An anthropologist's view of the practices involved in Mali's unique puppet masquerade tradition, which includes *sogo bò* puppetry. It analyzes how the form operates within its community.

Asch, Leslee. *Out of the Shadows: The Henson Festivals and Their Impact on Contemporary Puppet Theater*. Foreword by Cheryl Henson, Inform Press, 2020.

Written by the curator of the Henson International Festivals of Puppet Theatre that took place in New York from 1992 to 2000, this coffee-table style book offers an overview of the many talented, creative artists in the United States and internationally who took part in the festivals and outlines the legacy of those events. It is full of gorgeous, inspiring images that will quickly expand your views of what puppetry can be.

Astles, Cariad. "Puppetry training for contemporary live theatre." *Theatre, Dance and Performance Training*, vol. 1, no. 1, 2010, pp. 22–35.

Baird, Bil. *The Art of the Puppet*, Macmillan, 1965.

An older publication, written by a puppet master, this was, for a long time, an important introduction to a broad view and history of puppetry. It includes many photos. Other books have now taken the place of this one in providing this kind of introduction, but it is still a lovely volume if you can find a copy.

Bell, John. *American Puppet Modernism: Essays on the Material World of Performance*, Palgrave Macmillan, 2008.

I recommend anything written by John Bell, one of the most insightful puppetry scholars of our time. He is also a long-time puppeteer working with both Bread and Puppet Theatre and Great Small Works, and director of the Ballard Institute and Museum of Puppetry. This scholarly book shows the ubiquitous presence of all kinds of performing objects within US culture, beginning with practices from indigenous communities, including recognized puppetry troupes, and moving to the cultural performativity of objects like muscle cars. Bell finishes by discussing the work of Jim Henson, creator of the Muppets, and Peter Schumann, founder of Bread and Puppet Theatre, acknowledging them as significant pillars of US puppetry in the second half of the twentieth century, artists who made puppetry an integral part of the culture. The book functions as a kind of history of the United States through the eyes of object performance and applies theoretical analysis to these cultural practices. A must-read for anyone interested in the serious study of performing objects in the United States.

Bell, John. "Bread and Puppet and the Possibilities of Puppet Theater." *Restaging the Sixties: Radical Theaters and Their Legacies*, edited by James M. Harding and Cindy Rosenthal, University of Michigan Press, 2006, pp. 377–410.

An excellent introduction to the work of Peter Schumann's Bread and Puppet Theatre, one of the most significant companies in the United States, both for its political activism and its legacy of training and inspiring several generations of puppeteers. John Bell's essays on the company, which can be found in various publications, are excellent, providing analytic understanding of the company's practices and philosophy drawn from his years of working with the troupe.

Bell, John. "Louder Than Traffic: Bread and Puppets Parades." *Radical Street Performance: An International Anthology*, edited by Jan Cohen-Cruz, Routledge, 1998, pp. 271–81.

Another excellent article by John Bell on Bread and Puppet Theatre, this one analyzes the company's contributions to protest marches. Today, large processional puppets are a common sight at any protest march or political rally, an important legacy of Bread and Puppet's early activism and continued activities.

Bell, John, editor. *Puppets, Masks, and Performing Objects*, MIT Press, 2001.

Originally published as a special issue of the journal *TDR*, this book contains a collection of very helpful, critical articles on contemporary puppetry. Among them is Stephen Kaplin's "A Puppet Tree: A Model for the Field of Puppet Performance," which I refer to frequently. It offers a chart that usefully reconfigures how to think about the relationships of humans to different kinds of performing objects rather than seeing puppetry as an art that stands in contrast to human performance. Steve Tillis' "The Art of Puppetry in the Age of Media Production" is also very useful in its early thinking through of how puppetry relates to other technological media.

Bernier, Matthew, and Judith O'Hare, editors. *Puppetry in Education and Therapy: Unlocking Doors to the Mind and Heart*, AuthorHouse, 2005.

Blattner, Evamarie, et al. *In Praise of Shadows*, Charta Books, 2008.

Blumberg, Marcia. "Puppets Doing Time in the Age of AIDS." *Performing Democracy: International Perspectives on Urban Community-Based Performance*, edited by Susan C. Haedicke and Tobin Nellhaus, University of Michigan Press, 2001, pp. 254–68.

An account and analysis of Gary Friedman's project using puppetry in prisons in South Africa as a means of AIDS education. The wonderful documentary film *Puppets in Prison* (vimeopro.com/garyfriedmanproductions/film-archive/video/113823880) fills out the picture, showing how puppetry allowed inmates to address the prison conditions and interpersonal relationships that lead to the spread of AIDS while exploring their own creativity.

Blumenthal, Eileen. *Puppetry: A World History*, Harry N. Abrams, 2005.

This coffee-table-style volume is a wonderful introduction to the vast and varied world of puppetry. I have used it often in my puppetry class. It contains a cornucopia of beautiful and inspiring photographs and describes innumerable companies and productions from across the globe. Its chapters are organized thematically rather than offering a chronology as the title suggests. It is easy to read and jump-starts readers into an expansive view of puppetry. Sadly, it is now out of print.

Bogatyrev, Pyotr. "Czech Puppet Theatre and Russian Folk Theatre." *TDR*, vol. 43, no. 3, 1999, pp. 97–114.

One of several articles originally published in a journal issue of *Semiotica* devoted to puppetry that was foundational in applying semiotic analysis to puppetry.

Craig, Edward Gordon. "The Actor and the Übermarionette." *The Mask*, vol. 1, 1908, pp. 3b–16b.

An important, foundational article for puppetry theory. Anyone interested in puppetry should have some familiarity with Craig's views, which are referred to throughout puppetry literature. Actors tend to hate this article, which advocates for replacing actors with life-size puppets or "übermarionettes." But Craig's perspective on how puppets embody character in contrast to human actors has been an important point of departure for discussions on the unique aesthetics and values of puppetry. The writing style can seem a bit arcane.

Currell, David. *Shadow Puppets and Shadow Play*, Crowood Press, 2008.

An excellent guide to creating shadow theatre, clarifying various options of materials and techniques, with numerous instructive and inspiring photographs. I always bring this book to my puppetry class when we do our shadow puppet workshop to help students quickly apprehend how their shadow projects can go beyond simple cut out black forms on a white screen.

Diamond, Catherine. "Mending the Sky: Fighting Pollution with Bread and Puppets." *Asian Theatre Journal*, vol. 12, no. 1, 1995, pp. 119–42.

Emigh, John. *Masked Performance*, University of Pennsylvania Press, 1996.

Masks are included within today's expanded view of puppetry or what we might call performing objects or material performance. In this collection of essays, John Emigh, a specialist in Balinese mask performance with extensive experience in mask performance from other parts of Asia as well, brings analytic models from the field of performance studies and his personal experiences to bear on his critical analysis of masked performance.

Fernandez, Esther. *To Embody the Marvelous: The Making of Illusions in Early Modern Spain*, Vanderbilt University Press, 2021.

Fleury, Raphael, and Julie Sermon, editors.*Marionnettes et pouvoir: censures, propagandes, résistances* [The Puppet and Power: Censorship, Propagande, Resistance], Institut International de la Marionnette et Éditions Deuxième époque, 2019.

A wonderful collection of critical essays by scholars from around the world on disparate topics that explores puppetry's relationship to political power. Together the essays provide an in-depth exploration of this important theme. The publication is in French.

Foulc, Thieri, editor. *Encyclopédie Mondiale des Arts de la Marionnette*. Entretemps and UNIMA, 2009.

This encyclopedic guide to puppetry drew on the collected efforts of puppeteers throughout the world and took UNIMA twenty years to produce. Thanks primarily to the efforts of Karen Smith, there is now an online edition of *WEPA* (*World Encyclopedia of Puppetry Arts*) in English that continues to expand and update the material collected in this book. The hardcopy, published in French, is still a great resource, striving to give introductions to an extensive range of topics related to the field of puppetry. The online version offers more complete and updated coverage, continuing the original ambitions of this text.

Foster, Hal. *Prosthetic Gods*, MIT Press, 2004.

Ford, Hobey. *Rod Puppetry*. Hobey Ford Books, 2019.

Foley, Kathy. "The Dancer and the Danced." *Puppetry International*, vol. 8, 2001, pp. 14–28.

> I've found this short article helpful for the way it crystalizes the contrast between two ways of thinking about the puppet-puppeteer relationship: one, a traditionally Western view that sees the puppeteer dominating and controlling the object, and the other, emerging from Asian traditions, emphasizing how the puppeteer meets and works with the materiality of the object.

Francis, Penny. *Puppetry: A Reader in Theatre Practice*, Palgrave Macmillan, 2012.

> A very useful text offering a comprehensive introduction to puppetry, with chapters on techniques, dramaturgy, aesthetics, and history.

Geertz, Armin. *Children of Cottonwood: Piety and Ceremonialism in Hopi Indian Puppetry*, University of Nebraska Press, 1987.

Gross, Kenneth. *Puppet: An Essay on Uncanny Life*, University of Chicago Press, 2011

> A must-read book for puppetry lovers. Gross's eloquent, poetic prose interweaves his accounts of encounters with a diverse array of puppets and performers with his reflections on different aspects of the art, illuminating how puppets engage our hearts and minds.

Gross, Kenneth. *On Dolls*, Notting Hill Editions, 2018.

> A beautiful object in and of itself from a press that publishes unique, limited edition texts; the book is a collection of selected of essays from authors as diverse as Charles Baudelaire, Signmund Freud, and Franz Kafka, offering various, influential views on inanimate figures.

Guidicelli, Carole, editor. *Surmarionnettes et Mannequins: Craig, Kantor et leurs héritages contemporains [Über-Marionettes and Mannequins: Craig, Kantor and their contemporary legacies]*, Entretemps/Institut Internationale de la Marionnette, 2013.

> An extensive collection of essays, in both French and English in a single volume, that takes a close look at Craig's theories on puppetry and related arts. One section contains writings on "Esthetics of death and theatricality of simulacra," and another has essays that analyze such concepts within contemporary performance. The volume comes with a DVD of a short documentary video of a workshop given by the Polish director Tadeusz Kantor in

France in 1988 and discloses some of his views on material performance in the process.

Hayter-Menzine, Grant. *Shadow Woman: The Extraordinary Career of Pauline Benton*, McGill Queens University Press, 2013.

Pauline Benton studied shadow theatre in China and brought Chinese shadow puppets and their performance traditions to the United States. The book introduces readers to this interesting woman and the transplantation of the Chinese tradition.

Jiraskova, Marie. *The Puppet and the Modern*, Arbor Vitae, 2014.
Jurkowski, Henryk. *Aspects of Puppet Theatre*, Puppet Center Trust, 1988.

A seminal collection of critical essays by Jurkowski, a Polish professor, scholar, and critic of puppetry who, among his many other accomplishments, was a co-founder of the Institut International de la Marionnette and editor-in-chief for UNIMA's *Encyclopedia Mondial de la Marionette*. His essays here offer critical and historical perspectives and insights on puppetry, embracing semiotics as an analytical lens. To my knowledge, this is one of the few English language resources of Jurkowski's writings.

Kaplin, Stephen. "A Puppet Tree: A Model for the Field of Puppet Theatre." *TDR*, vol 43, no. 3, 1999, pp. 28–35.

I consider this an important, foundational article for understanding contemporary puppetry. It replaces thinking about puppets and actors in contrasting terms, as Edward Gordon Craig did, with acknowledging the presence of human performers in activating all puppets. Kaplin outlines a continuum of relationships between humans and different kinds of performing objects, beginning with actors using material elements, like wigs or red noses, to portray character and from there tracing human-object relationships through masks to a wide variety of puppets. He also sets up a useful diagram that tracks relationships of performers to performing objects, charting on one axis the distance between them and on the other axis the number of puppet manipulators to puppets.

Kominz, Laurence R., and Mark Levenson, editors. *The Language of the Puppet*, Pacific Puppetry Center Press, 1990.

A very helpful collection of short essays by scholars and puppeteers on a variety of puppetry topics. I particularly enjoy "Yoshida Bungoro – An Artist Remembers" (translated by Patricia Pringle), a personal account from the *bunraku* artist of how, as a novice performer, he struggled with the form's harsh training methods, but eventually gained a deeper understanding of that art and became a consummate puppeteer. A rare, personal account from a *bunraku* performer that gives a glimpse into the daily aspects of training and performance from an earlier period.

Kopania, Kamil, editor. *Dolls and Puppets: Contemporaneity and Tradition*, Alexsander Zelwerowicz National Academy of Dramatic Art, 2018.

Koss, Juliet. "Bauhaus Theater of Human Dolls." *Art Bulletin*, vol. LXXXV, no. 4, 2003, pp. 724–45.

A rich essay on the experiments in performance from artists at Germany's Bauhaus in the 1920s, emphasizing their work abstracting human form with constructed materials to turn human performers into doll or machine-like beings.

Kourilsky, Francoise. *Le Bread and Puppet Theatre*, La Cité, 1967.

Kuftinec, Sonja. "Go Have Your Life!: Self and Community in Peter Schumann's Bread and Puppet Theater" *Restaging the Sixties: Radical Theaters and Their Legacies*, edited by James M. Harding and Cindy Rosenthal, University of Michigan Press, 2006, pp. 359–76.

Levell, Nicola, editor. *Bodies of Enchantment: Puppets from Asia, Europe, Africa and the Americas*, Figure 1 Publishing, 2021.

A wonderful recent publication with essays on several specific puppetry traditions. A great resource for introducing students to a range of puppetry forms across the globe. It is full of beautiful photographs.

Mair, Victor H. *Painting and Performance: Chinese Picture Recitation and Its Indian Genesis*, University of Hawaii Press, 1988.

As I discuss in chapter 3, picture-storytelling is both historically related to traditional views of puppetry and deeply integrated within the work of contemporary puppet artists. This important text traces the history of picture storytelling in Asia.

Malkin, Michael R. *Puppets of the World*. Photographs by David L. Young, additional photographs by Alan G. Cook, A.S. Barnes and Company, 1943.

Mello, Alyssa et al., editors. *Women and Puppetry: Critical and Historical Investigations*, Routledge, 2019.

Our collection of essays by both scholars and practitioners from around the world bringings focus to the too often occluded work of women within puppetry. The book addresses important performers, the struggles and successes of women artists, and women's presence and absence within traditional forms. Practitioners offer insights into their creation processes and personal views on the art.

Meyerhold, Vsevolod. "The Fairground Booth." *Meyerhold on Theatre*, edited by Edward Braun, Hill & Wang, 1969, pp. 119–43.

> The Russian director Meyerhold was one of many theatre artists from the modernist era inspired by puppetry in thinking about revitalizing the human actor theatre. In this essay, Meyerhold outlines his excitement over Russia's fairground, popular hand puppet tradition and the inspiration it offers the avant-garde theatrical stage of his time.

Meschke, Michael. *In Search of Aesthetics for the Puppet Theatre*. Translated by Susanna Stevens, Indira Gandhi National Centre for the Arts, 1992.

> In this book, puppeteer founder and producer of the Marionetteatern (Marionette Theatre) in Stockholm takes readers through his own thoughtful process of conceptualizing and creating a puppet production, drawing on his years of experience, sharing his wisdom on numerous topics along the way. An inspiring text, particularly helpful when embarking on creating a performance.

Millar, Mervyn. *Journey of the Tall Horse: A Story of African Theatre*, Oberon Books, 2006.

> *Tall Horse* may not be Handspring Puppet Company's best known or most discussed production, but it was the product of a unique collaboration between Handspring and Mali's Sologon Puppet Troupe. Millar provides thoughtful insights and a record of the show's development from his close-up view of the production process.

Millar, Mervyn. *Puppetry: How to Do It*, Nick Hern Books, 2018.

> This how-to book lays out a clear process for sensitizing performers to the animate possibilities within ordinary objects, moving on to how to bring a *bunraku*-style puppet to life using a simple paper figure. It outlines a progression of exercises that culminate in creating scenes and stories. The influence of Handspring Puppet Company, from Millar's close work with the group, is evident here. It is an excellent resource for the classroom or for artists beginning puppetry work.

Myrsiades, Linda S. *The Karagiozis Heroic Performance in Greek Shadow Theater*. Translated by Kostas Myrsiades, University Press of New England, 1988.

Nelson, Victoria. *The Secret Life of Puppets*, Harvard University Press, 2001.

> Nelson takes readers on an expansive historical journey that charts shifting Western European views of uncanny life. She exposes how religious impulses related to animated matter have interacted with scientific thought, been suppressed, and re-emerged in the early twentieth century within horror and science fiction, manifesting as fearsome or apocalyptic visions.

Orenstein, Claudia. "Animated Objects in the Work of Ping Chong." *Elizabeth LeCompte, Ping Chong, Robert Lepage: Multi-Media Interrogations*, edited by Claudia Orenstein and James Peck, Great North American Stage Directors Series, Methuen, pp. 116–144.

> In this article, I offer insights into how the full corpus of Chinese-American avant-garde director Ping Chong's work can be understood through the lens of puppetry and performing objects. In so doing, I also outline many points I consider significant in thinking about performing objects generally.

Orenstein, Claudia. "Coming Full Circle: Performing Objects, New Media, and Interculturalism in New Puppetry." *Indian Horizons*, vol. 55, no. 2–3, 2008, pp. 172–88.

Orenstein, Claudia "The Danish Festival at the New Victory Theatre: Puppetry and A New Perspective on Family Entertainment." *TDR*, vol. 52, no. 3, 2008, 187–95.

> This article looks at how the innovative puppetry productions at New York's New Victory Theatre's festival of shows from Denmark, nominally addressed to children, could speak to spectators of any age. The festival demonstrated how children's puppetry can take on challenging themes, executed in imaginative performance styles that engage young and old alike.

Orenstein, Claudia "En temps et hors temps: l'animation selon Janie Geiser" [In and Out of Time: The Animated Art of Janie Geiser]. *Marionnette, cinéma et cinéma d'animation*, special issue of *Puck: La Marionnette et les Autres Arts*, vol. 15, 2008, pp. 129–34.

> The article gives insights into the imaginative stage and film work of Janie Geiser, an American puppeteer, who was active in the downtown New York puppetry scene before moving to a position at the California Institute of the Arts, where she teaches in the film department and also ran a puppetry program. This entire issue of *Puck* deals with the relationships of puppetry to film and film animation. Geiser's films are suggestive and surreal, foregrounding eclectic found objects.

Orenstein, Claudia. "Puppets Invade France: The XIVème Festival Mondial des Théâtres de Marionnettes." *Theater*, vol. 38, no. 1, 2008, pp. 132–41.

> The essay is an attempt to describe the amazing variety of innovative productions I saw on my first visit to the international puppetry festival in

Charleville-Mézières and to capture the excitement of the explosion of puppetry the festival brings to this small French town, a world center for the art.

Orenstein, Claudia "Kazuko Hohki: Objects of Contemplation." *Animated Encounters: A Review of Puppetry and Related Arts*, vol. 1, 2007, pp. 52–53.

Hohki is a Japanese-born singer, animator, theatre and puppet artist living in the UK, who creates quirky, imaginative, poignant shows that combine a variety of performance techniques. Here I describe some early works, including an installation featuring her guided tour of small objects presumptively created by tiny Borrowers, the small protagonists from a series of children's books by Mary Norton.

Orenstein, Claudia "Our Puppets, Our Selves: Puppetry's Changing Paradigms." *Action, Scene, and Voice: 21st Century Dialogues with Edward Gordon Craig. Mime Journal*, September 2016, pp. 65–84.

The article contrasts conceptualizations and uses of the puppet in the modernist period with those in our current moment. It is based on a short paper I gave at a conference on Edward Gordon Craig and addresses one of the main questions that motivated my early critical investigations into puppetry about the different nature of artists' interest in puppetry at these two historical moments.

Orenstein, Claudia, and Tim Cusack, editors. *Puppet and Spirit: Ritual, Religion, and Performing Objects*, Routledge, 2023. 2 vols.

A two-volume collection of essays from authors around the globe exploring the use of puppets and other performing objects in rituals and other performative contexts that relate to spiritual matters.

Orenstein, Claudia. "Thinking Inside the Box: Meditations on the Miniature at the Great Small Works Eighth International Toy Theatre Festival." *Theater*, vol. 39, no. 3, 2009, pp. 144–55.

Great Small Works injected new life into Toy Theatre performance in New York through their own productions and their organizing of annual toy theatre festivals, helping to transform a private nineteenth century parlor entertainment into an invitation to creative experimentation in small-scale puppetry. This article not only describes events at one of the festivals but articulates critical views of how shows in this genre operate.

Plassard, Didier, editor. *Les Mains de lumière: anthologie des écrits sur L'art de la marionnette* [Hands of Light, An Anthology of Writings on Puppetry Arts], Éditions Institut International de la Marionnette, 1996.

> A large, very useful collection of writings by theoreticians and artists throughout history on puppetry, for those who read French. It contains essential essays, like those by Craig and Kleist, alongside numerous others.

Posner, Dassia N., Claudia Orenstein, and John Bell, editors. *The Routledge Companion to Puppetry and Material Performance*, Routledge, 2014.

> A ground-breaking collection (if I do say so myself) bringing together twenty-eight essays on diverse topics to outline the contemporary landscape of critical approaches to puppetry.

Riccio, Thomas. "Kenya's Community Health Awareness Puppeteers." *PAJ: A Journal of Performance and Art*, vol. 26, no. 1, 2004, pp. 1–12.

> If you are unfamiliar with the important work Gary Friedman and his colleagues did in Africa, using puppets to address apartheid and then AIDS, this is a good place to start learning about it. You may also want to visit Gary Friedman's homepage, www.garyfriedmanproductions.com, to get further insights into this significant work and the impact it had and to see some videos from the projects.

Richards, Paulette. "Living Objects: How Contemporary African American Puppet Artists Figure Race." *Theater Symposium*, vol. 29, 2002, pp. 16–34.

Richards, Paulette, "Living Objects: Introduction." *Living Objects: African American Puppetry Essays*, OpenCommons@UConn, 2019, opencommons.uconn.edu/ballinst_catalogues/2

Richards, Paulette. *Object Performance in the Black Atlantic: The United States*, Routledge, 2023.

> An important contribution to scholarship, investigating various aspects of puppetry and mask, doll, and object performance by African and African Americans in the United States.

Rielly, Kara. *Automata and Mimesis on the Stage of Theatre History*, Palgrave Macmilan, 2011.

> An important critical investigation of automata, exploring the discourses around them and the metaphors that have contextualized them at different historical periods.

Rixford, Ellen S. *Figures in the Fourth Dimension: Mechanical Movement for Puppets and Automata*, Self-published, 2015.

Rixford drew on her own extensive experience in crafting mechanical figures for this comprehensive guide. The book contains over one thousand gorgeous photographs of mechanical puppets of all kinds and images explaining the intricacies of their designs. It is a treasure trove for anyone passionate about mechanisms and mechanical objects. Rixford self-published the text, which can be found in many university libraries or ordered directly from the author.

Schumann, Peter. "The Radicality of the Puppet Theatre." *TDR*, vol. 35, no. 4, 1991, pp. 75–83.

Searls, Colette. *A Galaxy of Things: The Power of Puppets and Masks in Star Wars and Beyond*, Routledge, 2023.

An exploration of the "thing aesthetic" in the use of masks, puppets, and other related objects within the vast *Star Wars* franchise.

Sherzer, Dina, and Joel Sherzer, editors. *Humor and Comedy in Puppetry: Celebration in Popular Culture*, Bowling Green State University Popular Press, 1987.

A unique collection of critical essays addressing the topic of comedy in a number of puppetry traditions globally from a variety of perspectives.

Silvio, Teri. *Puppets, Gods, And Brands: Theorizing the Age of Animation from Taiwan*, University of Hawaii Press, 2019.

One of my favorite books for how it characterizes the current period as an age of animation, with animation as the governing paradigm. Silvio contrasts this with the twentieth century as an age of performance. Silvio analyzes various current cultural practices in Taiwan, from folk religion to cosplay, through the lens of animation.

Segel, Harold B. *Pinocchio's Progeny: Puppets, Marionettes, Automatons and Robots in Modernist and Avant-garde Drama*, Johns Hopkins University Press, 1995.

This book explores numerous examples of modernist plays and productions that included puppets and related figures. The shows were more often written for and performed by human actors than actual puppets, but the book documents the widespread presence of these figures in modernist and avant-garde drama and serves as a helpful resource for learning about the playwrights interested in these figures and their work.

Shershow, Scott Cutler. *Puppets and "Popular"Culture*, Cornell University Press, 1995.

Shershow's book shows the connections and conflations between so-called popular and elite cultures through analysis of both the reality and the metaphor of the puppet within theatre from the Renaissance to the present.

Smith, Johanna. *Puppetry in Theatre and Arts Education: Head, Hands, and Heart.* Methuen Drama, 2019.

Smith not only gives a substantial guide to using puppets in the classroom, with plenty of concrete exercises and lesson plans, but also shows how puppetry connects to cognitive learning goals for children. Puppets are not just fun classroom activities but support core curricular values.

Taylor, Jane, editor. *Handspring Puppet Company*, David Krut Publishing, 2009.

A wonderful collection of insightful essays, most by the main artists of this important South African puppet company, about their work process and productions. A large, coffee-table style book, wonderfully illustrated.

Tillis, Steve. "The Actor Occluded: Puppet Theatre and Acting Theory." *Theatre Topics*, vol. 6, no. 2, 1996, pp. 109–19.

Tillis, Steve. *Toward an Aesthetics of the Puppet: Puppetry as a Theatrical Art*, Greenwood Press, 1992.

A foundational critical study of contemporary puppetry, importantly offering the idea of "double vision" in puppetry, of seeing the puppet simultaneously as object and living performer.

Veltruský, Jirí. "Puppetry and Acting." *Semiotica*, vol. 47, no. 1–4, 1983, pp. 69–122.

von Kleist, Heinrich. "On the Marionette Theatre." *TDR*, vol. 16, no. 3, 1972, pp. 22–26.

Williams, Chad. *50 Hand Puppet Techniques: Secrets and Tricks Revealed*, Self-published, 2022.

Periodicals, Special Issues, and Series

E Pur Si Muove: Puppetry Today

A magazine on puppetry published in French, English, and Spanish by UNIMA international between 2002 and 2008. Full of interesting articles on all aspects of the art.

Puck: La Marionnette et les Autres Arts

A series of 20 robust volumes, published in French from 1988 to 2014, under the direction of Brunella Eruli, focusing on different themes within puppetry.

Some volumes are still available from Editions L'entretemps in France, which has published several other texts devoted to puppetry as well.

Puppetry International

A magazine published biannually by UNIMA-USA full of interesting articles on all aspects of puppetry as well as book and performance reviews. Most issues focus on specific themes. The magazine is full of wonderful photos.

Puppetry Journal

A magazine published four times a year by Puppeteers of America. It has interesting articles and performance and book reviews, as well as information on festivals, puppeteers, and other topics of concern to puppeteers.

Puppetry Yearbook

Six volumes of diverse articles on puppetry, published from 1995 to 2005, edited by James Fisher from Edwin Mellen Press.

The Art Form of Contemporary Puppetry, special issue of *Critical Stages/Scenes Critiques*, vol. 19.

A special issue of this bilingual theatre journal from the International Association of Theatre Critics devoted to puppetry on the contemporary stage. The issue is published online at www.critical-stages.org/19/ and includes embedded video clips as well as photos.

UNIMA offers a comprehensive list of the serial publications of its many members around the world, in different languages, on its website at www.unima.org/en/projects-and-achievements/publications-directory-2/

Charlemagne Press

Established by puppeteer Luman Coad to fill a gap in publication, Charlemagne Press specializes in books on puppetry and related arts, emphasizing practical approaches and biographies.

Asian Puppetry
General
Asian Theatre Journal.

A scholarly journal published biannually by the Association for Asian Performance. As traditional Asian theatre has a strong emphasis on puppetry, and the journal was edited for 18 years by scholar and puppeteer Kathy Foley, this periodical has many puppetry-related articles in it. Two particular issues, the first and final issues edited by Foley, vol. 18, no. 1, 2001, and vol. 35, no. 1, 2018, are devoted to puppetry.

Journal of the Oriental Society of Australia, special issue *Asian Puppetry: Traditions and Transitions*, vol. 51

Foley, Kathy. "Puppets in Traditional Asian Theatre" *The Routledge Handbook of Asian Theatre*, edited by Siyuan Liu, Routledge, 2017, pp. 177–201.

The Routledge Handbook of Asian Theatre's robust coverage of traditional and contemporary theatre forms throughout Asia includes this full chapter on puppetry, giving an overview of forms throughout the region.

Chinese Puppetry

Bai, Yonghua. *The Glove Puppet Show in China*, Homa and Sekey Books, 2016.

Puppetry of China: A Rare Exhibition of Figures Which Illustrate the Four Styles of Chinese Puppet Theatre, Center for Puppetry Arts, 1984.

A thin volume with beautiful photographs from the exhibit.

Chen, Fan Pen Li. *Chinese Shadow Theatre: History, Popular Religion, and Women Warriors*, McGill Queens University Press, 2007.

An important scholarly study of Chinese shadow theatre shedding light on its history and links to religion. It brings focus to the theme of women warriors in plays and includes play translations.

Chen, Fan Pen Li. *Visions for the Masses: Chinese Shadow Plays from Shaanxi and Shanxi*, Cornell University, 2010.

A collection of translations of shadow plays with introductions to the history, from, and practice form the Shaanxi and Shanxi regions of China.

Jilin, Liu *Chinese Shadow Puppet Play*, Morning Glory Publishers, 1998.
Shaolong, Huang. *Quangzhou String Puppetry in China*, Homa and Sekey Books, 2015.
Zhong, Wu Liang. *The Shadow Puppet in China*, Shanghai Yuandong Press, 2007.

A Chinese language volume

Japanese Puppetry

Adachi, Barbara C. *Backstage at Bunraku: A Behind-The-Scenes Look at Japan's Traditional Puppet Theatre*, Weatherhill, 1985.

> An older book and now out of print, it is still a lovely guide to the tradition with personal views from the author and the artists on the form itself and the backstage work that goes into maintaining it and putting on productions. It is full of wonderful black and white photos of the artists at work on and offstage.

Ashmore, Darren-Jon. "Kiritake Masako's Maiden's Bunraku." *Electronic Journal of Contemporary Japanese Studies*, 17 Jun. 2005, www.japanesestudies.org.uk/articles/2005/Ashmore.html.

> One of the few publications in English that I have found about *otome bunraku*, or young women's bunraku. It provides detailed information about the form's history and practice, based on interviews with one of the form's most prominent practitioners, Kiritake Masako. The article's larger goal is to consider questions about the rights and responsibilities of artists to their traditions. Ashmore has written several other interesting articles on different Japanese puppet traditions and a dissertation on the topic.

Gerstle, Andrew C. *Circles of Fantasy: Conventions in the Plays of Chikamatsu*, Harvard University Asia Center, 1996.

> A close analysis of how the musical elements in the famous *bunraku* plays by Chikamatsu work with other aspects of the texts to structure the dramas.

Four Plays of Chikamatsu. Translated by Donald Kene, Columbia University Press, 1961.

> Translations by Donald Keene of important plays by Chikamatsu, one of the most significant playwrights in Japan, who wrote primarily for the *bunraku* puppet theatre.

Kimbrough, Keller R. *Wondrous Brutal Fictions: Eight Buddhist Tales from the Early Japanese Puppet Theater*, Columbia University Press, 2013.

> Kimborough's translations of puppet plays that predate the *bunraku* tradition, with a helpful introduction outlining the history and major themes of these works that puts the full history and later development of *bunraku* puppetry in context.

Law, Jane Marie. *Puppets of Nostalgia: The Life, Death, and Rebirth of the Japanese Awaji Ningyō Tradition*, Princeton University Press, 1997.

A significant study by an anthropologist of religion of the puppetry traditions of the Awaji area of Japan, which both nurtured and drew from the Osaka *bunraku* tradition. Law describes Awaji puppetry's history, the outcast status of early practitioners, the near demise of the region's traditions, especially during World War II, and their revival within the context of tourism.

Nash, Eric P. *Manga Kamishibai: The Art of Japanese Paper Theater*, Abrams Comicart, 2009.

A wonderful book, full of illustrations, about *kamishibai*, a form of Japanese picture-storytelling, particularly popular in the early to mid-twentieth century, when performers narrated tales to the images they showed from small stages set up on bikes that they rode from one venue to the next. The artists also sold or offered candy to their young audiences.

Orenstein, Claudia. "Class, Gender, and Ritual Puppetry: Negotiating Revival for the *Hakomawashi* Puppeteers of Tokushima, Japan," *Women and Puppetry: Critical and Historical Investigations*, edited by Alissa Mello, Claudia Orenstein and Cariad Astles, Routledge, 2019, pp. 101–14.

My article on a form of ritual puppetry in Japan, called *hakomawashi*, in which performers go house to house, blessing homes with their puppets at New Years.

Orenstein, Claudia. "Evolution of Puppetry Traditions and the Scholar's Role: The *Hakomawashi* of Japan and the *Nang Yai* of Thailand." *Evolution of Tradition: Interrogating Transformations in Traditional Folk Performing Arts*, edited by Anita Singh and Atasi Nanda Goswami, HP Hamilton Limited, 2022, pp. 173–83.

The article focuses on the contributions of three scholars who collaborate with the three current Thai *nang yai*, large shadow theatre companies, showing how partnerships between artists and academics can support the preservation of traditional performing arts.

Orenstein, Claudia "*Shank's Mare*: A Transcultural Journey of Puppetry Creation and Performance." *Asian Theatre Journal*, vol. 35, no. 1, 2018, pp. 1–26.

The article offers an introduction to the *kuruma ningyō* or cart puppetry tradition in Japan while recounting the creation of a new intercultural collaborative production.

Ortolani, Benito. "The Puppet Theatre." *The Japanese Theatre: From Shamanistic Ritual to Contemporary Pluralism*, E.J. Brill, 1990, pp. 200–18.

Ortolani's classic, detailed history of Japanese theatre has a substantive section on *bunraku*.

Pimpaneau, Jacques. *Fantômes manipulés: Le théâtre de poupées au Japon*, Université de Paris, Centre de publication Asie orientale, 1978.

In French, scholar Jacques Pimpaneau's extremely helpful study of Japanese puppetry, giving a view into its ritual origins, early forms, the flowering of the *bunraku* tradition, and contemporary puppetry (at the time of the writing). Wonderful black and white photos throughout. Now a rare find, there is to my knowledge no equally comprehensive book on the topic available in English.

Proschan, Frank. "The Semiotic Study of Puppets, Masks, and Performing Objects." *Semiotica*, vol. 47, no. 1–4, 1983, pp. 3–46.

Contained in an issue of *Semiotica* that offers a number of important articles analyzing puppetry through a semiotic lens, Proschan's article notably offers a foundational definition of the term "performing object."

Staub, Nancy L. "Besides Bunraku – The Incredible Variety of Japanese Puppetry." *Puppetry Yearbook*, vol. 3, edited by James Fisher, Edwin Mellen Press, 1997, pp. 21–42.

A good overview of the large variety of traditional forms of puppetry in Japan outside of the well-known *bunraku* tradition. It also outlines important contemporary puppetry troupes from the period when it was written. Some, like PUK, remain significant companies today.

South Asian Puppetry

Ali, Sarwat. *Animating the Inanimate: Puppet Theatre in Pakistan*, Ferozsons, 2005.

Banerjee, Utpal, K. *Millennium Glimpses of Indian Performing Arts*, Shubhi Publications, 2007.

Blackburn, Stuart H. *Inside the Drama-House: Rama Stories and Shadow Puppets in South India*, University of California Press, 1996.

An in-depth scholarly study of the *tholpavakoothu* shadow puppet tradition of Kerala, India, with a specific focus on the textual aspects of the form as well as attention to performance.

Chakravarti, Nisith, *Puppet Dance in India: Origin and Evolution*, R.N. Bhattacharya, 2003.

Contractor, Meher Rustom. *The Shadow Puppets of India*, Darpana Academy of Performing Arts: 1984.

Ghosh, Sampa. *Indian Puppetry and Puppet Stories*, Shubhi Publications, 2007.

Ghosh, Sampa. *Indian Puppets*, Abhinav Publications, 2006.

> This very large volume gives a comprehensive view of the many forms of puppetry in India. It's four sections, each containing numerous chapters, including "Overview of Puppets," cataloging the variety of forms; "Multiple Purposes of Puppetry," including its social role and role in education; "The Craft of Puppetry," dealing with making and manipulating figures; "Animation in Puppetry," a guide to creating contemporary performances; and "Beyond Puppets," which includes mask performance, juggling and other arts. The appendixes include a list of Indian museums housing puppet collections and a listing of puppet companies. It has many photos and drawings.

Hingorani, Alka. *Making Faces: Self and Image Creation in a Himalayan Valley*, University of Hawaii Press, 2013.

> A study of the craft of making *mohra*—faces from thin metal sheets representing deities—and the communities in Himachal Pradesh, India who do them.

Jairazbhoy, Nazir Ali. *Kaṭhputli: The World of Rajasthani Puppeteers*, Rainbow Publishers 2007.

> A very comprehensive book about the string puppetry tradition in Rajasthan that addresses its history, stories, changing practices, and contemporary performers. It includes many photos.

Kamath, Bhaskar Kogga. *Story of Kogga Kamath's Marionettes*, Regional Resources Centre for Folk Performing Arts, M.G.M. College, 1995.

> A comprehensive book, full of photos and drawings, about this troupe of Yakshagana puppeteers in India, with information on all aspects of this string puppet tradition and a personal view of the company.

Krishna, Nanditha. *Folk Toys of South India*, C.P. Ramaswami Aiyar Foundation, 2006.

Krishnaiah, S.A. *Karnatak Puppetry*, Centre for Folk Performing Arts, 1988.

Nanjunda Rao, M. S., *Leather Puppetry in Karnataka*, Karnataka Chitrakala Parishath, 2000.

A coffee table style art book about Karnataka, India's shadow puppet tradition. It has an abundance of large, color photographs of the puppets.

Orenstein, Claudia "Finding the Heart of Indian Puppetry." *Puppetry International*, vol. 36, 2014, pp. 16–19.

A short piece I wrote following a research trip to India, offering views on the ways some important traditional artists have created centers for puppetry arts around the country.

Orenstein, Claudia. "Women in Indian Puppetry: Negotiating Traditional Roles and New Possibilities." *Asian Theatre Journal*, vol. 32, no. 2, 2015, pp. 493–517.

The article, in a special issue of *ATJ* devoted to women in Asian performance, outlines the lives and careers of several significant women puppeteers in India—Rajitha Pulavar, Pankajakshi and Ranjini, Anupama Hoskere, Anurupa Roy, and Padmini Rangarajan—and their contributions to the art, giving attention to the often overlooked work of women artists.

Orenstein, Claudia. "Women in Indian Puppetry: Artists, Educators, Activists." *Gender, Space and Resistance: Women and Theatre in India*, edited by Anita Singh, DK Printworld, 2013, pp. 245–72.

The article outlines the lives and careers of several significant women puppeteers in India and their contributions to the art, giving attention to the often-overlooked work of women artists, with a different selection of artists from my article in *Asian Theatre Journal*.

Pani, Jiwan. *World of Other Faces: Indian Masks*, Publication Division Ministry of Information and Broadcasting Government of India, 1986.

A short text with a collection of images from mask performance traditions around the country.

Sabnani, Nina. *Kaavad Traditions of Rajasthan: A Portable Pilgrimage*, Niyogi Books, 2015.

This is a wonderful, comprehensive book about the *kaavad* box storytelling tradition that I discuss in chapter 2. Sabnani is the foremost scholar of this form and gives an in-depth view into all aspects of the tradition and the communities who practice and receive it.

Sarma, Nagbhushana M. *Tolu Bommalata: The Shadow Puppet Theatre of Andrah Pradesh*, Sangeet Natak Akademi, 1985.

A comprehensive introduction to the large Shadow puppet tradition of Andhra Pradesh, with color photos.

Schuster, Michael. "Visible Puppets and Hidden Puppeteers: Indian *Gombeyata* Puppetry." *Asian Theatre Journal*, vol. 18, no. 1, 2001, pp. 59–68.

Smith, Karen, and Kathy Foley. "Tradition and Post-Tradition: Four Contemporary Indian Puppeteers." *Asian Theatre Journal*, vol. 35, no. 1, 2018, pp. 70–84.

Sutradhar

A magazine published periodically by UNIMA-India, full of useful articles on Indian puppetry, both new practices and traditional forms.

Venu, G. *Puppetry and Lesser Known Dance Traditions of Kerala*. 2nd rev. ed., afterword by Mulk Raj Anand, Natana Kairali, 2004.

Venu, G. *Tolpavakoothu: Shadow Puppets of Kerala*, Sangeet Natak Akademi and Hope India Publications, 2006.

An introduction to all aspects of the shadow puppetry tradition of Kerala, India by Venu G., who has been instrumental in writing about, producing, and, in a variety of ways, promoting performing arts in Kerala, especially the dance-drama *kutiyattam*. It contains many lovely photos and a full synopsis of all episodes of the traditional *Ramayana* performance.

Vergati, Anne. *Gods and Masks of the Kathamandu Valley*, D.K. Printworld, 2000.

Beautiful photographs and a detailed study of a fascinating tradition of mask performance in Nepal.

Southeast Asian Puppetry

Brandon, James R. *On Thrones of Gold: Three Javanese Shadow Plays*, University of Honolulu Press, 1970.

Scholar James Brandon's translations of three Javanese shadow plays with an extensive introduction to all aspects of the tradition.

Chandavij, Natthapatra and Promporn Pramaualratana. *Thai Puppets and Khon Masks*, River Books, 1998.

A gorgeous book full of beautiful images of Thai puppets and masks, with a text introducing the performing arts, the main Ramakien (Ramayana) tales, and the characters in them.

Cohen, Matthew Isaac. "Global Modernities and Post-Traditional Shadow Puppetry in Contemporary Southeast Asia" *Third Text*, vol. 30, no. 3–4, 2016, pp. 188–206.

Matthew Cohen is a scholar of Indonesian performance and is himself a trained *dalang*, shadow puppet performer. He has many articles and books on Indonesian performing arts and all are worth reading. One of his contributions to puppetry scholarship is the distinction between what he calls traditional and post-traditional puppetry. The latter breaks more forcefully with traditional models than performances that merely adjust traditions to changing circumstances.

Cohen, Matthew. "The Dr. Walter Angst and Sir Henry Angest Collection of Indonesian Puppets: The Structure of the Conjuncture." *Asian Theatre Journal*, vol. 34, no. 2, 2018), pp. 300–28.

This article discusses the important collection of thousands of Indonesian shadow puppets and related materials amassed by Walter Angst with financial support from his brother, donated to the Yale Museum. Cohen, who is in charge of cataloguing the collection, offers background to Angst, and how, why, and what he collected. The article helpfully contextualizes this rich trove of performing objects.

Dhaninivat, H.H. Prince (Kromamun Bidyalabh Birdhyakorn) *Shadow Play (the Nang)*. 1954, Department of Fine Arts, 1968.

Dowsey-Magog, Paul. "Popular Workers' Shadow Theatre in Thailand." *Asian Theatre Journal*, vol. 19, no. 1, 2002, pp. 184–211.

Goodlander, Jennifer, *Puppets and Cities: Articulating Identities in Southeast Asia*, Bloomsbury, 2018.

Based on extensive field work, an exploration of the roles of puppetry within Southeast Asia's contemporary urban spaces. The book brings contemporary critical theories to bear on how traditional puppets within museums and other contexts are positioned to express national identities and negotiate past and present culture.

Goodlander, Jennifer. *Women in the Shadows: Gender, Puppets, and the Power of Tradition in Bali*, Ohio University Press, 2016.

Based on Goodlander fieldwork both researching women shadow puppeteers in Bali and training to become one herself, the book explores what's involved in becoming a *dalang* and the constraints that keep women from full participation in the art.

Herbert, Mimi. *Voices of the Puppet Masters: The Wayang Golek Theatre of Indonesia*, University of Hawaii Press, 2002.

A coffee-table style book with beautiful photographs. The fascinating texts offer the words of prominent *dalang*, who are both puppeteers and spiritual leaders in their communities, describing their unique perspectives on their art and its personal, ritual, and philosophical dimensions.

Hobart, Angela. *Dancing Shadows of Bali: Theatre and Myth*, Routledge, 1988.
Keeler, Ward. *Javanese Shadow Puppets*, Oxford University Press, 1992.
Keeler, Ward and Kathy Foley. *Aspects of Indonesian Culture: Puppetry (Puppet Theatre of The Javanese and Sundanese)*, The Festival of Indonesia Foundation, 1991.
Kravel, Pech Tum. *Sbek Thom: Khmer Shadow Theater*. Khmer version edited by Thavro Phim and Sos Kem, English Translation by Sos Kem. Abridged, adapted, and edited by Martin Hatch, Cornell University and the United Nations Educational, Scientific and Cultural Organization, 1995.

An excellent, comprehensive resource on the history and practice of the large shadow puppetry tradition of Cambodia.

Mattani Rutnin, editor. *The Siamese Theatre: Collection of Reprints from Journals of the Siam Society*, N.P. 1975.

A very helpful collection of essays on a variety of types of performance in Thailand, including articles on shadow puppetry. This older text give insight into earlier periods of performance.

Matusky, Patricia. *Malaysian Shadow Play and Music: Continuity of Oral Tradition*, Oxford University Press, 1993.
Mrázek, Jan. *Phenomenology of a Puppet Theatre: Contemplations on the Art of Javanese Wayang Kulit*, KITLV, 2005.

This book provides an excellent model for a phenomenological analysis of puppetry performance. It attends to all the aspects of a Javanese puppet performance, one at a time, first contemplating the puppets themselves and the role of the *dalang*, then the roles of the screen and the music. The second half of the book, which could be its own book, analyzes contemporary performances of the period. It shows how the cosmology set up by the traditional model is phenomenologically disrupted with new practices. I have found it a very valuable text for my own thinking about puppetry.

Mrázek, Jan. *Wayang and Its Doubles: Javanese Puppet Theatre, Television and the Internet*, National University of Singapore Press, 2019.

Here Mrázek builds on the work of his previous book (see previous citation) to analyze further transformations in the tradition of Javanese puppetry when presented through other media, especially television.

Mrázek, Jan, editor *Puppet Theatre in Contemporary Indonesia: New Approaches to Performance Events*, The Center for Southeast Asian Studies, 2002.

A collection of essays by prominent Indonesian performance scholars addressing a range of contemporary puppetry practices in Indonesia from a variety of perspectives.

Nicolas, René. "Le Théâtre d' Ombres au Siam." *The Siamese Theatre: A Collection of Reprints from the Journal of Siam Society*, edited by Mattani Rutnin, Siam Society, 1975. pp. 103–14.

Osnes, Beth. *The Shadow Puppet Theatre of Malaysia: A Study of Wayang Kulit with Performance Scripts and Puppet Designs*, McFarland and Company, 2010.

An excellent comprehensive resource on shadow puppetry in Malaysia, a form that rarely receives attention.

Purwoseputro, Ardian. *Wayang Potehi of West Java*. Afterhours Books, 2014.

Sears, Laurie J. *Shadows of Empire: Colonial Discourses and Javanese Tales*, Duke University Press, 1996.

An in-depth scholarly study, including literary, historical, and anthropological perspectives on the interplay between traditional Indonesian village practices in shadow puppetry, especially improvisation in performance, and colonial impositions on the form.

Singer, Noel F. *Burmese Puppets*, Oxford University Press, 1993.

An excellent small book on all aspects of Burmese string puppetry, including its history.

Smithies, Michael and Euayporn Kerdchouay. "Notes: The *Wai Kru* Ceremony of the *Nang Yai*." *Journal of Siamese Heritage*, vol. 62, no. 1, 1974, pp. 143–47.

Thanegi, Ma. *Illusion of Life: Burmese Puppets*, Orchid Press, 1995.

A lovely basic introduction to traditional Burmese string puppetry, with beautiful photographs.

Van Ness, Edward C., and Shita Prawirohardjo. *Javanese Wayang Kulit*, Oxford University Press, 1980.

An excellent comprehensive introduction to all aspects of the Javanese shadow puppetry tradition.

Weintraub, Andrew N. *Power Plays: Wayang Golek Puppet Theatres of West Java*, ISEAS Publishing, 2004.

Yousof, Ghulam-Sarwar, editor. *Puppetry for All Times: Papers Presented at the Bali Puppetry Seminar, 2013*, Partridge Singapore, 2014.

Punch and his Cohorts

Byrom, Michael. *Punch in the Italian Puppet Theatre*, Centaur Press, 1983.

> An engaging, detailed history of Pulcinella, the Italian puppet figure that fostered the Punch character in England, showing its complex origins, and its presence as a commedia character and marionette as well as a hand puppet.

Byrom, Michael. *Punch, Polichinelle and Pulcinella*, Millbrook Press, 2007.

Fournel, Paul. *L'Histoire véritable de Guignol*, Slatkine Resources, 1981.

> A detailed history of the Guignol hand puppet character in France, examining its birth within working class culture, its role in relaying news to illiterate factory workers, and its ultimate transformation into a form of children's entertainment.

Fournel, Paul, editor. *Les Marionnettes*. Preface by Antoine Vitez, Bordas, 1982.

Edwards, Glyn. *Successful Punch and Judy: A Handbook on the Skills and Traditions of Performing with the UK's National Puppet*, DaSilva Puppet Books, 2000.

Gross, Joan. *Speaking in Other Voices: An Ethnography of Walloon Puppet Theaters*, J. Benjamins, 2001.

> An interesting scholarly, linguistic study of the various roles of texts and oral transmission in passing on vocal skills for puppetry performance within the rod puppetry tradition in Liège, Belgium, an area where both French and Walloon are spoken and have different cultural and political significance. Among the author's fascinating revelations is that, while puppet play texts are valued as objects that confer authority on puppeteers, performers absorb the language and ways of speaking for their characters from apprenticing with and watching master performers more than from reading their cherished scripts.

Kelly, Catriona. *Petrushka: The Russian Carnival Puppet Theatre*, Cambridge University Press, 1990.

> A detailed, scholarly study of Petrushka, a Russian version of the Punch/Pulcinella character within Russian society and culture, from its early incorporation at fairgrounds to its demise under Stalin. Kelly analyzes Petrushka's presence in both popular and more elite cultural forms.

Leach, Robert. *The Punch and Judy Show: History, Tradition and Meaning*, Macmillan, 1989.

A comprehensive, scholarly, historical study of England's iconic hand puppet tradition of Punch and Judy, from its origins in Italian itinerant performances, to its absorption of English theatrical tropes, to its growth in popularity for its rebellious central character, to the taming of the form as it entered nineteenth-century playrooms, to its eventual transformation into a seaside entertainment.

McCormick, John, and Bennie Pratasik. *Popular Puppet Theatre in Europe, 1800-1914*, Cambridge University Press, 1998.

An exhaustive, detailed historical study of puppetry performers, their audiences, and the social and cultural contexts of their performances from 1800 to 1914.

Onofrio, Jean-Baptiste. *Théâtre Lyonnais de Guignol*. Preface by Marcel Maréchal, Illustrated by Eugène Lefebvre, Lafitte Reprints, 1978.

Orenstein, Claudia "Punch the Red." *Festive Revolutions: The Politics of Popular Theatre and the San Franciso Mime Troupe*, University Press of Mississippi, 1998, pp. 45–89.

A history and analysis of the politically activist theatre company, the San Francisco Mime Troupe's, their use of puppets in their performances, and of the radical nature of the popular puppetry they draw on in their work. It includes a discussion of their use of a Punch character in a commedia dell'arte-style production against the War in Vietnam and other projects.

Reeve, Martin John. *Contemporary Punch and Judy in performance: an ethnography of traditional British glove puppet theatre*, Royal Holloway, University of London, PhD thesis, 2010.

Speaight, George. *Punch and Judy: A History*, Vista, 1970.

An older, general history of the Punch and Judy tradition in England.

Books Not on Puppetry, but Useful for Critical Thinking

Appadurai, Arjun, editor. *The Social Life of Things: Commodities in Cultural Perspective*, Cambridge University Press, 1986.

A collection of scholarly essays bringing together historical, sociological, economic, and anthropological perspectives in analyzing how particular objects within specific, varied cultural contexts become socially and economically valuable.

Auslander, Philip. *Liveness: Performance in a Mediatized Culture*. Routledge, 1999.

An influential, theoretical text considering the realities and implications of live vs. mediated performance in contemporary culture. Questions and perspectives addressed here about what is live and what is mediated through various forms of technology in theater and rock concerts also bear on the use of technologies within puppetry.

Bachelard, Gaston. *The Poetics of Space*, Beacon Press, 1969.

Bachelard's poetic writing about the physical and emotional experiences of spaces throughout a home, nests, nooks and crannies, hidden areas, and places of personal memory, can be very useful for thinking through phenomenological experiences created on the puppet stage.

Bennett, Jane. *Vibrant Matter: A Political Ecology of Things*, Duke University Press, 2010.

Bennett's writings on the agency of material things, working in *assemblages* with human agents, rather than being dominated by them, has been extremely influential for puppetry scholars. Her examples include things like the electric grid and ingested foods.

Berger, John. *Ways of Seeing*, Penguin Books, 1990.

Berger's classic book about how to look at art and other imagery is instructive for thinking about the visual aspects of puppetry.

Biernoff, Suzanne. *Sight and Embodiment in the Middle Ages*, Palgrave, 2002.
Bleeker, Maaike. *Visuality in the Theater: The Locus of Looking*, Palgrave Macmillan, 2008.
Casati, Roberto. *Shadows: Unlocking Their Secrets, from Plato to Our Time*. Translated from the Italian by Abigail Asher, Vintage Books, 2003.

A thoughtful and wide-ranging history of human views on and relationships to shadows written by a philosopher. The insights and metaphors explored here can be inspiring and informative for work in shadow theatre.

Davis, Richard H. *The Lives of Indian Images*, Princeton University Press, 1997.

Through a series of case studies that offer the biographies of particular Hindu objects, the book shows how cultural, social, and historical forces and events can animate objects as much as any ritual actions or deities believed to inhabit them.

Eck, Diana L. *Darsan: Seeing the Divine Image in India*. 3rd. ed., Columbia University Press, 1998.

A Selective and Selectively Annotated Puppetry Bibliography 169

A classic text, it provides important perspectives on how to understand images, icons, and other ritual material culture in India, within their religious and social context.

Freedberg, David. *The Power of Images: Studies in the History and Theory of Response*, University of Chicago Press, 1989.
Gehman, Chris, and Steve Reinke, editors. *The Sharpest Point: Animation at the End of Cinema.* YYZ Book/Ottowa International Animation Festival/Images Festival, 2005.
Gray, John. *The Soul of the Marionette: A Short Inquiry Into Human Freedom*, Farrar, Staus and Giroux, 2015.

About human freedom rather than actual puppets, it can serve as a thoughtful prompt for how the metaphor of the puppet in this context operates in our relationship to ourselves and to real puppets.

Heidegger, Martin. "The Thing." *Poetry, Language, Thought*. Translated by Albert Hofstadter, Harper & Row, 1971, pp. 165–86.
Kentridge, William. *Black Box/Chambre Noir*, Deutsche Guggenheim, 2005.

The artwork of South African artist William Kentridge, who also worked with Handspring Puppet Company directing some of their important productions, spans a wide range of media including prints, animation, and opera direction, as well as many hybrid forms. To my mind, Kentridge's work stretches across the continuum of arts that reflect the scope of contemporary puppetry. This book contains critical essays about and is a documentation of the process and work of a mechanized art installation piece that developed from Kentridge's work directing Mozart's *The Magic Flute*: a black box that stands as a kind of model theater with moving parts and projections that both reflect Kentridge's designs for the production, and a unique artwork of its own.

Kentridge, William. *Thinking Aloud: Conversations with Angela Breidbach*, David Krut Publishing, 2006.

Insightful discussions with the artist about his work.

Knowles, Richard Paul. *Reading the Material Theater*, Cambridge University Press, 2004.
Latour, Bruno. *We Have Never Been Modern*, Harvard University Press, 1993.
Mack, John. *The Art of Small Things*, Harvard University Press, 2007.

A copiously illustrated book about miniatures that also contemplates the attraction of small objects and how they operate on the imagination.

Margolies, Eleanor. *Props*, Palgrave, 2016.

> This scholarly book, written by a puppeteer, considers the unique position of props in theatre, standing between actor and scenic design, alternately inert and enlivened performers.

McCauley, Gay. *Space in Performance: Making Meaning in the Theatre*, University of Michigan Press, 2010.

McCloud, Scott. *Understanding Comics: The Invisible Art*, Harper Perennial, 1993.

> A comic book itself whose pictures and words explicate how visual imagery and text function together and independently in storytelling in comics. I speak at some length about the book in chapter 3. An amazing, intellectual study of comics, clearly and imaginatively conveyed, it offers many insights for thinking about puppetry.

Meilach, Dona Z. *Box Art: Assemblage and Construction*, Crown Publishers, 1975.

> The images in this book of art objects constructed in boxes, an artform popularized particularly by Joseph Cornell, can offer inspiration to puppeteers. It is worth looking specifically at the extensive literature on the works of Cornell as well, although I haven't included any in this bibliography.

Miller, Daniel. *The Comfort of Things*, Polity Press, 2008.

Mitchell, W.T.J. *Iconology: Image, Text, Ideology*, University of Chicago Press, 1986.

Monaco, James. *How to Read a Film: The World of Movies Media and Multimedia*. 3rd. ed., Oxford University Press, 2000.

> I turned to this book when I felt that, in order to understand cinematic artistic expressions within contemporary puppetry, a film vocabulary would be useful. This book was useful, and there are no doubt many on the subject.

Moxey, Keith. "Visual Studies and the Iconic Turn." *Journal of Visual Culture*, vol. 7, 2008, pp. 131–46.

Nitsche, Michael. *Video Game Spaces: Image, Play, and Structure in 3D Worlds*, MIT Press, 2008.

> The avatars in video games can also be considered as puppets of a sort. This is one book I found as a way to start investigating this idea. There is no doubt a good deal of more recent literature on these ideas. I cannot claim to be an authority in this area, so I invite you to investigate the literature yourself.

Pattison, Stephen. *Seeing Things: Deepening Relations with Visual Artefacts*, SCM Press, 2007.

Rayner, Alice. "Presenting Objects, Presenting Things." *Staging Philosophy: Intersections of Theater, Performance, and Philosophy*, edited by David Krasner and David Z. Saltz, University of Michigan Press, 2006, pp. 180–202.

Robertson, Jennifer. *Robo Sapiens Japanicus: Robots, Gender, Family, and the Japanese Nation*, University of California Press. 2018.

>Robertson's critical analysis of the presence of and discourses pertaining to robots and related figures in contemporary Japanese culture. The author highlights social, political, and gender-related agendas embedded in the growing presence and promotion of robots.

Rosenthal, Mark, editor. *William Kentridge: Five Themes*, San Francisco Museum of Modern Art, Norton Museum of Art, in association with Yale University Press, 2009.

Schweitzer, Marlis and Joanne Zerdy, edited by Marlis Schweitzer and Joanne Zerdy. *Performing Objects and Theatrical Things*, Palgrave Macmillan, 2014.

>A collection of essays from theatre and performance studies scholars that investigate and theorize the performativity of material things such as props, costumes, and museum artifacts within theatre studies. The volume reflects the turn towards New Materialism within theatre scholarship. None of the essays, however, discuss puppets.

Schwenger, Peter. *The Tears of Things: Melancholy and Physical Objects*, University of Minnesota Press, 2006.

Sofer, Andrew. *The Stage Life of Props*, University of Michigan Press, 2003.

>An important, pioneering scholarly analysis on the role of props in theatre. It offers helpful insights for thinking about performing objects.

States, Bert O. *Great Reckonings in Little Rooms: On the Phenomenology of Theater*, University of California Press, 1985.

>A foundational, scholarly study applying phenomenological perspectives to analyzing stage performance. The overall perspectives here, and specifically distinctions between living and non-living things onstage, are helpful for contemplating how puppetry works on spectators.

Stewart, Susan. *On Longing: Narratives of the Miniature, the Gigantic, the Souvenir, the Collection*, Duke University Press, 1993.

Taylor, Joshua C. *Learning to Look: A Handbook for the Visual Arts*. 2nd. ed., University of Chicago Press, 1981.

A thoughtful guide to how to look at visual art that can help in considering the visual aspects of puppetry.

Turkle, Sherry editor. *Evocative Objects: Things We Think With*, MIT Press, 2007.

A collection of biographical essays, framed by literary and theoretical views, that express the emotional and intellectual power of ordinary objects in our daily lives.

Turkle, Sherry, editor. *The Inner History of Devices*, MIT Press, 2008.

Whitehead, Amy. *Religious Statues and Personhood: Testing the Role of Materiality*, Bloomsbury, 2013.

A scholarly theoretical and descriptive study underscoring the performative aspects of interacting with religious statues in Western European contexts.

Wood, Gaby. *Edison's Eve: A Magical History of the Quest for Mechanical Life*, Anchor Books, 2002.

A history of robotic and mechanical objects from the eighteenth century to the present, offering critical perspectives and contextualizing them within social, cultural, and philosophical views.

Index

Note: *Italic* page numbers refer to figures.

abstraction and structure 51–54
actions and emotions 23, 29
The Adventures of Charcoal Boy 27–28, *28*
advertisements 57
Alighieri, Dante 135–138
American Puppet Modernism (Bell) 16
American Society for Theatre Research (ASTR) 16
American theatre 3
animated/inanimate objects 19–21, 29–30
Anne Frank: Within and Without 109
Anywhere 44–45
"A Puppet Tree: A Model for the Field of Puppet Theatre" (Kaplin) 101
Aristotelian model 2
art of montage 23
Asche, Leslee 3
Aspects of the Puppet Theatre (Jurkowski) 6, 15–16
ASTR. *see* American Society for Theatre Research (ASTR)
ASTR Working Group on Puppetry and Material Performance 16
audiences 26, 66, 103; object-oriented 41; Toy theatre 119
Avenue Q 9

Balla, Frank 11
Ballard Institute and Museum of Puppetry 11
banners and cranks 75–79
Banzhaf, Pia 19–20, 25
Bass, Eric 54
Bell, John 4
Bennet, Jan 6, 7
Bennett, Jane 6
Blumenthal, Eileen 15, 21

Boerwinkel, Henk 45
Bogatryev, Peter 4
books 71
breathed stillness 22–23
Brentley, Ben 96
bunraku tradition 102–103, 120–121; three-person technique 103–104
Butler, Judith 30

cabinet boxes 32, *33*
California Institute of the Arts 12
The Cenotaph of Dan Wa Moriri 39–40, 54
Chicago International Puppet Theater Festival 10, 11
Chiflón: The Silence of Coal 119
cinematic techniques 6
Clark, Bradford 12
contemporary creative explorations 70–73
A Conversation with Frederick Douglass 27
COVID pandemic 10, 75, 86–87
crafted materials 25
Craig, Edward Gordon 5, 38
cranks 75–79
Cruz, Santa 12
CUNY Graduate Center's Doctoral Program in Theatre 3

designing process 26–27
Disfarmer (Hurlin) 107–108, *108*
diverse puppet 102–106
Dōjōji scroll performance 82
Dōjōji Temple scroll 63–64
Dolan, Clare 76–77, *77*
Domestic Resurrection Circus festivals 101
double-vision 79
dramaturgical moment 36–37
dramaturgy/dramaturgical 34, 35; choice of

174 Index

object and materiality 44; *kaavad* box 38–39; object and materiality 44, 54–56; storytelling 35; structure 39, 41
Dream Music puppet program 8–9

eclectic art form 43
The Emperor 42
Enlightenment ideologies 21
Esslin, Martin 5

Feathers of Fire 70
figurative character 25–26
Figurentheater Triangel 45, 46
Foley, Kathy 7, 12
French Puppetry 80
Freud, Sigmund 21

Geiser, Janie 9, 12
gender performance 30
Gesell Chamber 3
giant Olympic puppet 85–88, 87
Green, Jesse 96
Gross, Kenneth 15

habitual story makers 23
The Hairy Ape (O'Neill) 125–133
Handmade Puppet Dreams 9–10
Handspring Puppet Company 3, 19, 22
Handspring Puppet Company 15
Hand to God 9
Helen: Queen of Sparta 79
Henson Foundation 10–11
Henson International Puppetry Festivals 3–4
Henson, Jim 10, 121
Hindu tales 38
hitogata 103
human actors: with crafted materials 25; onstage performance 22–23; theatre 121–122
humanette 25
human interconnections in puppetry 102–106
Hunchback 71
The Hunchback of Notre Dame (Hugo) 71

identities 109–112
images/pictures 23, 57
Indian puppetry 32, 82, 83; *pattachitra* 61; scroll storytelling tradition 60–66, *61*, *62*, *65*; traditions 60
Inferno (Alighieri) 135–138

In Search of Aesthetics for the Puppet Theatre (Meschke) 6
International Puppetry festival 13
Introduction and Allegro for Strings (Elgar) 80
Italian Pulcinella hand puppet 118

Japanese: *bunraku* tradition 102–103, 120; screens 69–70; stomping feature 104–105
Jarry, Alfred 133–135
Jesus Christ story 38
Jones, Basil 22–23, 26
Jurkowski, Henryk 16

kaavad boxes 33, 33–34, 37, 45, 60; dramatic structure 38–39; Hindu tales 38; Jesus Christ story 38
Kaavad Traditions of Rajasthan: A Portable Pilgrimage. (Sabnani) 56
Kathputli: The World of Rajasthani Puppeteers (Jairazbhoy) 32
Kaplan, Bruce Eric 1
Kaplin, Stephen 101
Kentridge, William 3
King Kong 9, 94–99, 98
Kleist, Heinrich Von 5
kuruma ningyō (cart puppetry) 5, *104*, 104–105

language 119–120
The Language of the Puppet (Kominz and Levinson) 6
Law, Jane Marie 103
Lawrence, Sarah 12
Le Cri Quotidien (The Daily Cry) 71–72, *72*
Lee, Tom 5, 12, 54–55
Limbo, Agnès 42
The Lion King (Taymor) 9, 25, 99, 101
Little Amal project 85–86, *86*
Louis Riel: A Comic Book Stage Play (Refinery') 81–82

The Macanuda 78–79
material/materiality 26–27; choice of 27; culture 6; invitations 54–56
McCloud, Scott 23, 78
Metamorphoses 45
micromovements 29
Miyambo, Tony 39–43, *40*
modernity 21
movement in puppetry 79–82
Mrazek, Jan 4, 5, 23
Muppet projects 10, 17, 38, 121

Murakami, Haruki 52
museum exhibitions 10
music and poetic language 118–121

Nashville International Puppetry Festival 10–11
Nelson, Victoria 21
"New Puppetry" 6
The New Yorker 1
The New York Times 95–96

object dramaturgy *see* dramaturgy/dramaturgical
Object Movement Puppetry Residency and Festival 12
object-oriented audiences 41
object-oriented-ontologies 6–7
object performance 58–59, 59
objects: as books 71; and subject 112–114
object theatre 42
Oedipus Rex 36
Off-Broadway show 23–25
O'Neill, Eugene 125–133
onstage performance 22
"On the Marionette Theatre" (Kleist) 5

Pabuji ki phad 60–62, 61
Painting and Performance: Chinese Picture Recitation and Its Indian Genesis (Mair) 60
Paper Story 80–82
Parks, Suzan-Lori 121–122
Pasic, Inés 25
pattachitra 61, 79
performances 29–30, 118, 124; emotional journey 35–37; of human body 76–77, 77; Japanese screens 69–70; with object 42–43; sand-art 81; traditional 57–58
Peter and Wendy 108
Phenomenology of a Puppet Theatre:: Contemplations on the Art of Javanese Wayang Kulit (Mrazek) 4, 5
pictures *see* images/pictures
pilgrimage puppets 84–90
playing with expectations 49–50
pop-up books 71–73
Posner, Dassia N. 6
Pulcinella hand puppet 118
Puppet and Spirit: Ritual, Religion and Performing Objects 16
puppeteers 7, 12, 16, 18, 22; *see also* puppet/puppetry (shows); character development and storytelling 28–29; Teatro Dei Piedi 25
Puppeteers of America (P of A) 12
puppet/puppetry (shows) 1, 9; *see also* dramaturgy/dramaturgical; human actors; pilgrimage puppets; actions and emotions 29; arts, examination of 16–17; Banzhaf's scientific approach 20; breathed stillness 22–23; *bunraku* 120–121; degree programs 11–12; description of 19; double-vision in 79; festivals 10–12; human interconnections in 102–106; investigation 6, 7; joy of 48–49; movement in 79–82; in New York 1; object theatre and 32; onstage performance 22; onstage struggle 19; pedagogical handbook 16; and picture storytelling 59–69; pop-up books in 71–73; psychoanalytical perspective 21; to puppeteers 94–101; racial and other identities 109–112; semiotic approach for 4–5; storytelling 26; successes and failures of 3; theatre *vs.* 4; training programs 11–12; visibilities and presence 107–109; wooden 3
Puppetry: An Essay on Uncanny Life (Gross) 15
Puppetry: A Reader in Theatre Practice (Francis) 16
Puppetry: A World History (Blumenthal) 15, 21
Puppetry International (PI) 6
Puppetry Yearbook (Fisher) 6
Puppets Come Home! program 10
Puppet Slam Network 9
Puppets, Masks, and Performing Objects 4

racial and other identities 109–112
Rahmanian, Hamid 70
Rajasthani string puppets 32, 117
Reed, Larry 71
Richards, Paulette 27
Riel, Louis 81–82
The Routledge Companion to Puppetry and Material Performance 14

Sabnani, Nina 56
St. Ann's Puppet Lab 9
sand-art performances 81
Sandglass Puppet Theatre 54

Schweda, Brendan 10
scroll storytelling tradition 60–66, 61, 62, 65, 82, 83
Searls, Colette 12
Sesame Street 17, 22
Shahnameh 70
Shank's Mare 5
Simonova, Kseniya 81
sounds 117; dramatic punctuations/rhythm 118; musical accompaniment 118; objects and 117–118
South Africa 109–111
speaking puppets 23
spectators 23–24
stage performance 22, 35
Staub, Nancy Lohman 6
stomping 104–105
storytelling 23, 26, 35; see also puppet/puppetry (shows); scroll storytelling tradition
Suárez, Hugo 25

The Table 80
Takes After His Father (Buchen) 77
Teatro Dei Piedi 25
Teatro SEA's festival 11
Thailand companies 68, 69
"The Actor and the Ubermarionette" (Craig) 5
Théâtre de L'Entrouvert, France 44, 44
"The Dancer and the Danced" (Foley) 7
The World of Puppetry 45
Tomte show 54–55
Toward an Aesthetic of the Puppet: Puppetry as a Theatrical Art (Tillis) 5–6, 79
toy theatre 73–75

Ubu and the Truth Commission 109–110
Ubu Roi (Jarry) 133–135

Understanding Comics: The Invisible Art (McCloud) 23, 78
UNIMA (L'Union Internationale de la Marionette) 13–14
UNIMA-USA 6, 13–14, 16
United States: puppetry artists 1; racial and other identities 111–112; training programs in 11
ur-narrative 19, 25
US organizations and institutions 9–10

Veltruský, Jiří 4
Vibrant Matter: A Political Ecology of Things (Bennett) 6
visibilities and presence 107–109
visual qualities 57
vital materialism 6

War Horse 9, 15
We Have Never Been Modern (Latour) 21
Williams, Margaret 25–26
Wind-Up Bird Chronicle 18
Wind-Up Bird Chronicle (Earnhart) 52–54
Women and Puppetry: Critical and Historical Investigations 16
wooden puppets 3
The Woodsman (Ortiz and Karpen) 23–25
workshops 116–117
The World of Puppetry 45
Woyzeck on the Highveld 3
Woyzek on the Highveld and *Ubu and the Truth Commission* 15

Xu, Liqing 116–117

Zahhak: The Legend of the Serpent King 70
Zaloom, Paul 27
Zich, Otakar 4

For Product Safety Concerns and Information please contact our EU
representative GPSR@taylorandfrancis.com
Taylor & Francis Verlag GmbH, Kaufingerstraße 24, 80331 München, Germany

www.ingramcontent.com/pod-product-compliance
Lightning Source LLC
Chambersburg PA
CBHW052134010526
44113CB00036B/2145